Regional Economic Systems after COVID-19

NEW HORIZONS IN REGIONAL SCIENCE

Series Editor: Philip McCann, *Professor of Urban and Regional Economics, University of Sheffield, UK*

Regional science analyses important issues surrounding the growth and development of urban and regional systems and is emerging as a major social science discipline. This series provides an invaluable forum for the publication of high quality scholarly work on urban and regional studies, industrial location economics, transport systems, economic geography and networks.

New Horizons in Regional Science aims to publish the best work by economists, geographers, urban and regional planners and other researchers from throughout the world. It is intended to serve a wide readership including academics, students and policymakers.

Titles in the series include:

High Speed Rail and China's New Economic Geography
Impact Assessment from the Regional Science Perspective
Zhenhua Chen and Kingsley E. Haynes

Smart, Sustainable and Inclusive Growth
Political Entrepreneurship for a Prosperous Europe
Edited by Charlie Karlsson, Daniel Silander and Brigitte Pircher

Regions and Innovation Policies in Europe
Learning from the Margins
Edited by Manuel González-López and Bjørn T. Asheim

Diversity, Innovation and Clusters
Spatial Perspectives
Edited by Iréne Bernhard, Urban Gråsjö and Charlie Karlsson

Entrepreneurial Ecosystems Meet Innovation Systems
Synergies, Policy Lessons and Overlooked Dimensions
Edited by Alexandra Tsvetkova, Jana Schmutzler and Rhiannon Pugh

The Globalization of Regional Clusters
Between Localization and Internationalization
Edited by Dirk Fornahl and Nils Grashof

Unlocking Regional Innovation and Entrepreneurship
The Potential for Increasing Capacities
Edited by Iréne Bernhard, Urban Gråsjö and Charlie Karlsson

Regional Economic Systems after COVID-19
Actionable Insights for an Equitable and Resilient Recovery
Edited by Fred Olayele

Regional Economic Systems after COVID-19

Actionable Insights for an Equitable and Resilient Recovery

Edited by

Fred Olayele

Sprott School of Business, Carleton University, Ottawa, Canada

NEW HORIZONS IN REGIONAL SCIENCE

Edward Elgar
PUBLISHING

Cheltenham, UK • Northampton, MA, USA

Published by
Edward Elgar Publishing Limited
The Lypiatts
15 Lansdown Road
Cheltenham
Glos GL50 2JA
UK

Edward Elgar Publishing, Inc.
William Pratt House
9 Dewey Court
Northampton
Massachusetts 01060
USA

A catalogue record for this book
is available from the British Library

Library of Congress Control Number: 2023935496

This book is available electronically in the **Elgar**online
Economics subject collection
http://dx.doi.org/10.4337/9781802208214

ISBN 978 1 80220 820 7 (cased)
ISBN 978 1 80220 821 4 (eBook)

Printed and bound in Great Britain by TJ Books Limited, Padstow, Cornwall

Contents

Contributors

EDITOR

Fred Olayele's diverse career spans academia, government, finance, and international development. His research interests and practice areas cover trade policy, innovation, FDI, urban policy, political economy, and inclusive development. He has published and shared best practices in these areas at numerous conferences and institutions around the world. He has consulted widely and advised many public and private organizations in Canada, United States, Spain, and across several African countries. He has held academic positions and taught graduate and undergraduate courses at the University of Regina and Carleton University in Canada. He has served as a visiting professor and guest speaker across universities and academic institutions abroad. He was a Visiting Scholar at the World Trade Institute in Bern, Switzerland, and a Visiting Professor of Trade and Development at the University of Las Palmas de Gran Canaria, Spain. Fred previously served as Chief Economist and Senior Vice President with the New York City Economic Development Corporation, where he oversaw a wide range of economic research and policy initiatives. He has advised the Canadian provincial governments of British Columbia and Saskatchewan across the FDI, economic development, and energy policy domains. He earned his PhD in Economics from Lancaster University, United Kingdom, and his MA in Economics from the University of Victoria in British Columbia, Canada.

CONTRIBUTORS

Louise Anderson is Senior Director of Research at the International Economic Development Council. She has served in multiple roles since joining IEDC in 2001, consulting on dozens of projects for local governments and economic development organizations across the United States. Louise also is the author of numerous articles, research reports and publications on subjects that include inclusive economic development, economic transformation and workforce development, climate change, broadband access and more. She holds master's degrees in regional planning and public administration from the University of North Carolina at Chapel Hill and bachelor of arts degrees from Indiana University at Bloomington.

Harvey Brookes is Executive Director at the Waikato Wellbeing Project, New Zealand and has over 30 years' experience in public policy, environmental management, infrastructure, economic development and community wellbeing. He has worked at local, regional and central government levels, in private consultancy and in academia. Harvey has led regional economic development programmes across New Zealand, including Auckland, where he led the development of the region's first economic development strategy and the Waikato, where he designed and implemented the region's first regional economic development agency. He has taught at the Schools of Geography, Architecture and Planning, University of Auckland. Harvey earned his bachelor's and master's degrees from the University of Auckland, New Zealand. He is a member of the New Zealand Institute of Directors.

Bartomeu Deya Canals (Tomeu Deya) is a Spanish independent professional who combines tourism and heritage assessment with his own company, focused on agriculture and tourism maintaining a 400-year-old olive and orange plantation with a traditional oil mill. He graduated in Economics from Barcelona University and has an MSs in Marketing and PR from Stirling University in the UK. He was for 15 years the Mallorca Tourism Board director and for three years the World Heritage Site Serra de Tramuntana manager. Both positions together with his familiar commitment give him a very holistic and practical view of the different stakeholders involved. As Vice President with the ICOMOS International Cultural Tourism Committee, he shares insights related to heritage and tourism worldwide.

Jeffrey Dykes is an Analyst, with over eight years of economic modeling experience for REMI. He is based at the company's Amherst, MA headquarters, and has contributed to model development, policy research, and consulting with regional economic impact analysis in transportation and infrastructure, resilience, incentive analysis, and the development of linkages to external models. Jeffrey conducts research and evaluates data for consulting projects. He also evaluates new model versions for errors and discrepancies in economic forecasting simulations. Prior to becoming a staff member, he worked at REMI as an intern, helping economists with projects such as modeling the economic impact of casino building and immigration legislation. He holds a B.B.A. in finance and a B.A. in economics from the Isenberg School of Management at the University of Massachusetts Amherst.

Herb Emery is the Vaughan Chair in Regional Economics at the University of New Brunswick, Canada. An advisor to federal and provincial policymakers, Herb focuses his research on the development of the Canadian economy and the persistence of long-standing regional disparities. Aside from understanding the economic fundamentals of growth in a small open economy, his work incorporates political, historical, cultural, and other institutional factors that have shaped Canadian development processes. He holds an MA and PhD in Economics from the University of British Columbia. His academic career began at the University of Calgary where, from 1993 to 2016, he assembled a track record of demonstrated excellence in research, teaching, and leadership.

Bernadette Maria Antão Fernandes is a seasoned professional with extensive international experience in marketing, sales, business development, operations, human resources, risk management, and corporate leadership. In 2011, Bernadette founded The Varanda Network, an economic development organization. As the CEO and founder of The Varanda Network, Bernadette provides business services globally for start-ups, immigrant entrepreneurs, SMEs, and multinationals across various sectors. A dynamic, energetic and passionate leader, Bernadette has worked in the area of international market access since 2006, with a specific focus on exporting since 2013. Having worked closely alongside government, industry partners, and most recently academia, Bernadette is familiar with the nuances of the innovation ecosystem that allows bioscience companies to grow and thrive. Her work and travel have brought her across five continents, where she has developed successful public-private engagements and collaborations across all sectors, igniting and accelerating business and economic growth. Through this, she has built up an impressive and extensive network of trusted contacts all over the world.

Ifor Ffowcs-Williams is recognised globally as a leader in cluster-based economic development, and draws on his experience in over 50 countries. Among others, his clients include the World Bank, IFC, OECD, UNIDO, UNDP, and EU. Ifor has also assisted national and regional economic development agencies on six continents. He is the Founder and Past President of TCI Network, the global organisation for cluster practitioners, where he currently serves on the Board of Advisors. He has served on the Advisory Boards of the Danish Cluster Academy, European Cluster Observatory, Indian Institute for Competitiveness, Pan African Competitiveness Forum, and Sintonia – Mexico's competitiveness programme.

Swati Ghosh is Vice President, Insights and Innovations at NGIN. In this capacity, she leads NGIN's program delivery to deliver insights, best practices and innovations which will advance the field of inclusive economic development. Prior to NGIN, Swati served as the Senior Director of Research at International Economic Development Council (IEDC), where she led the research department in addition to contributing to technical assistance and training programs. Swati has nearly 15 years of experience in economic and community development, including analyzing and designing economic development strategies in entrepreneurship and workforce development, inclusive growth, economic recovery and diversification, and organizational capacity building, among others. She has authored several papers and articles on economic development and related topics. Swati has a Master of Government Administration from the University of Pennsylvania and a Bachelor of Urban Planning from the School of Planning & Architecture, India. Swati is also a Board member and Senior Fellow at the Institute for Work and Economy.

Poorvi Goel is a PhD candidate at New York University, specialising in development economics and public policy. Her research interests lie at the intersection of poverty, labor markets, and social protection. Her most recent research involved studying the impact of socioeconomic factors on older women's economic vulnerability and labor market outcomes in urban contexts. Poorvi has seven years of prior professional experience, and has held economic research and policy advisory positions with New York City Economic Development Corporation, Commonwealth Secretariat in London, United Nations Development Programme in Delhi, and Planning Commission in the Government of India. She holds an MPA in Development Practice from Columbia University, an MSc in Economics from London School of Economics, and a BA (Hons) in Economics from St. Stephen's College, Delhi.

Joyce Jauer currently serves as Vice President of the Economic Research & Policy department of the New York City Economic Development Corporation, overseeing monitoring and evaluation efforts and policy formation. Most recently, Joyce served as a Senior Revenue Analyst for the Texas Comptroller of Public Accounts tracking federal funds and leading projects on health care expenditures, state budget cost drivers, tax exemptions, and Hurricane Harvey costs and economic impact. She has experience in social enterprise, nonprofit management, and financial advising including having served as the CFO of a cycle rickshaw venture in Varanasi, India. Joyce holds a Master of Public Service and Administration from the Bush School at Texas A&M University and a Bachelor of Arts in Social Anthropology from Harvard University.

Jaclyn Kelly is Director of the NYC Labor Market Information Service (LMIS) research center at The CUNY Graduate Center, and an adjunct faculty member at City College (CCNY) where she teaches courses on public policy, evaluation, and research methods. She is passionate about research that promotes strong outcomes for mission-driven organizations and their clients, and has over two decades of experience working with educational institutions, nonprofits, and researchers to accelerate analysis-driven decision-making and practices. Jaclyn is trained in the Co-Active® model of leadership coaching, holds an Ed.M. in Measurement and Evaluation from Columbia University and Harvard Kennedy School's Public Leadership credential, and is a doctoral candidate at The Graduate Center.

Anindya Kundu is a sociologist and Assistant Professor of Educational Leadership at Florida International University. He researches how individuals navigate personal, social and institutional challenges to opportunity, in K through Workforce settings. In 2020, Anindya's book, The Power of Student Agency, was endorsed by Dr. Angela Duckworth and became a 2021 Association of American Publishers PROSE Award Finalist. From 2019 to 2021, Anindya led a research team at the New York City Labor Market Information Service. He received his Ph.D. from New York University where he was an award-winning educator. Anindya has two TED Talks that have more than five million views.

Billy Leung is the Senior Vice President of REMI, where he plays a leading role in U.S. and international consulting and support services. He has worked with government agencies and organizations throughout North America and the world, helping them achieve their planning and policy analysis goals. As part of REMI's global services, Billy has worked with the Chinese Academy of Sciences and the Korea Energy Economics Institute. In addition to his international efforts, Billy has assisted state and regional agencies, including Southern California Association of Governments. He has supported their long-term transportation and environmental planning initiatives. He holds a B.A. in Economics from the University of Massachusetts, Amherst and received his M.A. in Regional Economics and Social Development at the University of Massachusetts, Lowell. His master's thesis was on the research and development of incorporating transportation and land use with Input/Output economic modeling.

Fergus T. Maclaren is a Canadian sustainable tourism and cultural heritage management professional with 25 years of experience in Africa, North America and Asia. His current focuses are tourism to World Heritage sites and implementing the 2030 UN SDGs. He has a broad range on tourism planning, destination management and development experience including coordinating international meetings as the Director of the UN-funded International Year of Ecotourism; teaching sustainable tourism at Canada's McGill University and post-secondary institutions internationally. He serves in expert and professional capacities for UNESCO, UNWTO, ICOMOS, Organization of World Heritage Cities, World Monuments Fund, Economic Innovation Institute for Africa, and the Heritage and Cultural Society for Africa.

Kyle Marks is an Assistant Vice President at the New York City EDC where he specializes in labor market analysis. His recent research has focused on topics including economic mobility, neighborhood-level economic vulnerability, and sizing New York City's green workforce. Kyle has a B.A. from Tufts University and an M.Sc. from the London School of Economics.

Patrick McVeigh has more than 25 years' experience working across the public and private sectors in strategy development, policy formulation, research and evaluation, scenario planning and visioning. He has delivered a broad range of projects in a variety of subject areas and locations, bringing high-level political understanding and finesse. Patrick is a hands-on practitioner who focuses on the client's needs. Patrick's strong consultancy background is based on eight years' experience in public policy and economic development roles in London, where he worked with clients in local, regional and central government. Patrick has a BSc in Town Planning Studies, a Post Graduate Diploma in City and Regional Planning (Distinction), and a Post Graduate Diploma in Social Science Research Methods – all from Cardiff University.

Melissa Pumphrey is a Vice President at the New York City Economic Development Corporation (NYCEDC) where she leads the fiscal and economic impact pillar on the Economic Research & Policy team. Her group estimates the tax and job impacts of many of the projects that NYCEDC does, with a portfolio ranging from real estate developments to tax incentives to offshore wind. She also leads economic research for the women.NYC Childcare Innovation Lab, working to frame childcare as an economic development issue and as critical infrastructure for a robust, inclusive economy. Prior to EDC, Melissa spent seven years in the finance and consulting industries. Melissa has a B.A. and M.A. in economics.

Bertrand Teirlinck is a Policy Analyst at the New York City Economic Development Corporation (NYCEDC) where he works within the fiscal and economic impact pillar on the Economic Research & Policy team. His work includes providing estimates of the tax and job impacts for many of the projects that NYCEDC undertakes, from real estate developments to tax incentives to offshore wind. He also leads the team's monitoring and evaluation efforts for workforce development programs. Prior to EDC, Bertrand worked in legislative affairs for a non-profit and in the U.S. Senate. Bertrand has a B.A. in economics and history and M.Sc. in public policy.

David Wilson is Managing Director, Cities and Regions Limited, Auckland, New Zealand. Prior to that, he was Chief Executive Officer of Northland Inc, Northland's Economic Development Agency, Fellow and Chair of Economic Development New Zealand and a member of the New Zealand Government's Independent Advisory Panel for its new Provincial Development Fund – a NZ$1 billion/annum fund designed to lift productivity 'in the regions'. David holds a BA in Psychology and Social Policy, a Master's in Public Policy with first class honours, and a PhD in Governance and Regional Economic

Development. He was previously Director of the Institute of Public Policy at the Auckland University of Technology.

Yu Zhong is an Assistant Vice President at New York City Economic Development Corporation (NYCEDC), Economic Research and Policy department, where she specializes in fiscal and economic impact analysis and oversees the modeling process for many EDC projects – a portfolio that includes real estate development, tax incentives, infrastructure plan, and re-zoning. Her research covers a wide variety of topics ranging from industry analysis for fashion and the creative economy in New York City to the study of business closure during the COVID-19 pandemic. Prior to EDC, she attended the Urban and Regional Planning program at University of Illinois at Urbana-Champaign and worked as an urban planner in China. Yu holds a B.A. and M.A. in Urban and Regional Planning.

PART I

The economic redesign imperative

1. Introduction: the economic redesign imperative

Fred Olayele

Recovery from the economic crisis heralded by the COVID-19 pandemic will remain on the front burner of the economic development policy debate for a while. The pandemic triggered the most severe economic downturn since World War II, causing unprecedented disruptions in lives, economies, and societies. The virus has tested the limits of healthcare and economic systems across the world, with regional policy, supply chains, FDI, and tourism in many jurisdictions navigating uncharted waters. In the immediate aftermath of the crisis, business leaders and policymakers ramped up healthcare capacity and spending in a bid to save lives and contain the pandemic.

Since the crisis stems from a pandemic, understanding its impact on the economy and healthcare system remains critical for any interventions to deliver an equitable and resilient recovery. Unlike other economic crises in recent history, the source of the current recession is not financial. The pandemic-induced crisis is the outcome of an exogenous shock that triggered an economic crisis, with second order effects. While the scale of the economic and social disruptions caused by the pandemic is significant, with disproportionate impacts on marginalized groups, the potential silver linings in the crisis are the opportunity it presents for fixing the various ills associated with the pre-pandemic economy – in the context of structural barriers and unfair economic designs that allowed too many to be left behind. To the extent that economic growth and social inclusion are not mutually exclusive, interventions targeted at building a more inclusive economy must be centered on equity and economic mobility.

Healing the economic and social wounds inflicted by the pandemic will take time, but the long road to recovery presents a unique opportunity for regional business leaders, policymakers, civil society, and other key stakeholders to build back better. While accelerated vaccine development in the advanced and emerging economies offered a glimmer of hope for a quick recovery, new and emerging negative byproducts of the pandemic (e.g., supply-chain disruptions, labor market imbalances, and rising inflationary pressures) are prolonging the crisis, in addition to undermining recovery efforts. In the global context, unequal access to COVID-19 vaccines in low- and lower-middle income countries remains a major challenge.

To catalyze change and succeed in the post-pandemic era, economic development policy and practice must see the crisis as an opportunity to rethink and redesign regional economic systems. Among others, this will involve creating a shared understanding of, and policies to address, the differential impacts of the pandemic across occupations, industries, and socioeconomic groups.

To the extent that it is only a matter of when – and not if – the next crisis will happen, rethinking how existing economic development tools, frameworks, and practices can be optimized has never been more compelling. Even so, there will be no easy solutions; special attention must be given to interventions capable of accelerating desirable trends that are likely to shape the next normal. This is the preoccupation of this book. The various chapters present deductive arguments for deploying cutting-edge solutions, mobilizing resources, and engaging key stakeholders on the road to building a more inclusive, equitable, resilient, and sustainable economy.

The book is divided into four parts. The introduction sets the pace with contemporary discussion on the COVID-19 pandemic, regional economic systems, and the economic redesign imperative. Part II discusses the challenges and opportunities heralded by the virus in the broadest sense – with emphasis on occupational identity and economic mobility, regional responses, and the misunderstood role of population density. Part III examines several case studies and their associated pros and cons for equitable and inclusive economic recoveries vis-à-vis childcare provision, gender equality, and the future of work debate. An unprecedented reallocation of labor and capital in favor of industries that will thrive in the post-pandemic economy is expected in the coming years; it is therefore important to choose long-term recovery strategies carefully. The implications for regional innovation ecosystems in areas such as clusters, remote work, neighborhood infrastructure, the visitor economy, sustainable value creation, and the ocean economy are unpacked in Part IV. A summary of the different chapters is provided below.

THE CHAPTERS

In Chapter 2, Jaclyn Kelly and Anindya Kundu argue that underrepresented college students continue to navigate the unforeseen adversities of the COVID-19 pandemic – ones that exacerbate the inequalities that minority and low-income populations routinely contend with. Using both qualitative data from underrepresented young people as well as a comparison of current and past employer demand data, the authors provide new insight into the economic challenges and opportunities that are these young people's realities. To envision and subsequently achieve a more inclusive and healthy economy for all requires not only examining how the labor market is evolving but also including the perspectives of young people who are going through important college and career transitions during COVID-19, especially as they prepare to enter the workforce. Kelly and Kundu opine that learning from such young people's experiences is critical to better understanding the varied impacts of the pandemic and how to address them as we work toward a pathway to recovery. It is intended that this informs actionable, cross-sector recommendations for improving the conditions that lead to positive college and early career outcomes for young people who experience various structural obstacles, particularly those in urban settings like New York City, where the research was conducted.

Due to its geographic isolation, New Zealand adopted an elimination strategy in response to the pandemic. In Chapter 3, David Wilson, Patrick McVeigh, and Harvey Brookes unpack the myriad of reasons why in spite of the relative effectiveness of New Zealand's elimination strategy in reducing transmission, it has not been without risk, unintended consequences, and social and economic costs for the geographically isolated trading nation. The authors examine New Zealand's health and macroeconomic policies, spatial, structural and regional effects in the context of the pandemic, with five broad conclusions. First, the benefits of geographic isolation, seasonal variance, and economic structure provided time to plan and respond; second, high trust in government and health advice; third, a strong fiscal response; fourth, bespoke regional planning; and fifth, tension between "building back better" and rebuilding the economy. Wilson, McVeigh, and Brookes conclude that there have been unintended sectoral and structural economic effects due to heavy quantitative easing, but this has dampened negative effects overall.

How, and why, did population density become the *urban* culprit for the *transmission* of the *coronavirus*? Conventional wisdom simplifies the relationship between an area's population density and infectious diseases down to the following: higher population density means higher cases. In Chapter 4, Yu Zhong and Bertrand Teirlinck challenge the layman's theory of COVID-19 transmission and argue that density matters, but not that much. Using New York City data, the authors find that population density does not appear to play a critical role in the spread of the virus, contrary to widely shared belief. In addition to borough- and neighborhood-level correlation analyses associating higher population density with lower case incidence, Zhong and Teirlinck provide further insights into how international and domestic connections, timing, crowding, and socioeconomic background constitute the major drivers of an area's case incidence. They conclude that density has been more beneficial than harmful to New York City during the COVID-19 pandemic.

Why are we still talking about "gender equality as an economic imperative" in 2021? Maximizing female workforce participation is not just a moral imperative; it is smart economics. In Chapter 5, Bernadette Fernandes and Herb Emery make a case for gender equality in the post-COVID economy and society. The authors contend that to the extent that COVID-19's impacts on labor markets and the economy disproportionately impacted women, a resumption of pre-COVID-19 "business as usual" for the economy will fail any aspirations we may have for gender equality in society. Fernandes and Emery argue that the challenge of the pandemic should not be about returning to the pre-pandemic normal. COVID-19 laid bare the fragile base on which apparent economic and political gains for women were based. The most important lesson from the pandemic with respect to how we can "build back better" is to leverage the awareness of changes needed for greater economic inclusion leading to purposeful design of economic and social policies needed to achieve gender equality.

Pre-pandemic, working mothers already faced lower average wages than working fathers and non-parents, and already shouldered the burden of family caregiving responsibilities. The pandemic only exacerbated the childcare crisis; it did not create it. Leveraging a novel dataset by Upfront augmented with publicly available datasets to calculate demand–supply gaps in childcare provision in New York City, in Chapter 6, Melissa Pumphrey and Poorvi Goel analyze the impact of COVID-19 on the childcare market. The authors find stark disparities of access in center-based care for children under three, with more access concentrated in wealthier neighborhoods and greater prevalence of home-based care in less affluent areas. Pumphrey and Goel examine market failure sources in childcare provision, along with industry challenges. The channels through which the dual impacts of COVID-19 and caretaking responsibilities impact families, as well as the associated impacts on businesses, tax revenues, and the path of economic recovery are succinctly captured.

In Chapter 7, Swati Ghosh and Louise Anderson revisit the future of work discourse, albeit in an inclusive workforce development context. The authors explore trends in employment, automation, and their impacts on communities of color, and then highlight strategies in which economic development organizations (EDOs) in Dallas and Minneapolis-St. Paul are helping workers prepare for and connect to higher-skill, in-demand jobs. Triggered by the pandemic, Ghosh and Anderson opine that workforce trends in automation and digitalization will continue to eliminate low-skill jobs – and as this happens, displaced workers, who are overrepresented by people of color, increasingly need digital skills to get the good jobs of today and the future. They conclude with four suggestions for EDOs interested in advancing the workforce development efforts discussed: actively seek opportunities to address the needs of workers of color; prioritize existing regional demand for workers, with an eye on future demand; foster greater engagement between education/training providers and businesses; and promote the value of investing in a diverse workforce to regional businesses.

The labor theory of value has deep roots in both classical, free-market economics and traditional Marxism. In the neoclassical tradition, labor's marginal productivity and the price of its output are the key determinants of the *demand for labor*. Though largely theoretical, this has implications for labor access. The cyclicality of the labor share of output, especially following a recession, has received considerable attention in the literature. Among others, uncertainty and structural factors perpetuate wage depression in the aftermath of a recession. Contemporary evidence on the labor market effects of the pandemic, based on changes in labor costs, shows that low-wage, essential workers are worse off. In Chapter 8, Jeffrey Dykes, Billy Leung, and Fred Olayele examine the effect of decreased labor access resulting from fewer employees being available for in-person work, based on the unique industry makeup of the region in which work is located. Based on simulations in which each industry is assigned an Effective Potential – which ranks how well workers in a particular industry can perform tasks remotely – the authors derive a Labor Access Index policy variable which estimates the effect of access to labor choice and individual characteristics by occupation and industry on labor productivity. Since it has the greatest ability for workers to perform functions remotely, Dykes, Leung, and Olayele find that the finance and insurance industry experiences the smallest decrease in labor access at 24 percent, while the accommodation and food services industry witnesses the largest decrease at 92 percent. The implications of the results for policy are discussed, in the context of creating a more equitable labor market that unlocks the potential of more segments of society – especially historically marginalized demographics.

The history of government's impact at the neighborhood level is mixed, with the legacies of redlining, location selection for major highways, and discriminatory lending still visible today. In Chapter 9, Kyle Marks and Joyce Jauer argue that governments can use infrastructure and services to address inequalities and injustices through equitable provision of public transit, public parks, public libraries, and broadband infrastructure – which are vital tools for creating cities in which ZIP codes do not determine residents' economic outcomes. The authors advance the Critical Infrastructure and Services (CIS) framework to understand urban vulnerability through a neighborhood lens. By creating a single index value based on a weighted average of vulnerability across 12 variables, Marks and Jauer offer insights into which neighborhoods are most vulnerable through the lens of the CIS domain. They find that lower CIS vulnerability at a neighborhood level is associated with higher rates of air pollution, a higher share of the population age 25–39, and a higher share of the population born in a U.S. state other than New York. Through these and other findings, the implications for economic development policy, in the context of key demographic, environmental, and investment variables, are discussed.

In Chapter 10, Ifor Ffowcs-Williams cautions that building regional economies demands a focused approach, especially after external shocks such as COVID-19. To the extent that sectors and their businesses are not equal in terms of transformational potential, a starting point is within the traded side of a region's economy. The author explores how cluster development initiatives across Europe, and globally, have been able to assist businesses in responding with urgency to the pandemic – along with how resilient initiatives pivot to other challenges, addressing equitable growth, the circular economy, digitalization, evolving technologies and markets. Broad portfolios of needs-driven projects are the cluster initiatives' engine room, and resilient initiatives focus on endogenous growth, with investment attraction as a fill in. Ffowcs-Williams explains the roles of clusters as enablers and platforms, how resilient organizations integrate a clutter of piecemeal support from government agencies and academic institutions, and the nuances of facilitating change from agglomeration clumps to a co-opetition culture amongst businesses. Forward agendas include addressing critical issues with mission-type collaboration are covered, in the context of developing resilient clustering initiatives.

Prior to the advent of COVID-19, high profile destinations were more concerned about overtourism and the impacts on destinations and quality of life. The pandemic has fully exposed the fragility of the global visitor economy, and the dependence countries have placed on deriving benefits from tourism industry investments. In Chapter 11, Fergus Maclaren and Bartomeu Deya Canals explore the concept of sustainable tourism, its emergence and application over the past 30 years, and the new focus of the global tourism sector on a tandem recovery approach of sustainability and resilience. The authors argue that many popular destinations had been suffering under the weight of "overtourism," impacting local environments and quality of life, while also causing economic leakage to external businesses. A key example of this is Mallorca, a popular mass tourism destination which was being overwhelmed by visitors and was moving toward more high value and low impact forms of tourism. The pandemic accelerated these sustainable tourism initiatives and the Mallorcan response can serve as a useful case study for destinations trying to evolve and become more resilient in response to socioeconomic, environmental, and cultural challenges. Maclaren and Canals support practices and policies that foster a more sustainable and resilient visitor economy which balances out its risk exposure to tourism, while branching out into other sectors such as agriculture, traditional crafts, and longer-term experiences.

In Chapter 12, Fred Olayele underscores the innovation imperative for sustainable value creation in Canada's ocean economy. The ocean innovation economy cuts across many sectors and derives its primary value from digital technologies, the availability of top talent, startup and growth capital, intellectual capital, creativity, the presence of large firms, and a robust ecosystem that can connect startups to programs and funds for expansion. With abundant ocean resources and deep capabilities, Canada is a global leader in coastal and marine sciences, technology, and innovation. While this presents a huge opportunity, both commercially and in terms of its ability to influence the new global political economy, its lackluster performance on labor productivity growth in the last two decades, compared to its southern neighbor, remains a source of concern. Olayele argues that insofar as much of this lagging performance is due to sub-par innovation outcomes, mainly due to multifactor productivity gap, the case for deepening Canada's innovation economy by bringing together industry, research, investors, government, and Indigenous stakeholders remains compelling. This model underpins the Canadian innovation superclusters, anchored on robust private-public partnerships, with transaction costs at the core of the institutional design. This chapter explores these issues and draws lessons for policy and business modernization vis-à-vis unlocking value in the marine economy.

PART II

Occupational identity, regional responses, and population density

2. Striving despite disruption: young people's occupational identity and economic opportunity during COVID-19

Jaclyn Kelly and Anindya Kundu

2.1 CONTEXTUAL BACKGROUND, PROBLEM STATEMENT, AND MOTIVATIONS

A significant number of college students today represent groups that have been historically underrepresented in postsecondary education. They come from socially and economically challenged backgrounds while also embodying a number of additional identities: many are members of racial minorities, immigrants, and first-generation college attendees who are older than the traditional college student's age of late teens to early twenties. Predominantly, such students attend two-year college institutions, or community colleges, as stepping-stones on their way to obtaining bachelor's degrees or entry into their early career experiences. Though community colleges receive these diverse groups of students with open arms, a number of institutional barriers and programmatic limitations still exist, which can constitute obstacles for young people on their way to academic and professional success.

During the COVID-19 pandemic, when colleges and universities have had to abruptly shift to online learning—sometimes multiple times—faculty, staff, and student relationships have been disrupted, and student support and administrative services have struggled to engage and scaffold students at pre-pandemic levels. At the same time, the students, who already experience forms of marginalization, have shouldered additional immense financial, familial, and social burdens. The problem that we address in this chapter is as follows: the structural challenges that underrepresented young people contend with have been further exacerbated by the COVID-19 pandemic. Achieving fuller economic recovery requires intentionally including strategies that support these populations in their aspirations to succeed in higher education and the workforce. In order to realize what these supports may be, we must

10

include the perspectives and expertise of young people themselves as a complement to other more traditional ways of understanding the labor market; for example, through the lens of employer priorities and hiring trends.

Our goal in this chapter is to achieve a better understanding of the varied impacts of the COVID-19 crisis on young people and to contribute to addressing these pressing issues of educational and economic inequality. We conducted independent, mixed-methods research, assessing both qualitative data and aggregate overviews of employer demand. The results of this research include a number of actionable recommendations for postsecondary institutions to consider that we believe may substantially improve the college and early career outcomes of underrepresented young people, such as (1) bolstering structured student advising and offering more—and more-integrated—work-based learning opportunities; (2) facilitating stronger relationships between faculty, staff, and students while providing more wraparound and mental health resources; and (3) leveraging labor market data to help inform overarching programmatic and curricula decisions, but also commit to making labor market data accessible to students and an explicit part of their career planning process. These changes will go a long way toward improving educational and economic inclusivity for all.

The year 2020 shined a glaring spotlight on persistent racial and class-based inequities as the COVID-19 pandemic had a greater, disproportionate impact on marginalized communities. In particular, young people from minority and low-income backgrounds are largely underrepresented across the board in postsecondary and workforce settings, environments that are most closely tied to attainment social and economic stability. This lack of inclusion is a systemic and social justice issue that reflects deeply rooted opportunity gaps and became increasingly prominent during the initial phase of the COVID-19 pandemic in the United States. Such gaps are of consequence to more than young people's eventual educational and financial stability; they also impact their access to quality healthcare, social services, housing options, and ways of breaking cycles of intergenerational poverty (Blankstein, Noguera, & Kelly, 2016; Chetty et al., 2018; Jack, 2019; Kundu, 2020).

There is more we can and must do to create equitable environments and policies that promote the educational and workforce participation of these young people. As researchers, we were driven by a desire to highlight how these historically connected disadvantages are being experienced firsthand by young people in current times surrounding COVID-19 and to provide some hope during an otherwise bleak juncture in history. Through mixed-methods approaches, in this chapter we examine how students are confronting issues related to striving for academic and professional mobility and financial stability as well as potential ways to address and alleviate structural obstacles.

This investigation advances the field's current understanding of college and career transitions by providing (1) deeper insight on the types of multifaceted, complex challenges that surround the educational and professional journeys of young people who are navigating both systemic and institutional barriers as well as the challenges presented by the COVID-19 pandemic; (2) background on what matters to underrepresented young people as they develop their occupational identities and workforce training in these times; (3) insight into the opportunity gaps and barriers in the labor market, pre- and during COVID-19 in the United States; (4) a way to position young people who experience marginalization within an asset-based framework that highlights their unique perspectives, strengths, and potential contributions to institutions of higher education and workforce settings; and (5) recommendations on the supports that can aid underrepresented students in their college and career transitions and approaches for creating a more inclusive school-to-work pipeline, particularly in the aftermath of COVID-19.

Section 2.2 of this chapter describes some of the routine and structural challenges encountered by underrepresented college students working to improve their academic and professional trajectories, as well as how these are exacerbated in the climate of the pandemic. In section 2.3, we discuss challenges experienced by these young people related to securing work experiences and opportunities while also presenting analyses of employer demand, pre- and during COVID-19. Section 2.4 focuses on mediating factors and strategies for confronting structural obstacles and provides recommendations based on our data analyses for creating more inclusive pathways to mobility, again leveraging both the voices of community college students and labor market data. We believe this design provides a more complete picture as our qualitative research personalizes some of the aggregate employer-demand-based overviews through the much-needed perspectives of underrepresented young people. We also include relevant background literature throughout these sections to ground our research in the existing literature on the social and economic mobility of young people who face unique challenges and overcome them.

Guiding Research Questions, Setting, and the Young People Who Provided Voice

Some of the questions that guided the design of this research include:

- In their own words, how are underrepresented young people dealing with the impacts of COVID-19 and how has the pandemic affected their college and career experiences and goals?

- In their own words, what are the resources and support systems that are most helpful to underrepresented young people as they contend with and navigate the routine structural challenges they encounter as they strive for success in college and career?
- What do employment prospects and earnings look like for associate's degree holders compared to bachelor's degree holders, and has this shifted during the two years of COVID-19?
- What skills and credentials seem most "transferrable" and desired by employers across industries and are therefore most valuable to young people striving to climb different career pathways?
- In general, what are some of the various roles that community colleges can play as these individuals strive toward economic stability and social mobility, and how can higher education institutions support students with diverse needs?

Our qualitative research included interviews with young people who are representative of the population whose outcomes we examine at large. Specifically, our sample includes nine young people, five women and four men, between 21 and 28 years old. They represent a period of life often referred to as emerging adulthood—a promising yet critical stage when young people are still experiencing formative brain development, establishing critical relationships and social networks, and, of course, beginning to explore various life possibilities through key decisions (Hochberg & Konner, 2020).

Our participants are all persons of color, with six of the nine being immigrants coming from home countries such as Ghana, Haiti, Nigeria, the Philippines, and Myanmar. They are also all first-generation, or first-in-their-family, college attendees in the U.S. higher education system who also each come from low-income backgrounds. We believe including these perspectives is of utmost importance to presenting research that can influence practice and policy. The vantage points of underrepresented young people provide a necessary contextual background to our employer demand analyses, which examine trends over time but lack the narrative of how young people experience such phenomena themselves. To the goal of respecting their authority and identity in matters about them, these individuals were invited to choose their own aliases, which represent them throughout this chapter (for more detail regarding this project's methodology please see Appendix A).

Community colleges are a primary focal point of our research. Each of our participants attended a City University of New York (CUNY) junior college to earn their associate's degree, and eight of the nine have also gone on to obtain or pursue their bachelor's degree from a CUNY senior college.[1] In the United States, community colleges continue to be engines of mobility and stepping-stones for students who experience varied forms of marginalization.

At the same time, these institutions also directly reflect the challenges and constraints of their students, particularly during the resource-constrained period of economic contraction that has occurred during the COVID-19 pandemic in the United States. As such, community colleges present ideal environments for implementing targeted interventions that can promote greater economic opportunity for young people who embark on a journey toward college and career aspirations.

Specifically, the CUNY system provides an ideal setting for this research to identify what underrepresented students today need to thrive. CUNY is exemplary for demonstrating what inclusive, open-door admissions policies look like in higher education. The largest public urban university system in the United States, CUNY spans across 25 campuses throughout the five boroughs of New York City. When compared with national statistics, the CUNY university system openly welcomes, encourages, and admits a greater, disproportionately diverse body of students. In the fall semester of 2019, among CUNY senior colleges, 27 percent of students identified as White while 23 percent identified as Black, 26 percent as Hispanic, and 23 percent as Asian or Pacific Islander (CUNY Student Data Book, 2020). Among CUNY community colleges, minorities are even more prominently represented with 29 percent Black, 38 percent Hispanic, 17 percent Asian or Pacific Islander, and 15 percent students who identified as White. In other college institutions across the United States, the racial and ethnic composition of student populations is quite different, with less than half of students identifying as being a member of a minority group in the overall U.S. higher education landscape (National Center for Education Statistics, 2017).

CUNY's inclusion of diverse student populations also goes beyond racial categories. For 58 percent of senior college students, neither parent graduated from college, and this was the case for 65 percent of community college students (CUNY Student Data Book, 2020). And, in 2016, 42 percent of CUNY students lived in households that earned less than $20,000 in annual income, and 13 percent of CUNY students had dependents or supported children (Office of Institutional Research and Assessment, CUNY, 2018). All of the participants have contended with multiple, similar structural obstacles and responsibilities while navigating their studentship. They serve as examples that achieving in college and career often entails so much more than meeting standard benchmarks or expectations. We will elaborate more thoroughly on what confronting these multidimensional realities looks like in the sections that follow and how these challenges have been amplified or mitigated during the COVID-19 pandemic.

2.2   MULTIDIMENSIONAL STRUCTURAL DISADVANTAGES

Postsecondary Contexts and Challenges During COVID-19

In 2020, the New York City Department of Education (DOE) reported a 77.3 percent graduation rate for high school students across all boroughs (Algar, 2020). Yet, while graduation rates have increased over time in New York City (Farley, Stewart, & Kemple, 2022), there are still many shortcomings in how schools prepare underrepresented students for higher education and for the workforce. According to the College Readiness Index (CRI), only 35 percent of students are exceeding the target metrics and enrolling in postsecondary opportunities within 18 months of high school graduation (New York City Department of Education, 2020).

The National Center for Education Statistics (NCES) data reflect that overall, college enrollment among 18–24-year-olds has increased 5 percent over the last 17 years (Effiong, 2020). Yet the college enrollment for Black and Latinx young people between 18 and 24 still remains lower than for White students (Effiong, 2020), and when viewed in a more recent interval, it appears that Black student enrollment is dropping; compared to the 2014–15 school year, in 2019–20, we see that 200,000 fewer Black students enrolled in public colleges, which is close to a 9 percent drop in enrollment (CAP, 2020). As such, underrepresented, or "non-traditional," students within this group typically consist of those who are slightly older racial minorities, immigrants and international students, and first-generation college attendees. Though termed "underrepresented," this population of students remains sizeable and significant, with 46 percent of college students being first generation and 37 percent of students being older than 25 years of age (Lumina Foundation, 2019).

One of our research participants, "Sarina," a 24-year-old first-generation Filipina student, provided some of her own views about what factors might be responsible for such trends in decreased enrollment. She described feeling that current models of higher education, especially those implemented during the pandemic, might not resonate with students who have a deeper need to connect to the material while also dealing with a lot on their plate:

> Going back to school, that would be a hard "no" at the moment. … I feel so bad for students who are going through this right now … I'm not an expert at this obviously, but we've been sitting in classrooms for how long now, for how many decades, years, centuries? … I think learning has to be visceral in a way, because that way it kind of sticks to you more.

Students who face difficult decisions between prioritizing work or obtaining a postsecondary degree may feel that higher education is either outdated or unable to assist in providing the kinds of short-term reliefs that are needed in order to manage their multiple responsibilities at once. Students might be discouraged by newer approaches, such as distance learning, or be spread too thin among various commitments and obligations to take on college.

Community or junior colleges continue to be the primary entry points for many students into the world of higher education, though there are lingering challenges around how to best support students' success during matriculation. While the majority of Black and Latinx college students matriculate at community colleges, the majority do not complete their degrees on time (Anderson & Nieves, 2020). Junior college completion rates hover at approximately 36 percent and 28 percent for Black and Latinx students, respectively (Shapiro et al. 2018). Furthermore, in 2020, Black and Latinx students' completion rate of community college within six years declined. In fact, this six-year rate for graduation has dropped for all community college students despite showing previous growth. Today, less than 40 percent of junior college students receive a certificate or degree within six years of enrolling (Completing College, 2018). Across races, the graduation rate for two-year public colleges is about 39 percent (Anderson & Nieves, 2020; Shapiro et al., 2018), highlighting that community colleges are confronting a lot of different challenges. Though these figures could potentially call into question the effectiveness of junior colleges as a whole, there is more than meets the statistical eye as students often deal with an array of complex realities that require deeper attention.

For many underrepresented students, despite their actual abilities to achieve the standards of what is expected in college, they are routinely confronted with structural, institutional, and interpersonal barriers that make academic success much more challenging compared to others (Johnson & Joseph-Salisbury, 2018; Jack, 2019; Kundu, 2020; Waters, 2018). Beyond undermining academic success, feeling marginalized in these ways can also lead to adverse health outcomes for students whose confidence diminishes or who do not feel like they belong; mental health and wellness issues around the transition to college continue to be complex and below the surface. There is a strong correlation between the stress experienced during college and detrimental effects on immune system, sometimes culminating in the development of depression and anxiety over the long term (Fried & Irwin, 2016). "Carla" told a story about when she was the most depressed, and it felt like the many obstacles she faced were compounding:

> I ended up moving out of the [homeless] shelter. … That's when the struggle really started because I had to pay rent … The owners asked me to leave and I ended up staying at my friend's house for a couple of months. I was sleeping on her floor.

That's when I was in my deepest point. I started crying every day and I started regretting not taking school [more seriously] when I was first at the shelter. ... I didn't have the support system that I needed. ... When I was in my associate degree, I spent five years because I stopped going for a couple of years. And for two semesters, I even took classes, but I gave up and I did not take the final. I became very depressed.

Carla's story highlights the multidimensional nature of structural disadvantage that some students experience. She experienced housing instability and bouts of homelessness between the ages of 18 and 22. She was forced to navigate the extremely difficult tasks of figuring out where to live while also attempting to find her footing at school. Historically, the "traditional" college student did not have to contend with housing insecurity, financial struggles, and being a first-generation college student simultaneously. Often, these challenges may go unnoticed by staff and faculty, though these experiences place heavy pressures on the students who experience them. Recent research in psychology informs us that the allostatic load, or the aggregate amount of "wear and tear" the body takes due to natural responses to chronic stress, can be much higher for first- and second-generation college students of color who routinely experience multiple forms of discrimination and marginalization (Currie, Motz, & Copeland, 2020; Garsman, 2017). For students like Carla, dealing with such burdensome tolls can make finding one's footing in an unfamiliar higher education context exceedingly hard, if not impossible.

Educational Challenges Exacerbated by the COVID-19 Pandemic

The COVID-19 pandemic has disproportionately affected already marginalized communities and more adversely impacted the health of minorities and communities of color in the United States compared to White communities. According to the Centers for Disease Control and Prevention, approximately 22 percent of all positive COVID-19 cases were among African American groups and 34 percent were among Latinx populations, although they comprise only 13 percent and 18 percent of the national population, respectively. Additionally, 33 percent of hospitalizations were of African American patients (Centers for Disease Control and Prevention, 2020; Tai et al., 2020).

In the workforce, lower-income workers face more immediate and grave risks: whereas 31.4 percent of non-Hispanic Whites in the United States could work from home pre-pandemic, only 19.7 percent of African Americans were able to do the same, with even more striking differences for the numbers between low-wage and higher-wage workers, with higher-wage workers six times more likely to be able to work from home (Bureau of Labor Statistics, 2019). COVID-19 has only exacerbated this disparity. In New York City, three quarters of all essential workers are minorities, with more than half of them needing public transportation to commute to work (New York City Comptroller, 2020; Tai et al., 2020). For many of our research participants, these issues are close to home; they have held essential and frontline jobs (such as being a home health aide) or have family members who hold these positions.

These inequities in work are often mirrored in educational opportunities and settings. Students suffered as COVID-19 massively disrupted general learning routines around the globe. Roughly 1.6 billion learners were mandated to stay at home across 194 countries (UNESCO, n.d.). College students worldwide have been found to be preoccupied and worried about their career and professional prospects (Aristovnik et al., 2020). Researchers sampling 30,383 students across 62 countries reported that students experienced greater degrees of deteriorating mental health from anxiety, frustration, and depression while also feeling deficient in their computer literacy and unsure of their performance levels in the new online learning environment (Aristovnik et al., 2020). "Brianna" describes dealing with these changes in her own words, stating that she and other students are very aware of the constraints in education:

> I think the [way the] educational system is set up, they're not equipped to handle post-COVID. ... Online classes are a band-aid to learning. Some people do well in it, but I know for a fact there are a lot of students like me who hate online classes.

Brianna explained that many of her peers feel disengaged and unmotivated in these new online learning environments, where it feels much harder to form relationships with professors and classmates and absorb academic material. It stands to reason that COVID-19 is also more adversely affecting the already unpromising college completion rates for underrepresented students. "Cee," a 28-year-old recent junior college graduate, talked about his last semester of community college when the pandemic abruptly halted routines and posed a strong threat to his being able to graduate:

> I definitely wanted to give up because after a while, sitting down, my neck started to hurt. I started to get cranky. I didn't feel as motivated this spring ... [mind you], college got shut down. ... I started worrying about money and things like that. ... I'm actually grateful that I [completed] my degree, because I have a professor who let me know [that] a lot of my peers did not finish or made the attempt to drop out. ... People have to do what they have to do. You got to do what you got to do. I just told myself, I was just fortunate enough not to do anything like that.

Cee positions his own struggles as being more manageable than many of his peers', for whom the pressures of leaving school became too burdensome to ignore. He acknowledges that they simply may not have had any other options. "Idlia" elaborates on these stresses in her interview. When asked about how her college could improve or demonstrate a greater commitment to supporting students through these challenges, she replied:

> I guess they should be more lenient with payment plans or [finances]. Because I lost my job, right? And I paid for school out of pocket. And then, like, if it wasn't for my family savings, I wouldn't be able to afford my last semester and then that would have delayed my whole graduation.

For students who have immediate financial or familial strains, the ability to finish college might become nearly impossible. Planning around how to make college fit into a longer-term vision of professional success can become more of an abstract idea and a luxury they cannot afford. And beyond financial struggles, some of the most routine activities also became more cumbersome. "Arnel," a 23-year-old first-generation immigrant from the Philippines, described new hurdles to graduating on time:

> But the thing is that now everything has to be online. … You have to deal with the Registrar's Office a lot and they don't reply back to emails. Also, the Financial Aid Office. Everything is remote and I guess they were never prepared to for this change. And so now it's like, "God, I need to reach out to them and they're not replying." And everyone is going crazy.

Right before starting the last semester of his bachelor's program, Arnel realized he actually had to take two more classes than he had planned for, for a total of seven courses, in order to finish. If he had not closely read his degree audit, he might not have been as successful. For students like Arnel, who have to figure out course requirements as well as financial aid, sometimes the most basic processes can start to become more obscure and obstruct the path toward college completion. Yet Arnel also reminds us that the pandemic has been a crisis felt by everyone in higher education, including school staff, faculty, administrators, leadership, and, of course, students.

Aside from everything else, clearly the most drastic impact of the pandemic has been the loss of human life. Most of our research participants stated knowing someone or having a loved one—including parents, aunts and uncles, or siblings and friends—who were impacted by the coronavirus and were more directly affected. "Montana's" story was particularly sobering:

> I lost my father two months ago. That was a big blow because I couldn't … go back home. Being the only son, I had to make a … I would say it was a little bit emotional, but also very thoughtful decision in terms of, if we keep the body in the morgue and wait for me to come back. I don't know when this whole thing will be over for me to get back, so I told them to go ahead with the burial. … It's really sad for me because the last person I spoke to before leaving Ghana was my father. He told me, "Hey, you go out there. Whatever happens, make sure you get your education before you

come back." It was difficult because I was taking a full course load and some of the professors were not flexible. … I have to make sure my grades are good to be able to maintain my scholarship.

Montana's heartbreaking decision to miss his father's funeral seemed most practically necessary given everything he was juggling, but the trade-off was emotionally taxing. His story highlights the notion that navigating college entails so much more than simply meeting academic or professional benchmarks. For young people with multiple responsibilities and challenges, these periods and the decisions made within them are incredibly significant to their long-term identity formation—often they must press on despite setbacks or obstacles. Montana's father's passing raised structural constraints that the typical 26-year-old does not have to grapple with: having to maintain strong academic standing and a scholarship during a time of deep sadness and tension.

The widespread health and economic impacts of the pandemic have made achievement much more exhausting for many. As educational institutions continue to figure out their processes to make distance learning more effective and engaging, it is also important to look more deeply and acknowledge the many different realities that students who experience marginalization contend with. Though these are certainly stories of modern students' resilience, they also beg the additional question: What can colleges and universities do to better support diverse students, so they do not feel like they are facing a constant uphill battle in their basic pursuit of happiness, stability, and fulfilment? We shift our attention to answering this question in section 2.3.

2.3   CAREER ASPIRATIONS AND THE STATUS OF THE LABOR MARKET

Early Workforce Participation and Current Opportunity Barriers

In 2018 in New York City, between 117,000 and 136,000 young people, aged 16 to 24, were neither working nor in school (National League of Cities, 2018; The City of New York, 2021). This group is often referred to as "out of school, out of work" young people, or OSOW. Nationwide, one in seven youth are "disconnected" in this way from education and work—a combination that has grave implications for the stability of the future economy. And prior to COVID-19 making its way to U.S. shores, one out of eight New Yorkers between the ages of 16 and 24 were OSOW despite being an overall better educated group than a decade prior (The City of New York, 2021).

The long-term consequences of young people falling into OSOW purgatory are manifold, but one struggle faced by young people who do not receive the necessary supports to reengage school and complete at least a high school education will be the challenge of securing work that pays a living wage: $45,285 for a single adult with no children living in New York City.[2] The compounding financial benefits of achieving higher levels of education have remained present despite the disruption of COVID-19. As reflected in Figure 2.1, in New York City, advertised salaries for all educational-attainment groups dipped in 2020 from 2019 levels and rebounded to new highs in 2021 for the months of March through December.[3] Particularly striking though is how uniform the trend is across years and despite the exogenous shock of a pandemic—every successive increase in educational credentialing yields a higher average advertised wage. By contrast, the "rebound" of 2021 advertised wages surpassing those of 2019 and 2020, though present for all educational-attainment groups, varies significantly. As shown in Table 2.1, while associate's degree holders enjoyed the most pronounced percentage increase (13.72 percent), high school/vocational training advertised salaries increased less than 1 percent between 2019 and 2021, with the average advertised salary for this group falling several thousand dollars below a living wage for a single adult with no children in New York City ($40,000 versus $45,285). Both of these findings—advertised wages positively correlating with educational attainment and 2021 advertised wages surpassing those of 2019 and 2020 for all education groups but at an especially low percentage for high school/ vocational training holders—demonstrate the importance of supporting young people who are pursuing higher education credentials.

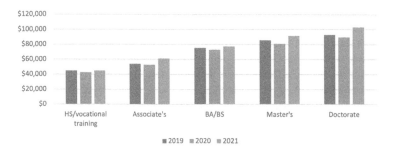

Figure 2.1   *Average New York City employer-advertised salaries by education level, March–December for years 2019–21*

*Table 2.1   Average salaries advertised in New York City-based job ads,
                 March–December, 2019–21*

Educational attainment	2019	2020	2021	% change 2019–21
HS/vocational training	$44,811	$42,747	$45,000	0.42
Associate's	$53,849	$52,783	$61,237	13.72
BA/BS	$75,368	$72,844	$77,274	2.53
Master's	$85,700	$80,975	$91,437	6.69
Doctorate	$93,030	$89,565	$102,868	10.58

There is also a growing education–workforce divide between high-skill and low-skill jobs. By 2024, 48 percent of all jobs in the United States will be "middle skill," meaning they require some level of postsecondary experience but not necessarily a four-year degree; however, there will be fewer Americans specifically trained for these positions than the demand for such workers (National Skills Coalition, 2015). Furthermore, jobs that were once attainable with high school credentials will likely demand some level of college experience and education (Selingo, 2017). Almost half of U.S. small businesses claim they are unable to locate the candidates with the right skills and talents needed for their open positions (Rampell, 2016). While percentage-wise employer demand for high school/vocational workers has bounced back more strongly than it has for workers with associate's or bachelor's degrees relative to 2019 demand, overall employers are more likely to be seeking a candidate with some level of postsecondary education for job openings in New York City (Table 2.2). These data suggest that, at least in large urban centers such as New York City, junior colleges should be not only preparing young people for jobs that are immediately accessible with an associate's degree but also equipping them with the learning skills and work-related experience to ultimately help them strive for bachelor's-level careers, thus giving them access to the most opportunities over their careers while also responding to the needs of the labor market.

Table 2.2   Number of job advertisements posted in New York City,

Educational attainment	2019	2020	2021
HS/vocational training	75,382	60,707	102,242
Associate's	31,947	23,186	36,668
BA/BS	316,894	205,160	310,300

Given the relatively high unemployment rate for young people, it is clear that the education and work-based training that young adults are receiving are out of date and misaligned to what is needed to succeed in a rapidly changing, global economy (Anderson & Kharem, 2010; Anderson & Nieves, 2020). Our research participants had a variety of perspectives on the status of the current labor market and their abilities to penetrate different industries. Brianna, who completed her associate's degree before obtaining her bachelor's, mentioned that she believes college students need more hands-on training to be adaptable to the needs of the workplace:

> Vocational courses would be a better option [for] a career right now than, I don't know, [having] an English major. Not that I'm dissing on that course at all. It just seems more practical to have a vocational course where you have a technical skill to offer ... that's not being done a lot these days ... it's easy to find people who have college degrees, but it's a lot harder to find people who have [those]technical vocational skills.

For colleges to be more (cost-)effective for students like her, Brianna suggests that they focus on providing technical skills foundations; otherwise they can leave graduates ill-prepared for success in the modern workforce. Brianna clarified that low-income students need to find employment—ideally something fulfilling with an upward trajectory—directly out of college. Whereas more privileged students can pursue a variety of broad interests, rely on their social networks and connections, and take their time, underrepresented students do not have these same luxuries. Brianna believes there is a place for vocational education to become more commonplace and desirable for students who seek to gain work experience in college.

Research findings in the education and career attainment fields substantiate Brianna's thinking that hands-on work experience for low-income students is linked to greater career opportunities. For example, the forecasted middle-skills jobs gap could be alleviated through junior college academic programming that is more directly reflective of workforce needs. As students develop transferable skills that translate between school and workplace settings, they become more valuable and less expendable (Gelber, Isen, & Kessler, 2016; Jacobs et al., 2017; Kemple & Willner, 2008). "Sarina" illustrated the concept by connecting it to her own experiences in school and work:

> Studying and [gaining] accounting [work experience] opened me up to a really stable job. Especially now, people don't always stay in the career that they set for themselves. They always change things, so I feel like I can at least enter a different field of study or industry and know that I have something to back myself on.

Sarina received an associate's degree in accounting at a CUNY junior college and her bachelor's in information systems and accounting at a CUNY senior college. She was also able to accumulate work experience, holding internships through CUNY Service Corps—a university program for community members to participate in social good initiatives—as a tax education associate, and she was a President's Society ambassador at her community college. Sarina is currently employed as a payroll administrator for a construction company at a Queens-based office, a job that she happily described as "highly stable" and "a blessing" during the pandemic. Interestingly, she stated that she was most proud of having developed a strong foundation of financial skills that she can fall back on and transfer across different industries if she someday chooses to explore her options in other lines of work.

Indeed, an analysis of the occupations most advertised for high school/ vocational, associate's-level, or bachelor's-level candidates in New York City reveals expected areas of divergence but also encouraging overlap among transferable workplace skills that employers most highly value (Table 2.3). Unsurprisingly, there was limited overlap in the occupations that were most frequently advertised to candidates of varying educational levels, though managers and sales representative opportunities were in the top 10 for all three groups (Table 2.4). However, overwhelming commonalities appeared when comparing the workplace skills that employers most often mentioned in job ads (Table 2.5, below). Across all three education groups, communication skills and Microsoft Office were the two most commonly mentioned desired skills by employers. "Organizational skills," "teamwork/collaboration," "detail-oriented," and "problem solving" also appear on all three groups' top-10 skills list. In fact, the only difference between the top skills most commonly cited in job ads for associate's-level candidates versus bachelor's-level candidates was "computer literacy" (#8 in job ads seeking associate's candidates) and "creativity" (#9 in job ads seeking bachelor's candidates). This significant overlap in priority skills presents an opportunity for community colleges to purposefully prepare their students by providing them access to settings such as work-based learning and internships. This will help students develop and practice the skills that can serve them in both the immediate and long term—upon graduation with their associate's degree or eventually for bachelor's-level jobs as well.

Table 2.3   Top-10 most frequent job ads by education level, New York City, March–December, 2021

HS/Vocational Training	Associate's	BA/BS
Security Guards	Registered Nurses	Managers, General
Customer Service Representatives	Secretaries and Administrative Assistants, General	Software Developers, Applications
Retail Salespersons	Customer Service Representatives	Computer Occupations, General
Secretaries and Administrative Assistants, General	Managers, General	Marketing Managers

HS/Vocational Training	Associate's	BA/BS
Medical Secretaries	Bookkeeping, Accounting, and Auditing Clerks	Sales Representatives, Wholesale and Manufacturing
Managers, General	Medical and Health Services Managers	Registered Nurses
Sales Representatives, Wholesale and Manufacturing	Human Resources Specialists	General and Operations Managers
Medical Assistants	Sales Representatives, Wholesale and Manufacturing	Financial Managers
First-Line Supervisors of Retail Sales Workers	Preschool Teachers, Except Special Education	Accountants and Auditors
Maintenance and Repair Workers, General	Computer User Support Specialists	Sales Managers

Table 2.4   Top-10 most frequently mentioned workplace skills in job ads by education level, New York City, March–December, 2021

HS/Vocational Training	Associate's	BA/BS
Communication Skills	Communication Skills	Communication Skills
Microsoft Office	Microsoft Office	Microsoft Office
Organizational Skills	Organizational Skills	Teamwork/Collaboration
Computer Literacy	Teamwork/Collaboration	Detail-Oriented
Physical Abilities	Detail-Oriented	Organizational Skills
Detail-Oriented	Problem Solving	Planning
Teamwork/Collaboration	Planning	Problem Solving
English	Computer Literacy	Research
Multitasking	Research	Creativity
Problem Solving	Writing	Writing

One study found that when students work part-time while in college (up to 15 hours a week), they develop the much-needed soft skills, such as time management and communication skills, to thrive later on in industry settings (Carnevale & Smith, 2018). Working more than 15 hours a week, however, can obstruct academic goals, implying that students need the built-in academic support to be able to take on and thrive in multiple roles. Carla described how she overcame her college-career limbo and depression while being housing insecure. She tells a story about a turning point when a friend insisted that she look into a specific type of work:

> My friend had advised me to take a job as a Home Health Aide. … I started being serious. … After two weeks, I finished the [Health Aide] course and I got a job.

After that, it has just been great. After I graduated from [CUNY Community College], I don't know how to explain it—it was very fulfilling because I finally did it. Because I started in 2013 and it was supposed to be two years. After that, I was like, "Nobody's going to stop me. I'm not going to waste my time. I'm not going to waste my life anymore." I started to take school seriously again, because school has always been my passion.

Finishing the home health aide certification sparked a chain of positive events in Carla's life. In time, the stable income from the occupation allowed her to find housing and get on her feet to go back to school. It remains a formative moment of immense pride and reassurance for her that she could accomplish what she set out to.

Carla gained the confidence to keep striving and continue her education straight through, despite the previous turbulence she experienced in early stages of community college. She started developing positive academic and occupational identities that were aligned with one another. After completing her associate's degree in business administration and management from a CUNY junior college, she went on to start and complete her BSc in health services and administration at a CUNY senior college. Her job as a home health aide, which she still holds part-time, helped Carla realize a passion for the field of healthcare. Today she is a master's candidate in the CUNY Graduate School of Public Health & Health Policy. Her story is a testament to the transformative power of career and educational opportunities being simultaneously available for young people.

Like Carla, many underrepresented young people are attending colleges and also seeking meaningful early work experiences with hopes of overcoming intergenerational poverty. At the same time, these students often manage multiple responsibilities and confront routine challenges simply to make ends meet. These burdens can be too heavy to shoulder by themselves. We turn now to considering some of the many potential options and policies that can be implemented in order to support them.

2.4   TOWARD MEDIATING FACTORS AND SOLUTIONS THAT PROMOTE EQUITY

Recommendations #1 & #2: Community colleges should bolster and provide hands-on academic and career advising followed by direct work-based learning programming. Relatedly, they should seek to leverage labor market data to inform programmatic and curricula decisions as well as commit to making labor market data accessible to students as part of their career planning process.

Our research participants have provided strong examples on how life changing it is when young people develop strong connections between their academics and career goals. There are many beneficial services junior colleges can provide to help students form deeper alignment between school and work. However, even more fundamental than community colleges' direct efforts toward building more career-focused programming, there are resources needed around providing more routine and structured advising. Most research participants mentioned having to largely self-advocate in order to learn and meet the requirements for graduation. Arnel, who needed to take seven classes in his last semester, said:

> I know they can't really scale it, the ratio of advisers to students … but I think that's the only downside of being in the CUNY system is that I have to navigate myself through. … I just want to graduate. … For instance, I was not aware of [not having enough credits] until I closely read my degree audit. [We need] more visible notifications, more systems established to see that, "Hey Arnel, this is an email saying [what] you still need to do," or, "We have a menu for your courses." I think just those [supports] will help tremendously.

The systematized advising Arnel describes is often offered at other college institutions and is especially needed at universities like CUNY where students balance a variety of simultaneous responsibilities in addition to attending school. Restructuring and providing extra advising resources can go a long way toward improving the college completion outcomes that predicate occupational attainment and success.

After ensuring that students are supported to achieve academically, community colleges should strive to offer and integrate more workforce-centric learning opportunities so that students can develop their academic and professional identities concurrently. One way that this can be accomplished is through helping students learn the ins and outs of locating and applying for jobs. Idlia described these kinds of helpful supports that were available at her community college:

> I learned through the school because they have different seminars on how to improve your resume, cover letter, and stuff like that. And they also tell me how to create my own online portfolio. I've always been current, thanks to the school. But I feel like I don't think there's enough resources online. They do teach you how to do your resume and cover letter, but sometimes we're all in different levels and the sample that you might get online might not [be] what you need. For example, you might get a resume for … for someone who has a career [already] … even though you're a college student and then you might hold back because you think that you need all those experiences to get a job.

Idlia praised these career programming resources but also lamented that they were not sufficiently tailored for specific student groups, each with different educational levels and work experiences. Though it is critical that students form a baseline understanding of what their occupational prospects could look like broadly, it is also useful for them to have access to more specific occupational trajectories to map their individual goals. These resources would allow students to develop both ambitious and accessible goals rooted in the realities of the labor market. In addition to providing general application support with resumes and cover letters, colleges should look to offer more targeted interventions such as job shadowing opportunities, career fairs, and webinars that highlight emerging occupations. Colleges could also leverage recent alumni connections to volunteer time and information to current students.

Many students and young people already do perceive school and work as related and consider both to be important to their well-being as well as to their formulation of self-identity, which positively correlates with academic performance, aspirations, and future earnings potential (Nieves, 2016; Anderson & Nieves, 2020). Though many college-going students, especially those from lower-income backgrounds, are already working out of financial necessity, there are class disparities in the types of early career experiences that are currently accessible to young people. "Henry" described how his academic interests were shaped by emerging economic trends he observed:

> I finished Bronx Community College in 2018 with my associate's degree. Currently I'm at CUNY Baruch College. I'm also continuing in the same program, Computer Information Systems, but now I'm focusing on cyber security. ... I was glad that this is a major that I'm doing. ... If you look at with the world we live in ... the future, the next generation ... everything's going to be technology. ... I think maybe for [a] masters, I'm going to probably do Health Information Systems, combining health with information systems.

Henry's recognition that the tech and healthcare industries are continuing to boom despite the pandemic led to his desire to go into a health-tech hybrid field. He is hopeful that his CUNY degrees and credentials will directly translate to work when he is job seeking after he graduates and that the pandemic's effects have started to lighten.

If more students are offered explicit opportunities to develop a baseline understanding of the economic landscape and in-demand industries, it can immediately impact their studies. Students would benefit from novel extracurricular resources such as labor market webinars and career coaching services. If these programs are reflective of economic circumstances and labor market realities, students can conceptualize more clearly how college can set them up for success in engaging, stable, and lucrative careers.

Additionally, when educational settings incorporate industry knowledge and work experiences into their curricula models, students learn how to better advocate for themselves professionally and integrate into professional environments, learning important things that all workers should know, such as acceptable working conditions and their protections (Booth, Budd, & Munday, 2010; Richey, 2014) and becoming more competitive applicants once they do seek to join the workforce. Recent New York City job ads suggest that while minimal professional experience is necessary for openings seeking candidates with a high school/vocational or associate's degree, employers hiring bachelor's-level workers are more likely to seek someone with several years of experience. As reflected in Table 2.5, almost two thirds of New York City-based job ads seeking high school/vocational or associate's-level workers indicated that zero to two years of job experience was desirable (66.7 percent and 60.7 percent, respectively) while that was only true for 30 percent of job ads seeking bachelor's-level candidates. By contrast, the most common years of experience employers were seeking for bachelor's-level candidates was three to five years (45 percent). By integrating work-based learning as a core component of preparing their students for success, junior colleges can help young people be more confident in their eventual career and also more likely to secure employment, particularly if they ultimately pursue a four-year degree.

Table 2.5   *Percentage of years' experience requested in New York City job ads by level of educational attainment, March–December, 2021*

Educational attainment	0–2 years	3–5 years	6–8 years	9+ years
HS/vocational training	66.70%	28.00%	3.50%	1.80%
Associate's	60.70%	31.10%	4.40%	3.80%
BA/BS	30.00%	45.00%	14.40%	10.60%

Recommendation #3: Community colleges should foster stronger relationships between staff and students and offer more accessible wraparound and mental health services.

The participants of this research also overwhelmingly credited their mentors throughout CUNY as influential in their ability to succeed academically and professionally. For young people navigating various structural and institutional barriers, such interpersonal relationships can be vital in helping them find their place in new environments. "Chu" is a 27-year-old who attended LaGuardia Community College and Queens College for her associate's and bachelor's degrees. She traveled to New York City from Myanmar on an immigration lottery system and credits her CUNY mentors as the most valuable influence in adjusting. She said:

> That's why I have affection for CUNY and the public school system in general because professors do care and now I'm in a huge public [university] in Colorado. I would say because it's more "American," but I had a culture shock when I moved [here] … I still write emails to [my CUNY professors]. I still write postcards to [them] because they are like my family here because I don't have close family in the U.S. … One professor taught English 101 and I remember visiting her office hours and [though] everybody was scared of her she told me … "You have a really interesting story. I can see you as writing a book in the future." It still [sticks] with me.

Positive reinforcement and support from her professors helped Chu develop greater motivation and confidence to form and achieve specific career goals. Even though she struggled with English, she remained a strong student. Given her interests, faculty encouraged her to apply to a doctoral program at CUNY, allowing Chu to go on to pursue her PhD in Colorado.

Montana, who lost his father in 2020, relayed similar sentiments when speaking about the Bronx Community College (BCC) community at large. He echoed the idea that staff at BCC felt like a family to him:

> Anytime I talk about Bronx Community College, I get super passionate … everybody there was like a family to me. I had days where public safety [officers] would open the gates for me to come to school early as 5:00 a.m. to go nap in the library … the ladies who work in the cafeteria, [when] I didn't have money, they literally would give me food or some leftovers from the cafeteria to eat. Sometimes the lady would be like, "Montana, come sit us for lunch," and I would go and have a whole lunch without paying. They told me, "Montana you're going to be great. … It's going to work." Having people like that who don't even know everything about your story tell you that you're going to be great means a lot. It became a fuel. … Regardless of what was going on, I went to school on time, did my homework, took a lot of honors classes … I wanted to tap into this academic journey. I always fall back on my community college experience, the people I met, from public safety to the college president … played a part in my life.

The BCC staff helped Montana in a way that went beyond academic support. These adults noticed the various nonacademic obstacles that Montana faced on a regular basis—including food and housing insecurity—and used the resources they had at hand to help this young man find stability. Supporting people in such a holistic manner, one that acknowledges and then addresses nonacademic barriers, has often been referred to as providing "wraparound" services (Hill, 2020). Wraparound services have been effective at helping students succeed academically and professionally, as well as improving socioemotional well-being. For Montana, the kindness and encouragement from CUNY staff boosted his academic performance and drive. He often looks back on these experiences as motivating and reinforcing factors as he strives to complete his bachelor's degree at an Ivy League institution.

To be most effective, wraparound services need to be formally and systematically available to students. Sarina said she was "amazed" by the resources offered at her community college, including day cares for student parents, numerous scholarships without strict grade requirements, and tutoring services for students to help other students. For Sarina, some of the most important services were around mental health. She described feeling overwhelmed in her early days at community college while she juggled a full course load, a job, and extracurricular activities:

> I had literal breakdowns. I would go into the bathroom stall and cry for five minutes like nothing happened. One day I was hyperventilating on the seven train, so then I [admitted], "I need help." Funny enough, I got off [the train] and at the [campus] common area they had a booth for mental health services offered for free. I don't know if it was a coincidence but I immediately [signed up]. I would tell other students I go to counseling sessions and they were so surprised, but they also become interested in those services so I would talk openly about it to anyone who would listen. ... I think as an immigrant it is hard to accept you need help. Our mantra in life is to "power through."

For many college students, and especially for those who are underrepresented like first-generation or immigrant students, using mental health resources can carry a negative stigma. It is important that junior colleges not only widely promote their wellness resources, but do so using marketing and language that prompts students to not feel ashamed when accessing them. As students develop positive wellness practices, they can improve their academic outcomes while lessening the allostatic load they take on, improving their health in the long term. If junior colleges can create environments that facilitate forming stronger relationships between faculty and staff and students while continuously offering wraparound services, college performance and completion outcomes can improve for students with diverse needs.

2.5 CONCLUSION: PROGRESS AFTER COVID REQUIRES INTENTIONALLY IMPROVING CONDITIONS FOR YOUNG PEOPLE TO THRIVE IN COLLEGE INTO CAREER

Promoting more equity in higher education and the labor market for underrepresented young people is necessary to achieve social and economic progress. There is too much at stake to leave such large pools of diverse talent untapped. By creating conditions conducive for college students and early career professionals to thrive, we essentially work to build more cohesive communities and a prosperous future for all. Carla puts this into perspective, by stating her deeper motivations behind pursuing a healthcare career:

> I don't have much experience in the public health field [yet], but wherever that leads me, I am okay with it as long as I feel like I'm involved with the community, doing something that could make a positive change. … Before I became homeless myself, I thought people *chose* to be homeless. I think I didn't have the understanding how the system works. … But learning and going to school, I learned that is not by choice. … Nobody wants to be outside in the cold, and nobody wants to sleep in the subway. It's because they don't have the resources.

Carla's commitment to civic duty and her desire to contribute back to her community directly stem from the struggles she experienced firsthand. Now, she wants to use her experiences and credentials to directly help other people lead improved, self-sufficient lives. Promoting the success of underrepresented young people requires acknowledging the varied backgrounds they come from in order to better understand their challenges and provide holistic supports. These efforts become investments toward creating a more inclusive society. Community colleges are ideally situated to implement more of these approaches as they are deeply knowledgeable regarding the evolving and multifaceted issues that their students face on a regular basis.

A primary takeaway from this chapter is that we must create more explicit bridges between higher education and the workforce, particularly leveraging the position of junior colleges. Of all college students, 64 percent are employed on some level, and students from low-income backgrounds make up 43 percent of all college students who work, yet they are also more likely to be working full-time in jobs unrelated to their academic aspirations (Carnevale & Smith, 2018; Lumina Foundation, 2020). This is an equity concern because these jobs do not typically put students on a path to social mobility and higher earnings but rather hinder their ability to complete college on time as they are spread too thin among various obligations and scarcities (Goldrick-Rab, 2016). These students often have to make difficult choices about their immediate financial obligations at the expense of laying the groundwork that will allow them to deliberately pursue a fulfilling career trajectory.

A more just system would reward students' diligence and work ethic so they do not have to make costly trade-offs between going to school or taking a job unconnected to a career pathway. Some specific recommendations for junior colleges around this goal include providing more structured and routine advising to students, increasing the likelihood that they can both complete their college requirements on time and also locate tailored work opportunities responsive to their goals; offering students labor market-focused resources such as webinars and networking opportunities, perhaps with alumni, giving them the necessary information to develop realistic and informed expectations for their careers; and enabling students to develop transferrable skills by incorporating work-based learning opportunities into existing college curricula.

Academically sponsored and encouraged employment has long-term benefits for junior college students who are transitioning into adulthood. In recent research, Anderson and Nieves (2020) find that "young people [display] a greater level of personal agency through their [work experiences]" (p. 86).[4] Promoting students' agency allows them to take more ownership over their educational and professional outcomes rather than being at the mercy of the structural disadvantages they encounter. By learning important skills such as effective verbal, written, and online communication; asking for help; and finding solutions to problems through their work experiences, students develop greater agency to thrive in college and career while developing an appetite and confidence for learning and self-improvement (Anderson & Nieves, 2020; Kundu, 2020). A greater sense of agency also benefits students by helping them develop more positive senses of self and improved mental health and wellness outcomes as well (Kundu, 2020).

Junior colleges can prioritize a school culture beneficial to agency through community-based and all-hands-on-deck approaches. Specifically, faculty and staff should feel empowered to form genuine relationships and connections with students; they should be encouraged to see nurturing students as a rewarding and critical part of their work. Colleges should foster these relationships through offering various and informal networking events that allow faculty and students to interact outside of the traditional classroom setting.

Ultimately, we must expand our notions of what effective higher education and early career pathways look like in order for them to be more inclusive. Especially in the wake of COVID-19, there is a greater obligation on institutions to get creative in order to be more engaging and useful to underrepresented students who take on a gauntlet of responsibilities and obligations while also striving for self-improvement and stability for their families. When education and workforce are responsive to these needs, young people can better visualize their future options and find alignment between their educational foundation and career trajectories.

We hope that this preliminary research has served to amplify often-excluded voices and elicit new perspectives on how to contend with structural challenges with a sense of hope and optimism for the future. Though the impacts of COVID-19 will likely be felt for years to come, if we can implement some changes to the educational system now, we ensure that young people will have a productive and positive role in the different phases of post-pandemic economic recovery by better integrating them into the workforce. This will provide them more opportunities to positively impact both their own future and that of society as a whole.

ACKNOWLEDGMENTS

The authors thank the inspiring young people who shared their time, perspectives, and insights with us for this research, JPMorgan Chase Foundation for their generous support of this work, and Jenn Bennett-Genthner for her copyediting prowess.

NOTES

1. The ninth participant is enrolled in an Ivy League institution for his undergraduate studies.
2. Massachusetts Institute of Technology's (MIT) Living Wage calculator, 2021 estimates for New York City.
3. See Appendix A, "Methodology," for a discussion of why this interval was used for each year's data set.
4. Agency theory refers to an individual's ability to understand their circumstances, navigate obstacles, and find and utilize resources in order to create positive change (Anderson & Nieves, 2020; Kundu, 2020).

REFERENCES

Algar, S. (2020, January16). NYC high school graduation rate increases to 77.3 percent. *New York Post*. https://nypost.com/2020/01/16/nyc-high-school-graduation-rate-increases-to-77-3-percent/.

Anderson, N. S., & Kharem, H. (2010). *Education as freedom: African American educational thought and activism*. Lexington Books.

Anderson, N. S., & Nieves, L. (2020). *Working to learn*. Springer.

Aristovnik, A., Keržič, D., Ravšelj, D., Tomaževič, N., & Umek, L. (2020). Impacts of the COVID-19 pandemic on life of higher education students: A global perspective. *Sustainability, 12*(20), 8438.

Blankstein, A. M., Noguera, P., & Kelly, L. (2016). Excellence through equity: Five principles of courageous leadership to guide achievement for every student. ASCD.

Booth, J. E., Budd, J. W., & Munday, K. M. (2010). Never say never? Uncovering the never-unionized in the United States. *British Journal of Industrial Relations, 48*(1), 26–52.

Bureau of Labor Statistics (2019, September 24). *Job Flexibilities and Work Schedules—2017–2018, Data from the American Time Use Survey* [press release]. https://www.bls.gov/news.release/pdf/flex2.pdf.

CAP (2020, September 8). *It's time to worry about college enrollment declines among Black students*.

Carnevale, A. P., & Smith, N. (2018). Balancing work and learning: Implications for low-income students. https://files.eric.ed.gov/fulltext/ED590711.pdf.

Centers for Disease Control and Prevention (2020). United States COVID-19 cases, deaths, and laboratory testing (NAATs) by state, territory, and jurisdiction. COVID data tracker. https://www.cdc.gov/coronavirus/2019-ncov/cases-updates/cases-in-us.html.

Chetty, R., Hendren, N., Jones, M. R., & Porter, S. R. (2018). *Race and economic opportunity in the United States: An intergenerational perspective*. National Bureau of Economic Research.

Completing College National and State Reports (2020, December 3). *National Student Clearinghouse*. https://nscresearchcenter.org/completing-college/.

CUNY Graduate School of Health & Health Policy (2018, February 2). *Healthy CUNY*. https://sph.cuny.edu/wp-content/uploads/2019/02/Promoting-Health-for-Academic -Success.2.12.18_-FINALpdf-2.13.18.pdf.

CUNY Office of Institutional Research (2020, April). *CUNY Student Data Book (Current & Historical), Current Student Data Book by Subject*. http://www.cuny .edu/about/administration/offices/oira/institutional/data/current-student-data-book -by-subject/#Race.

Currie, C. L., Motz, T., & Copeland, J. L. (2020). The impact of racially motivated housing discrimination on allostatic load among indigenous university students. *Journal of Urban Health, 97*, 365–76.

Effiong, I. (2020). *Rethinking how to support males of color for postsecondary success* (White paper). UnlockED.

Farley, C., Stewart, K., & Kemple, J. (2022). *How have NYC's high school graduation and college enrollment rates changed over time?* New York University. https:// steinhardt.nyu.edu/research-alliance/research/spotlight-nyc-schools/how-have-nycs -high-school-graduation-and-college.

Fried, R. R. & Irwin, J. D. (2016). Calmly coping: A motivational interviewing via co-active life coaching (MI-VIA-CALC) pilot intervention for university students with perceived levels of high stress. *International Journal of Evidence Based Coaching and Mentoring, 14*(1), 16–32.

Garsman, L. (2017). The role of social support on acculturation stress and allostatic load among first-and second-generation immigrant college students (doctoral dissertation). Rutgers University Graduate School, Newark, New Jersey.

Gelber, A., Isen, A., & Kessler, J. B. (2016). The effects of youth employment: Evidence from New York City lotteries. *Quarterly Journal of Economics, 131*(1), 423–60.

Goldrick-Rab, S. (2016). *Paying the price*. University of Chicago Press.

Hill, R. A. (2020). Wraparound: A key component of school-wide culture competence to support academics and socio-emotional well-being. *Peabody Journal of Education, 95*(1), 66–72.

Hochberg, Z. E., & Konner, M. (2020). Emerging adulthood, a pre-adult life-history stage. *Frontiers in Endocrinology, 10*, 918.

Jack, A. A. (2019). *The privileged poor: How elite colleges are failing disadvantaged students*. Harvard University Press.

Jacobs, E., Anderson, C., Hossain, F., & Unterman, R. (2017). *An introduction to the world of work: A study of the implementation and impacts of New York City's Summer Youth Employment Program*. U.S. Department of Labor.

Johnson, A., & Joseph-Salisbury, R. (2018). "Are you supposed to be in here?" Racial microaggressions and knowledge production in higher education. In *Dismantling race in higher education* (pp. 143–60). Palgrave Macmillan.

Kemple, J. J., & Willner, C. J. (2008). *Career academies: Long-term impacts on labor market outcomes, educational attainment, and transitions to adulthood*. MDRC.

Kundu, A. (2020). *The power of student agency: Looking beyond grit to close the opportunity gap*. Teachers College Press.

Lumina Foundation (2020). *Today's Student.* https://www.luminafoundation.org/wp -content/uploads/2019/02/todays-student.pdf.

National Center for Education Statistics (NCES) (2017). Digest of education statistics, 2017. https://nces.ed.gov/programs/digest/mobile/.

National League of Cities (2018, September). *The future of work for opportunity youth.* Andrew O. Moore. https://www.nlc.org/article/2018/09/21/the-future-of-work-for -opportunity-youth/.

National Skills Coalition (2015, November 15). *Rethinking the mission: Community colleges and workforce education.* https://nationalskillscoalition.org/news/latest/ rethinking-the-mission-community-colleges-and-workforce-education/.

New York City Comptroller (2020). *New York City's frontline workers.* Bureau of Policy & Research.

New York City Department of Education (2020, May 18). *School quality reports: Educator guide.* https://infohub.nyced.org/docs/default-source/default-document -library/2018-19-educator-guide-hs---11-13-2019.pdf.

Nieves, L. (2016). Breaking the tradeoff between school and work: Community college voices on navigating work and school roles. https://repository.upenn.edu/ dissertations/AAI10164181/.

OIRA CUNY (2018). *CUNY 2018 student experience survey.* https://public.tableau .com/app/profile/oira.cuny/viz/2018StudentExperienceSurvey/CoverPage.

Rampell, C. (2016, February 10). Opinion: Where are the workers? *The Washington Post.*

Richey, J. (2014). The effect of youth labor market experience on adult earnings. *Journal of Economic Development, 39*(1), 47. https://www.washingtonpost .com/news/rampage/wp/2016/02/10/where-are-the-workers/.

Selingo, J. J. (2017, June). There is life after college. *Phi Kappa Phi Forum, 97*(2), 28–9).

Shapiro, D., Dundar, A., Huie, F., Wakhungu, P. K., Bhimdiwala, A., Nathan, A., & Hwang, Y. (2018). Transfer and mobility: A national view of student movement in postsecondary institutions. *Higher Education Policy for Minorities in the United States.*

Tai, D. B. G., Shah, A., Doubeni, C. A., Sia, I. G., & Wieland, M. L. (2020). The disproportionate impact of COVID-19 on racial and ethnic minorities in the United States. *Clinical Infectious Diseases, 72*(4), 703–6.

The City of New York (2021). Disconnected youth task force, connecting our future. https://www.nyc.gov/assets/youthemployment/downloads/pdf/dytf-connecting-our -future-report.pdf.

UNESCO (n.d.). *Covid-19 impact on education.* https://en.unesco.org/covid19/ educationresponse.

Waters, J. L. (2018). In anticipation: Educational (im)mobilities, structural disadvantage, and young people's futures. *Journal of Intercultural Studies, 39*(6), 673–87.

APPENDIX A: OVERVIEW OF METHODOLOGY

The sample of student participants included in the qualitative component of this research was selected based on their participation in a fellowship program for first-generation college attendees and their varying characteristics being reflective of those common to community college students at CUNY (i.e., a mix of gender, ethnicity, and country of origin but all first-generation college attendees and low-income). Of the 12 students invited to participate in the study, nine did. The qualitative data and analysis that we present are intended to offer findings regarding CUNY students and their experiences, which may provide useful insights generalizable to other community and senior colleges that serve diverse populations. This work is an introductory small-*n* case study, rather than a representation of all possible student experiences.

Individual hour-long structured video interviews were conducted with each study participant via Zoom during the fall of 2020 and subsequently transcribed by a third-party transcription service (Rev.com). The nine participants' identifying information was removed before uploading the transcripts to qualitative coding software Dedoose to analyze the interviews for themes and findings. The interviews included five related research questions exploring the crucial and evolving role that community colleges play in providing opportunity and access (the full interview script can be found in Appendix B):

- How do community college students—many of whom are first-generation college attendees from economically disadvantaged backgrounds or members of historically excluded groups—perceive the rapidly changing world of work in the world of COVID?
- What do they hope to gain from their community college experience?
- What skills do they have?
- What skills do they think they will need?
- What opportunities and supports can help them bridge existing gaps between their goals and skills?

New York City employer-demand data were accessed and analyzed using Burning Glass Labor Insights software, a software that aggregates all publicly available job postings (and will merge to become part of EMSI software in 2022). Three comparable intervals of time were analyzed to provide insight into how employer hiring priorities in New York City have evolved in response to the COVID-19 pandemic. These include a pre-COVID interval (3/1/2019–12/31/2019), the initial phase of the COVID-19 pandemic (3/1/2020–12/31/2020), and New York City employers' efforts to learn to adapt work to a COVID-19 reality (3/1/2021–12/31/2021). March through December is used instead of a full 12 months for each year's interval to align with COVID-19's arrival in New York City. Specifically, January and February are excluded, since to include them in the 2020 data set would obscure the full impact of COVID-19 on employer demand for that year (March 15–16, 2020, New York City closed public schools, bars, movie theaters, restaurants, and gyms, and on March 22, 2020, New York State issued the PAUSE order, both of which had profound effects on New York City's labor market). These same months are excluded from 2019's and 2021's data sets to keep the time intervals consistent across years.

The Graduate Center, CUNY's Institutional Review Board, reviewed the protocol and provided an exemption for this research on July 30, 2020 (#2020-0565).

APPENDIX B: INTERVIEW PROTOCOL FOR EXPLORING CAREER INTEREST AND PATHWAYS: AN INVESTIGATION INTO THE OCCUPATIONAL IDENTITY OF FIRST-GEN COMMUNITY COLLEGE ATTENDEES

Introduction
My name is Dr. Anindya Kundu and I'm a researcher at the New York City Labor Market Information Service (LMIS), which is at the CUNY Graduate Center. I am working on a research project around understanding college and career access and pathways for young adults of color from underrepresented backgrounds. We're looking for young people who have attended community college and are either now in a senior college or recently graduated and looking for work to learn about navigating college and career given the COVID-19 crisis.

With your permission, this conversation will be audio and video recorded by LMIS/CUNY for use in this project. We will make our best efforts to maintain confidentiality of any information that is collected during this research study, which can identify you.

Your participation in this project is entirely voluntary. You can decide to withdraw your consent and stop participating in the research at any time or ask that we destroy the data after your interview. Is it okay if we record this conversation?

How would you describe yourself as a person?

a. How would you describe yourself as a student? As a professional?
b. What are your career interests and goals and how did you come to form these?
c. What did you study in college and why?
d. Tell me a little about your upbringing. What were unique circumstances that you faced growing up that other college students might not typically experience?
e. What is it like being a first-generation college goer in your family?
   i. What does it mean to your family, broadly?
f. How did being first-generation impact your college and career goals?
g. What does your family think of your goals? Are they supportive? Why or why not?

What are some of the largest challenges you experienced on your way to college or during your college experience?

h. How did this affect you?

i.   How did you overcome this challenge?
j.   If someone was in a similar position, what advice would you give them to overcome this type of obstacle?

What are some of the largest challenges you experienced on your way to getting a job or working in the field of your interest?

k.   How did this affect you?
l.   How did you overcome this challenge?
m.   If someone was in a similar position, what advice would you give them to overcome this type of obstacle?

What would you consider some of the biggest successes in your life?

n.   How does it feel? Why do you consider this a great achievement?
o.   What have you learned from this experience? How will you keep this in mind as you experience new challenges in the world of work?
p.   How have you stayed motivated when things get really hard?
q.   What advice would you give others who have similar challenges?

I'd like to talk a little about health and wellness. Is wellness and mental health important to you, and in what sense?

r.   Have you ever had any particularly big stresses in your life and how did you handle them?
s.   How do you pay attention to and foster good mental health for yourself? What practices do you think others can use to stay happy and healthy?

And finally, can we talk a little about COVID-19? How has the pandemic affected you personally?

t.   How have you dealt with the related challenges?
u.   What about those around you? How has the crisis affected others that you know?
v.   What have you learned from this experience and what advice would you give others who are experiencing challenges related to this pandemic?
w.   Has the crisis affected your college and or work? In what ways? How have you worked around the challenges?

Is there anything else you feel like is worth mentioning as we reflect on successes and challenges, that you would like to mention at this point?

Thank you for your time. Please reach out to me if you have any follow-up questions.

3. COVID-19 in New Zealand: consequences, policies, and regional responses

David Wilson, Patrick McVeigh and Harvey Brookes

3.1 INTRODUCTION

New Zealand is a small South Pacific nation of approximately five million people. Due to its geographic isolation, the country quickly adopted an elimination[1] strategy in response to the SARS Coronavirus-2 pandemic, which included:

- controlling entry at the border
- disease surveillance
- physical distancing and hygiene measures
- testing for and tracing all potential cases
- isolating cases and their close contacts
- broader public health controls.

As of 30 December 2021, over 90 per cent of the eligible population (4.35 million) had been fully vaccinated or booked to be fully vaccinated with the Pfizer vaccine, a remarkable turnaround from August 2021 when approximately 30 per cent of the eligible population were double-dosed. After the arrival of the Delta variant, the government was heavily criticized for the slow roll out of vaccines, which, with low intensive care hospital capacity, and higher transmission rates the Delta variant, led to a more than four-month lockdown period for the country. Currently, New Zealand is transitioning from an elimination strategy to an approach where highly vaccinated regions can operate more freely under a traffic light system. The Omicron variant has arrived in New Zealand with cases in isolation and the first case in the community.

The 'go hard go early' strategy since early 2020 was not without economic costs. New Zealand heavily relies on exports and the free flow of goods, ideas, and people to maintain its standard of living. Chief among these are primary industries – farming, horticulture, viticulture, forestry, and fishing – alongside tourism. Prior to COVID-19, international tourism was New Zealand's number one export industry, ahead of dairy products; however, tourism and related sectors have been reduced to a fraction of their previous size with more than a year of heavy falls in GDP. A recent 'travel bubble' (quarantine free travel) with Australia was closed by outbreaks in Australia and subsequently New Zealand of the Delta variant after long periods of minor COVID-19 incursions. At present the near-term prospects for international tourism to and from New Zealand remain uncertain.

This chapter provides an overview of the effects of COVID-19 on New Zealand's economy, its economic structure prior to the pandemic, health response, macroeconomic policy response, and structural (sectoral) and spatial (regional) effects. We then review regional planning responses, including a national guide for regions and economic development agencies (EDAs) and regional workshops. This is followed by an examination of differentiated regional responses drawing on examples of three regional typologies: a city region, a rural region, and a tourism town.

3.2   CORONOMICS AND NEW ZEALAND

Karl Popper (1902–1994) characterized New Zealand as 'not quite the moon, but after the moon … the farthest place in the world' (see Kierstead, 2019). Since initial European colonization, population growth has been relatively modest and sporadic, though rates of immigration in the five years before COVID-19 had increased significantly to over 70,000 per annum. New Zealand still has a population density approximately 14 times less than the UK ($279/km2^2$ vs $19/km2^3$) and its largest city Auckland's population density is 1,210/km2, compared to 1,500/km2 in Melbourne, or 7,800/km2 in Singapore.

Following the first refrigerated shipment of frozen meat from New Zealand in 1882, New Zealand has diversified its economy from a heavy reliance on primary agriculture to a more elaborate, service-based economy. However, primary production (dairy, meat, and wool) still accounts for more than 45 per cent of merchandise exports. As other parts of the economy have developed, the contribution of agriculture to New Zealand's GDP has reduced from 12 per cent in 1972 to 7 per cent in 2018 (Figures 3.1a and 3.1b).

Since the mid-1980s, the New Zealand economy has also changed from being one of the most regulated in the OECD to one of the least. There have been winners and losers from these reforms, and while for many, economic well-being has improved, productivity has remained low by international standards, and inequality has increased.[4]

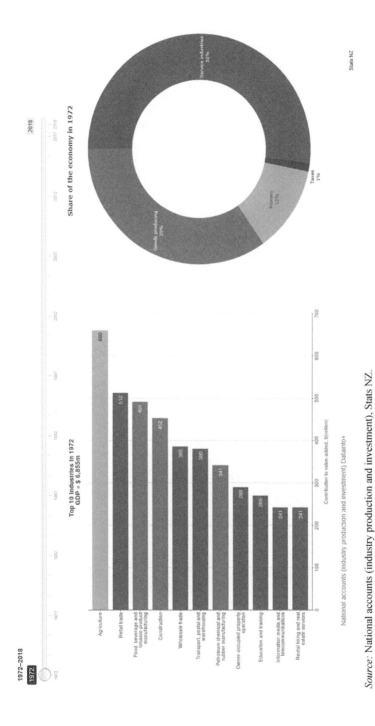

Source: National accounts (industry production and investment), Stats NZ.

Figure 3.1a *New Zealand GDP by industry (top 10 industries in 1972)*

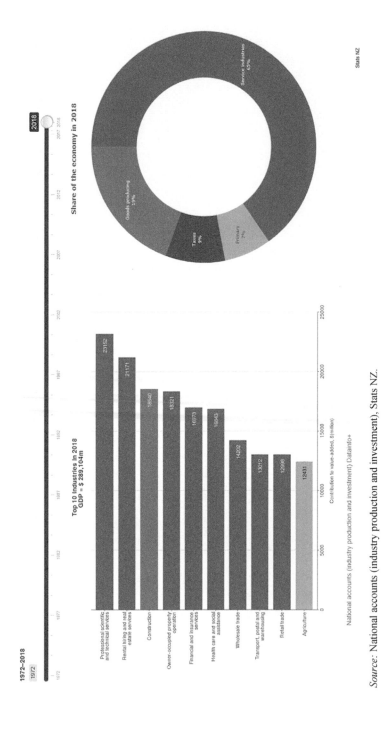

Source: National accounts (industry production and investment), Stats NZ.

Figure 3.1b   New Zealand GDP by industry (top 10 industries in 2018)

Prior to COVID-19, tourism had become New Zealand's biggest export industry, contributing 20.4 per cent of total exports (6 per cent of GDP) and directly employing 8 per cent of the New Zealand workforce. The 2020 lockdown saw international tourism halted overnight, severely impacting many regions and forcing the previously very profitable national airline Air New Zealand to seek capital assistance from the government to avoid insolvency.

Recent forecasts have indicated that international tourism may never rebound to its pre-COVID-19 levels, forcing many regions to either (a) focus more heavily on domestic tourism opportunities or (b) redeploy labour and capital into other sectors. For the government, this pause in the rate of tourism growth has provided an opportunity to further reflect on the 'quantity versus quality' dilemma which saw some of the country's most popular destinations reaching their social and environmental carrying capacity prior to the epidemic. Not only has it precipitated a rethink of the role of tourism, but industries with a heavily reliance on seasonal migrant employees such as hospitality and horticulture.

Health Response

New Zealand's international border closed to most non-citizens/residents except essential health workers on 25 March 2020 when a national state of emergency and Level 4 border lockdown was declared.[5] Government restrictions required all New Zealanders to remain at home within close contact 'bubbles'. Most businesses were closed, and people worked from home, facilitated by high levels of social compliance, good broadband penetration, and the high uptake of applications such as Zoom.

New Zealand's first case of COVID-19 community transmission was detected on 28 February 2020, and all international arrivals were required to self-isolate for 14 days from 14 March 2020. Level 4 lockdown was eased on 27 April 2020 and by 4 May new cases of community transmission reached zero, and New Zealand was declared COVID-free on 8 June 2020. The following day, government reduced alert levels to Level 1 – at which point most activities returned to relative normality. However, the border remained closed. Returning New Zealand citizens and residents were required to isolate at a government-mandated managed isolation and quarantine (MIQ) facility (typically requisitioned city hotels) for 14 days prior to release. The system was gradually tightened with MIQ attendees COVID-19-tested on days three and 12 to ensure they were not infectious at release.

The Delta variant outbreak saw a return for the country to Level 4, with Auckland remaining at Level 4 while the rest of the country reduced to 3, then 2 on 7 September, 2020. The country then moved to a less stringent traffic light system in early December 2021, although movement in and out of Auckland remained extremely restricted until 15 December. MIQ requirements are now being loosened with shorter stays and home-based isolation for returning New Zealand citizens being introduced.

Since the initial outbreak, the level of community transmission has remained low by international standards, with occasional small-scale outbreaks associated with casual transmission among border and MIQ workers. In many cases, the exact chain of transmission from the border has been difficult to identify, with short duration partial lockdowns, especially in Auckland where the majority of MIQ facilities and cases have been. The Delta outbreak in late 2021 saw the highest daily number of cases since the start of the epidemic (222 on 16 November), but still very low caseloads relative to other countries. Deaths related to COVID-19 have doubled to 47 in total due to the Delta outbreak, still amongst the lowest per capita in the OECD.

Management processes at the border have gradually been strengthened, both in terms of employee hygiene but also with all new arrivals requiring a negative COVID-19 test no less than 72 hours before departure for New Zealand. Testing of local wastewater has also increased health officials' ability to isolate potential outbreaks. A more targeted approach to high-risk arrivals has also been taken, with migrants (including New Zealand citizens and residents returning) from countries with uncontrolled outbreaks being temporarily prevented from entering the country.

Since early 2021, international restrictions have begun to ease in line with the rollout of vaccines in New Zealand and internationally, but with periodic restrictions when major outbreaks occur (for example in Australian states). New Zealand commenced quarantine-free travel with Australia in April 2021 but this was closed again when Delta was found to have been introduced by an arrival from Sydney. At this stage, there are no plans to reinstate the travel bubble concept until the global pandemic is more under control. New Zealand's COVID-19-related death rate is currently 5.3 per million people which compares favourably with many other developed nations (USA – 1,825; United Kingdom – 1,917; Australia – 35.9; and Singapore – 6.0[6]). This relatively low fatality rate reflects the strategies developed and deployed by health agencies, the strong community backing for the 'team of five million' campaign championed by the prime minister, and a degree of luck.

The country's relative isolation, some lead time for preparation, low population density, a culture of willing (but now rapidly waning) compliance with government directions and high broadband penetration contributed to the country's relative success. That the country's two outbreaks happened in autumn and spring/summer also reduced the burden on the health system. Paradoxically, the incidences of seasonal flu, which usually kills up to 500 people per year in New Zealand has reduced to almost zero. The question of whether the measures taken to save less than 50 lives over two years are efficient, when usually up to 1,000 might die from seasonal flu, let alone other unintended health consequences, remains an open political and policy question. The paradoxes of this flow in both directions. In June 2021, the Economist Intelligence Unit declared Auckland the most liveable city in the world,[7] a prize its civic leaders had coveted for over a decade. The status of Auckland as one of the few world cities where business, civic, and community life has been able to go on largely unimpeded saw it leapfrog to the top of the rankings (usually ranked in the top 10–15 cities) even though there are no major changes in many of the factors which had previously held the city's global ranking back (e.g. traffic congestion, high house prices, moderate GDP per capita, low innovation rates). Auckland, however, has seen dramatic housing and construction inflation, with the median wage to house price ratio as high as 12. The four-month lockdown in late 2021 due to Delta has dented Auckland's newfound reputation and left the city struggling to recover.

Macroeconomic Policy Response

Initial scenario modelling from the New Zealand Treasury in early 2020 indicated severe falls in annual GDP ranging from 13 per cent to more than 30 per cent if lockdowns persisted. Peaks in the unemployment rate were forecast between 13 per cent and 26 per cent[8] – akin to the Great Depression.

Fiscal responses

The January 2020 New Zealand Upgrade Programme, a $12 billion pre-pandemic programme of fiscal infrastructure stimulus, was announced in response to concerns of a slowing economy. Following lockdown, the government's COVID-19 response package in March included $5.1 billion in wage subsidies for affected businesses in all sectors and regions, a $2.8 billion income support package for the vulnerable, including a permanent $25 per week benefit increase, a doubling of the Winter Energy Payment for 2020 to address energy poverty, $2.8 billion in business tax changes to free up cashflow, including a lift in the provisional tax threshold, the reinstatement of building depreciation and writing off late payment interest and extensions for tax payments.

As part of Budget 2020, the COVID-19 Response and Recovery Fund (CRRF) of $50 billion was established – comprised of more than 250 individual programmes across most areas of government spending. By far the largest single source of spending in the CCRF was the Business Support (wage) subsidy of $16 billion. A small business cash flow loan scheme allocated $5.2 billion, with a further $3.44 billion allocated for the write-down cost of the loans. A further $3 billion infrastructure investment package aimed to support hundreds of projects around the country. An Infrastructure Reference

Group (IRG) was established to receive and assess proposals for projects. Approximately $20 billion of the Recovery Fund was set aside in the event of further outbreaks, some of which has been allocated in the May 2021 budget towards other general social well-being programmes. This was called on in the COVID-19 (Delta) resurgence.

Monetary responses

Following lockdown, the Reserve Bank quickly lowered the Official Cash Rate (OCR) from 1 per cent to 0.25 per cent (its lowest level ever) and committed to keep it there for at least the next year. A low OCR at the beginning of the pandemic saw a lowering of the OCR by 75 basis points, compared to 550 basis points during the global financial crisis (GFC). Further decreases to a negative OCR were debated and rejected at the time by the governor of the Reserve Bank and revisited early in 2021. Pandemic interest rates were further suppressed by the bank buying up to $100 billion of bonds in the secondary market through a large-scale asset purchase (LSAP) programme. A Funding-for-Lending Programme (FLP) also allowed eligible banks to borrow from the Reserve Bank at the OCR. Loan to value ratio (LVR) restrictions on home lending were scrapped to encourage more low deposit and first-time buyers to enter the market. This has resulted in a booming housing market and concerns that asset classes and those with assets (like houses) have benefitted the most from both fiscal and monetary policy. In the face of house price inflation of more than 45 per cent in two years, the government has since reinstated LVRs and has gone further removing some of the tax write-offs previously available to landlords, such as interest payments on housing investments.

As the pandemic progressed, direct economic impacts have been far less than initially expected, but long-term effects are now of greater concern. The country's economy grew 1.6 per cent in the first quarter of 2021, far higher than the 0.5 per cent predicted by the Reserve Bank. Also in late 2021, unemployment fell to 3.4 per cent, very close to full employment. Export prices for the country's major commodities (e.g. dairy/milk, beef, lamb, and timber) have remained high and in some cases have increased. Low consumer interest rates and rising property prices through 2020 and the first half of 2021 have created a wealth effect and associated consumer spending for many asset-rich New Zealanders. Meanwhile imports are under significant logistic constraints and price rises exacerbating, for example, manufactured construction supplies. Building materials have been in very short supply further inflating hosing costs.

The unprecedented economic stimulus above was successful in avoiding major short-term damage but has come at a price. In September 2021, inflation jumped from persistently low levels (less than 1 per cent) to an annual rate of 4.9 per cent, forecast to peak at 5.6 per cent in the March 2022 quarter. Setting aside temporary effects due to rises in goods and services tax (GST), this was the fastest increase in headline inflation in New Zealand since the early 1980s, whilst at 0.75 per cent the OCR is still historically very low. As a result, the Reserve Bank has begun lifting the OCR further and faster than was previously indicated and may continue to do so through 2022 in an attempt to dampen demand. Banks are tightening lending rules and increasing mortgage rates leading to talk of a credit crunch. Pressure is now coming on employers and the government to increase wages and salaries – with the attendant risk of further increasing prices and inflation pressure.

Macroeconomic impacts
The fiscal, economic, and social dividend from these responses is an economy which, while still volatile, appears to be far more resilient than was expected. Key statistics include:

- Prior to the outbreak, total unemployment had risen to 5.3 per cent (pre-COVID-19) but is now significantly below the earlier predictions at 3.4 per cent and expected to fall to 3.1 per cent by March 2022.
- GDP dropped by 11 per cent in the June 2020 quarter, its largest drop on record; however, in its December 2021 fiscal update, the government reported GDP rose by 4.1 per cent over the first half of 2021 (driven by inflation effects) and the unemployment rate fell to 3.4 per cent in the September 2021 quarter.[9]
- Stronger economic activity and the need for less fiscal support measures have assisted the government's fiscal position; however, an operating balance before gains and losses (OBEGAL) deficit of $20.8 billion is expected in the current year, which is $16.2 billion more than the deficit reported in the 2020/21 fiscal year. OBEGAL is expected to return to surplus in the 2023/24 fiscal year and reach $8.2 billion by the end of the forecast period.[10]
- In year to October 2020 visitor arrivals to New Zealand were 1.90 million, down by 2.01 million on the previous year. Following lockdown, the number of international visitors plunged to virtually zero, forcing tourism operators to market themselves to the domestic market, which responded positively with no international destinations on offer. Total tourism expenditure decreased 37.3 per cent in the year to 31 March 2021. Those regions highly dependent on international tourism, therefore, were heavily affected. With the long Delta lockdown, many regions are now expecting many tourism operators to be permanently lost.
- Aided by accommodating monetary policy, inflation was 4.9 per cent at the end of September 2021, with expectations of further increases. Such

rates are beyond the upper limit of the Reserve Banks policy range (1–3 per cent) and will lead to further interest rate increases in 2022.

- In the June 2021 quarter, total exports reached its highest ever value, $17.2 billion, driven by two record export months in May and June. This was up $1.5 billion (9.2 per cent) from same quarter last year. Imports were up $3.4 billion (27 per cent) compared with the June 2020 quarter, to $16.1 billion. June 2021 provided a monthly trade balance surplus of $261 million.
- House prices have defied predictions and are now as much as 45 per cent higher than they were in early 2020, driven by historically low interest rates, the government's LSAP programme, return migration of expatriate New Zealanders, discretionary spending diverted from international travel, and continued low levels of supply.

In late 2020, Treasury forecasted a volatile 2021 as the wider effects of the economic shock played out. However, the general trend has been that the economy has performed better than expected notwithstanding the dramatic effects on GDP caused by lockdowns.

3.3 SECTORAL, REGIONAL, AND COMMUNITY IMPACTS

Initial estimates of impact included:

1. Tourism and related industries such as accommodation, food and beverage services, and transport industries would be hit hardest and would take longer to recover compared with other sectors.
2. Regions with a high proportion of affected service industries and a high proportion of international migrant flows (temporary workers as a proportion of workforce, international students, recent residents) would also be most affected.
3. Output would decrease, less sharply, in the primary sector and manufacturing, construction and other services due to a decrease in available labour and capital.
4. Real annual GDP loss (in percentage terms) will be highest in tourism-centric regions (Queenstown Lakes, Rotorua, and Auckland).

Regional variations reflect underlying labour markets and industrial structures across the country and these have variously been impacted by the pandemic. The changes in the employment by industry are also reflective of the impacts of the pandemic. The industries which experienced growth included health, construction, and public administration, while transport, accommodation and food, and administration and support have seen the greatest falls in employment.

These changes have also driven job variations, with Waikato, Wellington, Bay of Plenty, and Manawatū-Wanganui all seeing positive job growth, while only Southland, Auckland, Marlborough, and Otago experiencing a fall in numbers of filled jobs. Beyond these variations in regional performance, it is also apparent that the economic impacts of the pandemic are being experienced differently by different groups, with some groups faring less well than others. Females and younger people have been hit the hardest. In addition, New Zealand's Pasifika (Pacific Island Peoples) population has been hit hardest by the pandemic, with rates of unemployment continuing to rise, while levelling off for other ethnicities.

The recent outbreak of the Delta variant centred in Auckland disproportionately affected Pasifika. The disproportionate impacts of the pandemic on females, youth, and ethnic minorities have longer-term implications. As such, policy and programmatic interventions must pay attention to these demographics to ensure the ongoing economic recovery is more equitable and resilient.

3.4   DIFFERENTIATED REGIONAL RESPONSES

As New Zealand has had a different experience of COVID-19 internationally, so have regions within the country. In this section we look at three regional typologies: a city-region (Auckland), a rural region (Taranaki), and a tourism region (Queenstown (Lakes District)). Some regions have simply adjusted priorities in their regional strategies, some were underprepared, and many lacked institutional capacity to respond optimally. Central government moved to address local deficiencies, but COVID-19 did expose what has been an historical lack of subsidiarity in economic development efforts in New Zealand (Wilson, 2020).

New Zealand's relatively small size and geographical isolation mean that a physical lockdown, when compared to other nations, was relatively easy to achieve. However, the impacts of the COVID-19 pandemic differed from place to place and from sector to sector. Some businesses, such as those in the tourism sector, saw an immediate contraction, and many workers lost their jobs. In other sectors, particularly the primary industries and other essential services, demand increased and there was a shortage of workers.

Consequently, different regions and localities have been forced to think and act differently and tailor responses. A key factor is the variation in local industrial structures across regional New Zealand, which influenced how quickly the impacts became visible and is determining how deep and long-lasting the impacts will be.

The majority of New Zealand's population lives in three major metropolitan centres: Auckland, Wellington, and Christchurch. However, many settlements sit within regions that are rural in nature and where the primary sector and tourism are important features of the regional economy.

With the surge in tourism in New Zealand over the previous 10 years, the sector accounted for approximately 10 per cent of New Zealand's GDP. In the year to March 2019, tourists (both international and domestic) spent about NZ$41 billion; international visitors, then New Zealand's largest export earner, amounted to over NZ$17 billion in export earnings. The impacts on tourism and related industries have been stark, with the sector dominated by a few large businesses and many small businesses running on narrow margins and tight cashflows.

In many rural regions, domestic tourists account for a greater share of the visitor economy than international tourists. Prior to the emergence of COVID-19, many rural regions were seeking to grow their share of international tourists in recognition of tourism's national growth trajectory. However, the food and fibres sector – which includes farming, horticulture, viticulture, forestry, fishing, food and beverages, and fibres (primarily wood and wool products) – is New Zealand's largest export sector.

While the primary sector is an important feature of rural economies, the total number of people employed in this sector has declined over time. Consequently, while the economies of New Zealand's rural regions have, like the rest of the country, been impacted by COVID-19, particularly during a national Level 4 lockdown,[11] many of these areas bounced back quicker than was expected. However, the immediate and ongoing impacts of COVID-19 on New Zealand's rural regions are of significant concern, particularly in their ability to access labour and the resilience of global supply chains. These constraints are a focus for regional economic development across the country.

Regions that have a strong primary industry sector, and perhaps more domestic than international tourism, have been more resilient. Lockdowns, subsequent reopening and renewed lockdowns, and lockdown level variations across regions, have generated business uncertainty. Increased demand across the primary sector has also put pressure on supply chains and distribution networks both within New Zealand and internationally. Labour shortages and frictional unemployment have become apparent, as demand increases and temporary labour, often supplied by temporary migrants, slowed to a trickle.

Larger cities, particularly Auckland, Wellington, and Christchurch, saw significant impacts, with service industries hit hard as the economy contracted. However, the scale and diversity of the cities, as well as the ability of many businesses to adopt flexible working arrangements have aided recovery. New Zealand's capital city Wellington, for example, has been somewhat shielded by its high level of public-sector knowledge-intensive employment.

Regional economic impacts, while varied, will be far-reaching and enduring. In all regions, local government, EDAs, Chambers of Commerce, Business

Representative Organizations, and other agencies worked with central government to support local businesses and communities.

Economic Development New Zealand (EDNZ) commissioned 'A guide to local and regional recovery and reimagination' and facilitated online regional workshops to promote tailored regional and local responses. Common features included:

- Gathering up-to-date economic intelligence on the performance of the regional economy and the impacts of the pandemic on key industries and businesses – including undertaking rapid surveys of businesses to better understand the impacts and tailor responses
- Ensuring that there was a constant flow of relevant information so that businesses could plan and adapt to the changing circumstances
- Facilitating national and local support programmes and services such as the Regional Business Partnerships
- Organizing and hosting online webinars and information sessions for advice and support virtually, providing opportunities for these businesses to keep up to date and connect with other local businesses and organizations
- Supporting displaced workers and local labour markets and encouraging employers to retain as much of their workforce as possible by facilitating access to wage subsidies, connecting displaced workers to job matching services and re-training programmes.

Examples of regional initiatives emerging during the early stages of the pandemic include:

- Queenstown Lakes District Council set up a taskforce to prepare a Council package to support business and community recovery, such as bringing forward spending that supports local jobs. The taskforce included the economic development unit, tourism organizations and Chambers of Commerce.
- Working with local business advisory experts, the Waikato Economic Development Agency Te Waka published regular business survival and continuity tips. Making sure business owners were aware of the support packages available, as well as facilitating professional advice.
- Auckland Unlimited's 'Go with Tourism' programme was redirected to support employees that had been displaced, tourism businesses, and workers wanting to explore education pathways into tourism during the lockdown or self-isolation.
- With the Ministry of Social Development, many regional EDAs set up job-matching schemes to match recruiting businesses with available employees as quickly as possible.

- The Auckland Chamber of Commerce worked with key agencies to put employers in touch with assistance, including cashflow support, tax relief, employee assistance, exporter support, and tourism operator assistance.
- Venture Taranaki secured additional investment from its local government funders which was then matched with in kind support from local business support providers to assist small and medium businesses to access legal, accounting, business continuity, or HR advice.
- The Nelson Regional Development Agency facilitated Project Kōkiri, the 'Nelson Tasman Economic Response & Regeneration Action Plan,[12] a collaboration between Nelson City Council, Tasman District Council, Nelson Regional Development Agency, Nelson Tasman Chamber of Commerce, Iwi/Maori, and regionally-based government agencies. The aim was to progress work-rich projects in key sectors within their overarching strategic framework Te Tauihu.[13]
- Enterprise North Canterbury created a local database of food producers to help sell produce locally to compensate for the loss of traditional markets.
- The Employers and Manufacturers Association (EMA) operated an 'AdviceLine' to help employers with key questions and to link them to supporting agencies. The EMA also enabled businesses to band together and share information and knowledge through a private Facebook group set up for its members and others in the 'BusinessNZ' network.

Auckland

Despite its low population density and rural reputation, New Zealand is a highly urbanized country. In 2019, 86 per cent of New Zealanders lived in urban areas, with 51.2 per cent in five major urban areas. Auckland with a population of 1.7 million comprises 33 per cent of the national population. This level of concentration in a primate city is high by international standards and means that Auckland's economic performance has a large impact on New Zealand.

These factors meant that when COVID-19 arrived in New Zealand, it was much more likely to occur in Auckland before other parts of the country. Indeed, of the 9,401 cases of community transmission reported in New Zealand, 8,509 or 90 per cent have been in Auckland.

The composition of the economy towards services, retail activity and real estate also meant that its economy was highly exposed to the impacts of lockdown-enforced reductions in business activity. As shown in the data from the Auckland Council's Chief Economist, the city's economy responded to the COVID-19 crisis in a complex way. Since September 2019, unemployment had risen 1.4 per cent to 5.6 per cent (about 1 per cent higher than the rest of NZ), and retail sales dropped 4.5 per cent to zero growth (same as rest of NZ).

Surprisingly, median house price growth increased from 4.1 per cent to 12.6 per cent (slightly lower that rest of NZ – 15.4 per cent).

In contrast to other major urban areas such as Christchurch or Wellington, Auckland did not develop a specific COVID-19 response or recovery plan. The Auckland Council is by far the largest local council in New Zealand after amalgamation of seven territorial and one regional council in 2010. It dwarfs other councils for asset base, employment, and operations. Its EDA, Auckland Unlimited (Formerly Auckland Tourism Events and Economic Development), also dwarfs other regional development agencies and regional EDAs in New Zealand relative to the size of the Auckland region. Auckland, however, relied on its general civil defence and emergency management powers to coordinate the initial COVID-19 response functions, and to distribute services and information. The Auckland Council established an emergency committee and its 2020/21 emergency budget included:

- Increasing council borrowing to 290 per cent of annual revenue
- Delaying capital investment, but still maintaining $2.5 billion in capital projects to continue asset development
- Reducing operating expenditure by $200 million in the 2020/21 fiscal year
- Increasing asset recycling by selling $244 million of non-core assets
- 1,100 temporary and permanent positions were removed from the council to reduce costs
- $50 million was set aside to fund rates postponements and deferrals for households in financial distress
- Voluntary pay cuts for high-earning staff
- A targeted rate on visitor accommodation was suspended
- Council set up a food distribution centre to help with the delivery of 20,000 food parcels and handled more than 30,000 calls to welfare support and emergency helplines
- Library staff made 15,000 calls to check in on residents over the age of 70
- A Māori-focused team worked alongside iwi, hapū, whānau and marae to bridge gaps in the delivery of welfare services and parcels
- Assisting with managed isolation and quarantine facilities
- Auckland Unlimited developed a Destination AKL Recovery Plan to guide the tourism industry's response and recovery from the pandemic.

Taranaki

The Taranaki region is illustrative of a rural region not dependent on tourism with strong primary sector and energy-related industries such as engineering. Located on the western coast of the North Island, the resident population has grown steadily over the last decade, although the rate of growth has typically been lower than the national average. In 2020, resident population grew by 1.5 per cent to 124,600 compared to a national rate of growth of 2.1 per cent.

The region's economy is relatively specialized with mining, agriculture, forestry and fishing, manufacturing and electricity, gas, water and waste services accounting for over 50 per cent of total regional output. Taranaki has the highest GDP per capita in New Zealand, with around 3 per cent of New Zealand's GDP and 2.3 per cent of New Zealand's employment. While the long-term performance of these sectors has been strong, looking forward, disruptions from technology and regulation pose major challenges.

From a jobs' perspective, the region's employment is more evenly distributed across a wider range of sectors. A more even employment distribution is important in terms of economic resilience and retaining and attracting talent.

Spatially, there are disparities across the region, with GDP and employment growth being primarily driven by the New Plymouth District, host to the region's largest town New Plymouth. In addition, there are differences in economic outcomes for Māori with higher unemployment rates and lower average incomes.

A combination of these dynamics and a subsequent global pandemic underscored the need to revisit and renew regional development planning.

The region's current economic strategy Tapuae Roa: Make Way for Taranaki was published in 2017 and is supported by a separate action plan published in 2018 developed through a partnership consisting of the region's four councils, Ngā Iwi o Taranaki, EDA Venture Taranaki, local business leaders, and central government.

'Four Futures' consist of three sectors with global opportunities where Taranaki has a competitive advantage – energy, food, and tourism, and the Māori economy. The Maori economy encapsulates eight iwi that whakapapa[14] to the maunga[15] progressing their own economic aspirations, within their rohe.[16]

Venture Taranaki is responsible for delivering economic development services and projects, strategic economic growth initiatives, sector growth projects, regional tourism marketing, destination development and promotion, district marketing for New Plymouth district, and the management of New Plymouth District Council's major event fund.

As well, coordinating the implementation of the Tapuae Roa strategy and action plan, Venture Taranaki, has led to the development of the Taranaki 2050 Roadmap, which was part of the region's response to the New Zealand's government's cessation of new permits for offshore oil and gas exploration. The Taranaki 2050 Roadmap was co-created with stakeholders and the communities to put Taranaki at the forefront of global efforts to support a just transition to a low-emissions world.

The Tapuae Roa strategy and action plan, together with the Taranaki 2050 Roadmap, set the strategic context for Venture Taranaki's response to COVID-19 and their key components are being integrated into the region's 'return to better' plan which is being developed in response to the impacts of the pandemic.

Venture Taranaki's response to the impacts of COVID-19 on the regional economy can be grouped into three phases:

- The immediate short-term response to the emergence of COVID-19 in the community and the associated Level 4 lockdown that was imposed across the country
- A strategic medium-term response which considers existing regional plans and strategies and reflects on where there is a need to adapt or change these to reflect the impacts of COVID-19
- A future focused longer-term response focused on regional resilience and building back better.

As the pandemic took hold, businesses across the region had to manage the sudden shock as they were forced to adapt to the nation-wide lock down and the shift to remote working. While essential services were able to continue to operate with some restrictions, many businesses were forced to close their doors and where possible switch to remote working which saw a dramatic change to their revenue and cashflow positions.

Venture Taranaki's immediate response was similar to the response of other EDAs across New Zealand in that their first concern was to understand the impacts on their local businesses. In April 2020, they conducted a COVID-19 impact survey which found that 90.3 per cent of respondents were experiencing revenue reductions or stoppage, 55.9 per cent had cashflow difficulties, and 44.8 per cent had concerns about their ongoing financial viability. In addition, 33.5 per cent of respondents reported stress and anxiety and 29.7 per cent faced challenges retaining or paying staff.

Venture Taranaki moved quickly to provide targeted advice and guidance to impacted businesses, including stepping up communication efforts and professional advice. This included newsletters, a dedicated webpage, and webinars. In addition, Venture Taranaki was able to quickly mobilize local business support providers, with some matched funding from their local government partners, to provide small and medium-sized businesses with access to legal, accounting, business continuity, and HR advice. The Venture Taranaki Professional Services Support programme provided two hours of free support from business support professionals. Venture Taranaki also established the Go Local, Go Taranaki campaign to stimulate spending in the local economy.

This immediate support was focused on cushioning businesses within the region from the short-term impacts of COVID-19. In March 2020, the New Zealand government rolled out a $16 billion package of subsidies and support to keep businesses operating, people employed, and the health system functioning. As in other regions, Venture Taranaki connected businesses to these services, which included wage subsidies and leave payments, and targeted support for tourism businesses through the Tourism Transitions Fund.

Beyond this immediate response, a three-year tactical 'Return to Better' plan to lead a green and inclusive recovery in Taranaki has been developed. The plan incorporates and integrates actions from Tapuae Roa, the Taranaki 2050 Roadmap, COVID-19 response, and the national policy objectives with a focus on economic recovery.

The longer-term focus is framed by Venture Taranaki's Impact Strategy, an outcomes-based framework that articulates the intervention logic between activities delivered and desired outcomes for Taranaki over the short, medium, and longer term. The Impact Strategy is a tool for guiding investment and resourcing decisions, prioritizing activities, and communicating to stakeholders and the region.

Queenstown

Queenstown is New Zealand's foremost international tourist town. With a resident population of just over 16,000, it sits within the Queenstown Lakes District with a population of just over 40,000. Queenstown itself is a hub for the Queenstown Lakes District and Otago regions in the South Island of New Zealand. It is a picturesque alpine town with world class natural capital surrounded by similar towns and scenic attractions such as Wanaka, Arrowtown, Cardrona, the Mt Aspiring National Park, and Cardrona, Coronet Peak and 'the Remarkables' ski fields. Queenstown and the Queenstown Lakes District (QLD) had successfully moved from a reliance on high winter seasonality in snow sports and recreation to smoothed shoulder seasons and another visitor peak during summer through diversifying its visitor offerings in adventure tourism and other activities taking advantage of its natural capital. It is the birthplace, for example, of the world-famous 'Bungy Jump', the Shotover jet (adventure jetboat ride), scenic ziplines, and gondola ride. Queenstown has capitalized on tourism with exceptional nightlife, food, entertainment, and events.

QLD's exceptional natural capital resulted in the highest reliance on tourism, and international over domestic tourism, of any region in New Zealand prior to COVID-19. Two thirds of its $3 billion GDP and 65 per cent of all jobs were tourism-related.

Prior to COVID-19, Queenstown was experiencing both GDP and population growth above New Zealand averages. However, it also has had the challenge of employment dependence and cyclicality in tourism and related industries such as construction. Post-GFC, Queenstown's employment growth dipped, consistent with national and international trends.

Because of Queenstown's heavy reliance on international tourism, it has been disproportionately affected by COVID-19. In recent years, QLD resident population[17] averaged around 42,000 with seasonal variance and increases at peak times, while visitors more than doubled Queenstown's overall population during high seasons and sometimes tripling that on peak days. This trend was predicted by the Queenstown Lakes District Council (QLDC) to continue prior to COVID-19.

This has the all-too-common consequence in resort towns and regions of putting pressure on infrastructure, a limited tax revenue source at the local level, high real estate prices, and a high cost of living for residents, who in many cases are working in lower-paid service jobs. The cost of residential property had continued to rise in line with national and international trends for desirable holiday properties and commercial property values in line with tourism demand exacerbating cost-of-living conditions for locals. A somewhat perverse effect is that residential housing sales and property values have continued to rise, and in parts of the region accelerated during COVID-19, despite reduced tourism demand. This is a combination of factors including low interest rates and government's temporary lowering of LVR ratios in line with national and international trends.

These factors have propelled plans to diversify the economy, highlighted in QLDC's Regional Economic Development Strategy (2015), to increase resilience, reduce the impacts of events outside of Queenstown's control and seek to address resident incomes and cost-of-living issues.

It is clear when comparing employment growth competitive share analysis with location quotients that Queenstown has comparative and competitive advantages in tourism and related industries when compared to Auckland and Taranaki, or New Zealand as a whole. This paints the picture of a strongly tourism-dependent economy.

Patterson compares Queenstown to the wider Otago region, Rotorua (another famous international tourist town), and New Zealand on an export diversification index. Tellingly, Rotorua has a considerably more diversified economy than Queenstown which is consistent with most other regions in New Zealand where tourism is a key sector. Nonetheless Rotorua, as a key visitor destination in New Zealand, was similarly affected with international visitor spend down 89 per cent in the year to May 2021, with Queenstown, not including the lakes districts, down 92 per cent for the same period. However, Queenstown fared better with domestic spending up 57 per cent compared to

13 per cent for Rotorua for the same period, substantially due to Aucklanders changing their travel habits during international travel restrictions.

Diversification, however, is not only challenged by a strong path-dependency[18] in tourism and tourism-related activities, but there are also geographic, human, demographic, structural, and institutional factors to deal with moving forward. The COVID-19 interregnum, with strong border controls and severe lockdowns in source markets for visitors, severely affected the local economy. Even domestic tourism in Queenstown, which was strengthened by an increase in visitors from its largest domestic market, Auckland, has been affected by Auckland being locked down more often, at higher levels, and longer than all other regions. The start/stop travel bubbles with Australia only adding to uncertainty.

Patterson (2020) suggests several strategies for Queenstown in diversifying its economy based on the literature:

- Enhance the skills and capacity of the area's workforce
- Foster smart specializations and clusters
- Encourage entrepreneurship and support small business
- Invest in infrastructure and take advantage of outside funding
- Recirculate local capital
- Innovate and adapt to new ways of doing things
- Support a clean and healthy environment
- Embrace diversity and youth.

The contexts – physical, built, human, social, cultural, institutional, and economic – will shape what is possible. It will also require, due to such strong path-dependency, outside examples of success. However, endogenous opportunities for economic development, diversification and long-term resilience will need to be developed in partnership with higher tiers of government, neighbouring territories, and local communities; both geographical and functional, such as business sectors and organizations, environmental and research organizations, and experts from strategic and related spheres.

Whether Queenstown continues in its path dependency, or manages to diversify, is the key question. There are strong signs that there is a lack of willingness to diversify away from tourism and that markets will open up to throw Queenstown a lifeline to recovery.

There are opportunities to diversify within tourism using a 'related variety' approach that may enable new market opportunities (e.g. mountaineering and rescue expertise or scalable and exportable adventure tourism expertise and technology). The appointment of a hospitality and tourism technology cluster manager is one such example. Other viable pathways include looking to build clusters of economic activity based on amenity value, high human capital, and entrepreneurship, digital start-ups, high mobility and connectivity, and a local source of highly skilled and high-net-worth individuals. The latter is under way through a new initiative called The Home for Healthier Business.[19] The campaign promotes the advantages of the unique Queenstown Lakes lifestyle, entrepreneurial community spirit, and progressive business attributes.

According to QLDC Economic Development Manager, Peter Harris:

> Queenstown Lakes district has a global reputation as a spectacular place to visit and holiday, but we want to challenge the perception of our district as a place simply to come on holiday … We have an exciting and progressive community of talent and innovation here which we want to build on. The Home for Healthier Business is a campaign to showcase Queenstown, Wānaka and surrounding communities as thriving places to live and do business while forging a regenerative economy.

Further, the development of a Research and Innovation Tech Hub has been announced, capitalizing on resident tech entrepreneurs and businesses. A Research & Innovation advisory board will be formed chaired by Austrian entrepreneur Sir Hermann Hauser, who co-founded businesses including Acorn Computers, and is vice chairman of the European Innovation Council's €10 billion Tech Fund.

Queenstown has been hit hard by COVID-19 socially and economically. The fundamentals are there to build back better, but path-dependencies and thinly resourced local institutional arrangements will require strong partnerships and innovative and entrepreneurial efforts (Wilson, 2020). It will require a strong partnership with central government, the private sector, researchers, and local leadership to build back better in a region severely and disproportionately affected by the pandemic.

3.5 CONCLUSIONS

New Zealand suffered similar adverse macroeconomic impacts to its trading partners with logistic constraints, tourism and related industry downturns, and asset inflation. It also used heavy fiscal spending over monetary responses to the pandemic. It has suffered increased inequality as those with assets, including housing, have benefitted from low interest rates and asset inflation over those without. That New Zealand bounced back quickly has been aided by geography and high social capital, but the pandemic has exposed vulnerabilities in both health responses and the economy. High-level macroeconomic trends have masked endemic underlying issues such as low productivity growth and a decades-long gradual reduction of exports as a percentage of GDP. These combined factors are borne out in employment outcomes, between population groups, and regional economies.

New Zealand's regional response to COVID-19 had three elements that came together. Firstly, leadership in the initial stages, when the need for good leadership and good governance was obvious and urgent. Economic development organizations needed to ensure they had the right people around the table to lead cities and regions in their recovery efforts. In many cases necessity became the mother of invention, but this should not detract from significant regional efforts at coordination and collaboration to address the pandemic.

Secondly, strategy. Life changed enormously and continued to change in unexpected ways, at pace. No economic commentators, for example, predicted a significant rise in asset prices –which in retrospect, with the largest fiscal response in New Zealand's history might have been better predicted. However, except for hard-hit sectors like international tourism and related sectors, many of the basic factors and structures of regional economies have remained, providing for varied regional outcomes. Economic strategies most often remained relevant and central to planning, even for regions like Queenstown who had diversification plans in place prior to the pandemic. A focus on shoring up significant sectors, bringing forward significant job-rich projects, such as infrastructure projects, and endeavouring to redeploy hard hit workers, all played roles in addressing the pandemic at the regional level.

Thirdly, action. Economic development leaders needed to balance speed with well-designed responses. Responses proportional to local circumstances usually did not have unintended negative consequences. The scale of action from central government averted what would have been an even worse shock across the national economy. Tailored regional responses complemented central government's approach. The government used its balance sheet to stimulate investment in the economy, especially in industries that could soak up and recycle capital, employ large numbers of people, and stimulate further economic activity. Infrastructure, construction, and housing remained strong and are currently booming in the domestic economy creating labour shortages and despite supply chain hindrances and inflationary pressures. Primary sector exports are leading the recovery even though they are somewhat constrained by global supply chain challenges and domestic labour shortages. Regional responses took advantage of macroeconomic settings and fiscal spending, often matching those with local government spending and private sector investment to activate local responses.

These responses put necessity ahead of new strategic approaches to building back better. Balancing pandemic response with climate change response was, and remains, difficult. That said, many regions were already on the zero-carbon journey prior to COVID-19 and these strategies played a part in national and regional responses.

Five key themes emerged from our research that typify New Zealand's response to the COVID-19 pandemic: First, the benefits of New Zealand's geographic isolation, seasonal variance, and lag time provided a breathing space to consider its response and learn from others. Second, high trust in government and health institutions meant that New Zealanders acceded to stringent rules associated with an elimination response. This response is severely challenged by the fact that New Zealand, as a small trading nation that relies on global connectivity for its prosperity, cannot continue to remain closed off. Third, a strong fiscal response buffered the income shock and insulated New Zealand long enough to take advantage of irrepressible market forces that allowed construction and New Zealand primary exports to lead recovery. Fourth, bespoke but nascent regional disaster planning aligned central government efforts with regional responses. It allowed for the strong fiscal response to be deployed locally and targeted programmes to local conditions. Lastly a tension between 'building back better' and simply rebuilding the economy is still playing out but the pandemic shock has opened opportunities for new thinking. Climate change responses and policy developments in New Zealand have progressed in earnest during the pandemic and, perhaps, a demonstration of resilience through the pandemic has helped in that regard.

We conclude that there have been significant unintended sectoral effects due to heavy quantitative easing, an elimination strategy, and lockdowns, but that fiscal policy dampened negative effects overall. New Zealand has benefitted from its reliance on primary products, but structural distortions remain challenging and key goals prior to COVID-19 – such as increasing productivity growth, higher value exports, inclusive growth, and addressing climate change – have had severe setbacks, even if still strongly on the agenda.

NOTES

1. Defined by the Ministry of Health as being confident that chains of transmission have been eliminated for at least 28 days and can effectively contain any future imported cases from overseas.
2. See https://population.un.org/wpp/Download/Standard/Population/.
3. See https://www.stats.govt.nz/indicators/population-of-nz.
4. See https://www.treasury.govt.nz.
5. Level 4 being the highest level of a lockdown in NZ. See initial rules at https://www.health.govt.nz/news-media/media-releases/additional-guidance-alert-level-4-rules.
6. See https://www.statista.com/statistics/1104709/coronavirus-deaths-worldwide-per-million-inhabitants/.
7. Auckland tops the Global Liveability Ranking – Economist Intelligence Unit (https://www.eiu.com/n/campaigns/global-liveability-index-2022/#:~:text=The%20Global%20Liveability%20Index%20quantifies,liveable%20city%20in%20the%20world).
8. See https://www.treasury.govt.nz/publications/tr/treasury-report-t2020-973-economic-scenarios-13-april-2020-html.

9.   Half Year Economic and Fiscal Update 2021 – 15 December 2021 (https://www
     .treasury.govt.nz/system/files/2021-12/hyefu21.pdf).
10. Ibid.
11. The highest level of lockdown in New Zealand's COVID-19 management
     response system.
12. Project Kokiri.
13. Te Tauihu: Intergenerational Strategy.
14. Have historical connections.
15. Sacred mountains.
16. Traditional tribal lands.
17. Resident population varies in line with cyclical employment related to tourism
     demand.
18. Where the concentration of industry has a self-reinforcing and cumulative effect
     and can create dependency.
19. See https://healthierbusiness.org/.

BIBLIOGRAPHY

Auckland City Council (2021Jan.) 'Auckland Emergency Management Plan: Unite
   against Covid-19', https://www.aucklandemergencymanagement.org.nz/covid-19.
Brookes, H., Leung-Wai, J. and McVeigh, P. (2020 Mar. 30) 'COVID-19 and our
   regions: Responding to the urgent, planning for the long term', Martin Jenkins
   and   Associates,   https://medium.com/from-the-exosphere/regions-and-covid-19
   -responding-to-the-urgent-planning-for-the-long-term-5828b90783dc.
Brookes, H., McVeigh, P. and Wilson, D. (2020), 'A guide to local and regional recovery and reimagination', Economic Development New Zealand, Martin Jenkins and
   Assoc., Cities and Regions Ltd, Auckland (May).
Cave, D. (2020 May 23) 'Coronavirus in New Zealand: How Jacinda Ardern sold
   a drastic lockdown', *New York Times*, https://www.nytimes.com/2020/05/23/world/
   asia/jacinda-ardern-coronavirus-new-zealand.html.
ChristchurchNZ (2020 Dec.) 'Ōtautahi Christchurch Recovery Plan', Christchurch
   City Council, https://ccc.govt.nz/assets/Documents/The-Council/Plans-Strategies
   -Policies-Bylaws/Plans/STR3913-Otautahi-Christchurch-Recovering-Plan-WEB
   .pdf.
Easton, B. H. (1994) 'Economic and other ideas behind the New Zealand reforms',
   Oxford Review of Economic Policy, vol. 10, no. 3 pp. 78–94.
Economist Intelligence Group (2021 June 9) 'Auckland tops the Global Liveability
   Ranking', https://www.eiu.com/n/auckland-tops-the-global-liveability-ranking/.
Fonseka, D. (2021 June 12) 'Our "hermit Kingdom" needs to get serious about supply
   chain issues', *Stuff*, https://www.stuff.co.nz/business/opinion-analysis/125410556/
   our-hermit-kingdom-needs-to-get-serious-about-supply-chain-issues.
Infometrics (2020 Dec.) 'Taranaki region economic profile', https://ecoprofile
   .infometrics.co.nz/Taranaki%2bRegion/Infographics/Overview.
Kierstead, J. (2019 June) 'Karl Popper's The Open Society and its Enemies', *Journal of
   New Zealand Studies* (NS28), https://doi.org/10.26686/jnzs.v0iNS28.5418.
Martin, S. and Maharaj, S. (2020 Nov.) 'Auckland Economic Quarterly: Journey to
   the centre of the city', Auckland City Council, https://www.aucklandcouncil.govt
   .nz/about-auckland-council/business-in-auckland/docsoccasionalpapers/auckland
   -economic-quarterly-november-2020.pdf.

McDonald, L. (2021) 'Queenstown to establish $45m research and innovation hub, with Government backing', *Stuff* (May 28), https://www.stuff.co.nz/otago/125278678/queenstown-to-establish-45m-research-and-innovation-hub-with-government-backing.

Ministry of Business Innovation and Employment (n.d.), Tourism data, https://www.mbie.govt.nz/immigration-and-tourism/tourism-research-and-data/tourism-data-releases/tourism-electronic-card-transactions/data-download/.

Ministry of Health (2021 Nov.) *Covid-19: Minimisation and protection strategy for Aotearoa New Zealand*, https://www.health.govt.nz/our-work/diseases-and-conditions/covid-19-novel-coronavirus/covid-19-response-planning/covid-19-minimisation-and-protection-strategy-aotearoa-new-zealand.

Nelson City Council, Tasman District Council, Mana Whenua, Nelson Tasman Chamber of Commerce, Nelson Regional Development Agency and the regionally based government agencies (2020) *Project Kokiri*, © 2021 Project Kōkiri—kokiri@nelsontasman.nz.

Olsen, B. (2021 May 27) 'Key Trends for Covid-19 and New Zealand's recovery', presentation to Economic Development New Zealand Annual Conference, https://economicdevelopment.org.nz/about-3-1.

Otago Daily Times (2021 Feb. 18) 'Tourism must be more sustainable: Commissioner', https://www.odt.co.nz/news/national/tourism-must-be-more-sustainable-commissioner.

Patterson, B. (2020) 'Diversification in Queenstown-Lakes: Context and what others have done', People and Places Ltd, Queenstown.

Queenstown Lakes District Council (2020) 'Queenstown Lakes District COVID-19 Recovery Intelligence Report', QLDC, Queenstown.

Queenstown Lakes District Council (2021 Sept.) 'Community and economic development', https://www.qldc.govt.nz/community/economic-development.

Queenstown Lakes District Council (2021 Dec.) 'Local businessman appointed to lead cluster development', https://www.qldc.govt.nz/2021/july-2021/21-07-13-local-businessman-appointed-to-lead-cluster-development.

Queenstown Lakes District Council: Economic Development Unit (2021 Sept.) 'Home for Healthier Business: Queenstown Lakes', https://healthierbusiness.org/.

Radio New Zealand (2020 Mar. 20) 'Coronavirus: Government offers $900m loan for Air NZ', https://www.rnz.co.nz/news/political/412197/coronavirus-government-offers-900m-loan-for-air-new-zealand.

Radio New Zealand (2021 Jan. 26) 'Dumb good luck: no Outbreak after Covid-19 community case – health expert', Checkpoint, https://www.rnz.co.nz/national/programmes/checkpoint/audio/2018781065/dumb-good-luck-no-outbreak-after-covid-19-community-case-health-expert.

Rosenberg, B. (2016) 'New Zealand's low value economy: An analysis of New Zealand's productivity paradox', *Prime Economics and the Policy Observatory, AUT*, https://thepolicyobservatory.aut.ac.nz/__data/assets/pdf_file/0004/75928/Bill-Rosenberg-on-NZs-productivity-paradox-v3.pdf.

Statista (2021 July) *Population density of Singapore from 2011 to 2020*, https://www.statista.com/statistics/778525/singapore-population-density.

Statista (2021 Dec.) *Coronavirus (COVID-19) deaths worldwide per one million population as of December 13, 2021, by country*, https://www.statista.com/statistics/1104709/coronavirus-deaths-worldwide-per-million-inhabitants/.

Stats NZ, Tatauranga Aotearoa (2021 June) *2018 Census population and dwelling counts*, https://www.stats.govt.nz/information-releases/2018-census-population-and-dwelling-counts.

Stats NZ, Tatauranga Aotearoa (2021 June) *Estimated Population of NZ*, https://www.stats.govt.nz/indicators/population-of-nz.

Stats NZ, Tatauranga Aotearoa (2021 July) *Primary products push exports to a new high*, https://www.stats.govt.nz/news/primary-products-push-exports-to-a-new-high.

Stats NZ, Tatauranga Aotearoa (2021 July, Nov.) *Covid-19 data portal: Total cases for the Auckland, Waitematā and Counties-Manukau District Health Board areas*, https://www.stats.govt.nz/experimental/covid-19-data-portal.

Stats NZ, Tatauranga Aotearoa (2021 Dec.) *Tourism satellite account: Year ended March 2021*, https://www.stats.govt.nz/information-releases/tourism-satellite-account-year-ended-march-2021#topic.

The Treasury, Te Tai Ōhanga (2020 Dec.) *Half Year Economic and Fiscal Update 2020*, https://www.treasury.govt.nz/system/files/2020-12/hyefu20.pdf.

The Treasury, Te Tai Ōhanga (2021 June) *New Zealand Economic and Financial Overview 2016*, https://www.treasury.govt.nz/sites/default/files/2010-04/nzefo-16.pdf.

The Treasury, Te Tai Ōhanga (2021 July) *T2020/973: Economic scenarios – 13 April 2020*, https://www.treasury.govt.nz/publications/tr/treasury-report-t2020-973-economic-scenarios-13-april-2020-html.

The Treasury, Te Tai Ōhanga (2021 Dec.) *Half Year Economic and Fiscal Update 2021*, https://www.treasury.govt.nz/publications/efu/half-year-economic-and-fiscal-update-2021.

Tourism Industry Aotearoa (2021 Sept.) 'Quick facts and figures', https://tia.org.nz/about-the-industry/quick-facts-and-figures/#:~:text=Tourism%20is%20New%20Zealand's%20biggest,of%20New%20Zealand's%20total%20GDP.

Tyler-Harwood, L. (2015) 'Wealth and income inequality', University Challenge Essay, University of Auckland, https://www.treasury.govt.nz/sites/default/files/2017-10/uc-laurentylerharwood.pdf.

United Nations Department of Economic and Social Affairs: Population Dynamics (2021 June) *World Population Prospects (2019)*, https://population.un.org/wpp/Download/Standard/Population/.

Venture Taranaki (2018) 'Tapuae Roa: make way for Taranaki', http://www.makeway.co.nz/media/1028/tapuae-roa-action-plan-6-april-2018.pdf.

Venture Taranaki (2020 July) *Taranaki Business Survey June 2020*, https://www.venture.org.nz/assets/Uploads/Venture-Taranaki/Taranaki-Business-Survey-June-2020.pdf.

Wakatu Incorporation (2019) *Te Tauihu Intergenerational strategy*, https://www.tetauihu.nz/#mihi-welcome.

Wellington City Council (2021 Jan.) 'Annual Plan 2020/2021 Appendix 1: Pandemic response and recovery plan', https://wellington.govt.nz/-/media/your-council/plans-policies-and-bylaws/plans-and-policies/annualplan/2020-21/wcc-annual-plan-2020-21.pdf?la=en&hash=DA0F36FEBC44C7827E413FFB90BFE8ABF6F63D79.

Wilson, D. (2020) 'Powering up the regions: Improving the mechanisms to achieve a productive, sustainable and inclusive economy', Cities and Regions Ltd, Auckland.

4. The overblown role of population density in the COVID-19 pandemic in New York City

Yu Zhong and Bertrand Teirlinck

4.1 INTRODUCTION

COVID-19 (SARS-CoV-2) is not New York City's first encounter with a highly transmissible virus. Back in 1918, when the influenza pandemic swept through the United States, New York City, with the help of its experienced public health experts and practitioners, fared better than its regional neighbors (Aimone, 2010). The city leveraged its large public health infrastructure to establish control strategies, mount public health education campaigns, and mandate certain behaviors through ordinances. Over a century later, the city faces another enormous challenge in the COVID-19 pandemic and combated with even more drastic mitigation efforts including stay-at-home orders and the closure of public schools during the first wave.

This new virus and the subsequent measures such as social distancing and mask mandates spurred an acute awareness of density and crowding. Some commentators named high population density as a primary factor in high case incidence (Schoichet and Jones, 2020; Kotkin, 2020). However, numerous studies note the absence of a causal link between the two (Fang and Wahba, 2020). And as the pandemic continued to spread globally, we have seen the curve in New York City being flattened, while other less dense areas began to see higher case incidence. Much like in 1918, it appears other factors are more predominant than population density in the spread of a virus.

Laying blame at the feet of population density alone also ignores the practical inability to keep people apart and conditions where people might have little option but to live in a crowded household or a packed workplace. In fact, some argue that these are more prominent factors in identifying hotspots (Bhardwaj et al., 2020). Furthermore, there are reasons to believe large urban centers are more resilient to such shocks. In the case of New York City, the city's robust public health infrastructure was better equipped to absorb a large influx of patients and contain the spread, especially in the early stage of the pandemic. The city was also able to quickly leverage its resources and robust innovation ecosystem to facilitate a speedy and seamless production of essential equipment while simultaneously imposing social distancing measures.

Using neighborhood-level COVID-19 data from New York City, we seek to bring our own analysis to the existing literature and undertake a review of other factors that have played a critical role in the spread of COVID-19 from a local perspective. Our analysis finds no strong correlation between an area's population density and its case incidence, measured as number of cases per 100,000 residents. In fact, we find the opposite is true – higher population density is associated, albeit weakly, with lower case incidence – regardless of which time period we look at. When this analysis is repeated for other factors, we find that case incidence tends to be higher in low-income neighborhoods and family communities where average household size is bigger. It appears that the overall population density does not matter much – it may in fact be helpful – while crowding within one's home or workplace and the socioeconomic factors leading to such crowding are the main culprit.

The remainder of the chapter is organized as follows. We first discuss our methodology, including data sources and definitions used in this analysis. The next section focuses on the relationship between population density and COVID-19 case rates. We then explore other prominent factors behind the spread of the virus, including international and domestic connections, crowding, and socioeconomic factors, as well as the role of timing and public health response during the pandemic. Finally, we discuss ways in which New York City and other urban centers benefited from their population density when dealing with the challenges of COVID-19.

4.2   METHODOLOGY

Our analysis mostly relies on correlation analysis to study the impacts of population density and other factors in the spread of COVID-19. Although it does not imply causation, correlation shows the direction and strength of the relationship between two variables and can help us understand the factors of COVID-19 transmission. Consequently, we do not seek to establish causal links between socioeconomic factors but provide a descriptive review of associations in New York City.

Despite the limitations, correlation analysis remains a useful tool in public health studies and has been utilized to examine the relationship between socioeconomic factors and health outcomes or prevalence of a certain disease, as demonstrated, for instance, by Song et al. (2011) and Gant et al. (2012). This approach is also commonly found in the literature exploring social determinants of health and COVID-19, such as Abrams and Szefler (2020), Singu et al. (2020), Turner-Musa et al. (2020), and De Jesus et al. (2021).

In this study, we use case data from New York City Department of Health and Mental Hygiene (DOHMH), which publishes cumulative COVID-19 cases and deaths daily. The granularity of this data is one of its main strengths as it provides access to data down to zip code level, which we then aggregate into Public Use Microdata Areas (PUMAs) for further analysis.[1] To calculate case rates per 100,000 people, DOHMH relies on 2019 population estimates from the United States Census Bureau.

Most variables used in this analysis are from the United States Census Bureau's American Community Survey (ACS) 2015–19 five-year Public Use Microdata Sample (PUMS) estimates, which provide a vast amount of demographic and socioeconomic information down to the PUMA level including income, education, occupations, and commuting patterns. While most variables are directly available through the survey, some factors related to crowding – specifically the "number of people per room" and "occupancy coefficient" – required some aggregation and transformation. We create the "number of people per room" variable using "number of persons" and "number of rooms" information for each household and construct the "occupancy coefficient" variable using the occupants per room data directly from the Census website.

To study the impact of working from home in COVID-19 transmission, we rely on the telework definition put together by Dingel and Neiman (2020) along with ACS PUMS data. Based on O*NET's Work Context Questionnaire and Generalized Activities Questionnaire, certain activities are identified as ones that cannot be performed at home. If any such activity is an important part of a given occupation, they code it as not telework-capable. We slightly alter their work and convert the 2010 Standard Occupational Classification (SOC) codes used in their work to be ACS compatible. Using employment figures from Bureau of Labor Statistics' May 2020 Occupational Employment Survey (OES), we then conclude a sensitivity analysis looking at the share of New York City residents employed in "telework-capable" occupations. While we note some disparities, our findings generally align with their work (Table 4.1). The difference could also be due to the different occupation compositions at the local and national level.

Table 4.1   Percentage of workforce deemed "telework-capable" by
              occupational group

Standard Occupational Classification (SOC)		Percentage of workforce coded as "telework-capable"		
SOC	Title	Teirlinck & Zhong	Dingel & Neiman	Difference
11	Management Occupations	88	88	0.00
13	Business and Financial Operations Occupations	88	87	0.01
15	Computer and Mathematical Occupations	100	100	0.00
17	Architecture and Engineering Occupations	62	54	0.08
19	Life, Physical, and Social Sciences Occupations	49	61	0.12
21	Community and Social Service Occupations	36	28	0.08
23	Legal Occupations	97	97	0.00
25	Educational Instruction and Library Occupations	99	98	0.01
27	Arts, Design, Entertainment, Sports, and Media Occupations	74	65	0.09
29	Healthcare Practitioners and Technical Occupations	7	6	0.01
31	Healthcare Support Occupations	1	2	0.01
33	Protective Service Occupations	6	5	0.01
35	Food Preparation and Serving Related Occupations	0	0	0.00
37	Building and Grounds Cleaning and Maintenance Occupations	0	0	0.00
39	Personal Care and Service Occupations	45	37	0.08
41	Sales and Related Occupations	30	26	0.04
43	Office and Administration Support Occupations	71	76	0.05
45	Farming, Fishing, and Forestry Occupations	1	0	0.01
47	Construction and Extraction Occupations	0	1	0.01
49	Installation, Maintenance, and Repair Occupations	0	1	0.01
51	Production Occupations	1	1	0.00
53	Transportation and Material Moving Occupations	6	3	0.03

Sources: Dingel and Neiman, 2020; New York City Economic Development Corporation Economic Research and Policy analysis using U.S. Census Bureau 2015–19 ACS five-year PUMS.

4.3   DENSITY MATTERS, BUT NOT THAT MUCH

Conventional wisdom often simplifies the relationship between an area's population density and infectious diseases down to the following: higher population density means higher cases. At first pass, this makes sense as population density increases the contact rate of an individual, thereby increasing the reproduction number (also called R by epidemiologists) of the virus and leading to larger outbreaks. This idea seems to hold merit. County-level data in the United States from March to June 2020 highlights that transmission rates of COVID-19 are higher in regions with high population densities. As seen in Figure 4.1, case incidence was higher in seemingly densely populated areas in the United States in the early months of the pandemic.

A closer look, however, suggests that density is not the only or even the primary factor in COVID-19 spread. For example, Sun et al. (2020) find no significant relationship between COVID-19 case rates and population density. Another statistical analysis looking at Chicago cases finds no correlation between population density and infection rates (Coryne, 2020). Similar findings are also observed in France and in other parts of the United States, although the researchers note that initial cases are more likely to appear in transportation hubs, themselves often high-density areas (Le Bras, 2021; Carozzi, 2020). The issue with population density as the culprit is that it ignores the dynamic nature of a virus' transmission. The public health responses including local regulations and behavioral changes like working from home and social distancing are far more critical than population density itself.

While New York City emerged as one of the earliest hotspots for COVID-19, giving credence to the idea that density is key, a more granular look within the city suggests a more nuanced take. In fact, the association between density and confirmed COVID-19 cases is negative regardless of which point in time we study. Using cumulative case data from New York City DOHMH from May 2020 (the first wave), January 2021 (the second wave), and September 2021 (the Delta wave), we find that the correlation between population density and case rates is −0.43 in May 2020, −0.49 in January 2021, and −0.50 in September 2021.[2]

We observe similar trends at the borough level (Table 4.2). These negative correlations between population density and COVID-19 case rates yield one critical question: if density is the answer, why does Manhattan, the most densely populated borough of New York City, have the lowest case rate at either point in time? Conversely, we might also ask: why does the least densely populated borough, Staten Island, have the highest case rate during both the second wave and the Delta wave?

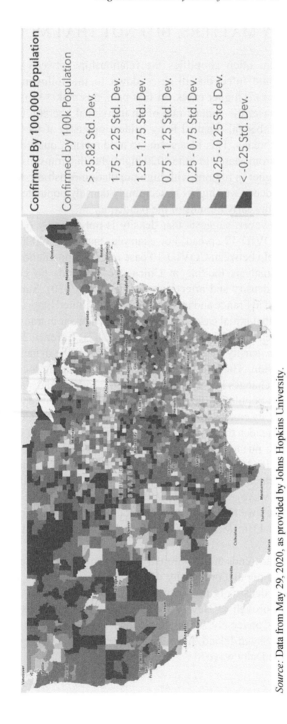

Source: Data from May 29, 2020, as provided by Johns Hopkins University.

Figure 4.1 COVID-19 cases per 100,000 population throughout United States counties

Some people argued that the low case incidence in Manhattan was due to population outflow in 2020, which had significantly lowered the borough's population density during the pandemic. To account for the outflow, we assume a 20 percent population loss in Manhattan, which was even higher than the high estimate from the *New York Times*.[3] This does not change the conclusion: Manhattan still stands out as the most densely populated borough in New York City with the lowest case rates (Table 4.2).[4]

Table 4.2   Borough analysis of case rate and population density

Borough	Population Density (per sq. mile)	Case Rate (Confirmed + Probable)		
		5/18/2020	1/15/2021	9/15/2021
Bronx	33,607	2,987	6,298	14,112
Brooklyn	36,886	1,959	5,056	12,267
Manhattan[a]	57,399	1,736	4,750	12,008
Queens	20,735	2,554	5,834	13,423
Staten Island	8,281	2,707	7,845	17,768

Note: [a] Assumes a 20 percent population outflow for Manhattan.
Source: Population from U.S. Census Bureau; cases data from New York City DOHMH as of 5/18/2020, 1/15/2021, and 9/15/2021.

4.4   WHAT MATTERS THEN?

International and Domestic Connections

The literature notes that three types of places confer outbreaks, all intertwined in some capacity (Florida, 2020). The first is "superstar" cities like New York and London. These cities have large inflows of visitors, both for leisure and business purposes. The second type is industrial centers like Wuhan, Detroit, or the region of Lombardy, among others, which are largely connected globally through supply chains. Finally, there are popular tourist spots like the ski slopes of Italy, Switzerland, and France, and their counterparts in the Colorado Rockies.

There is abundant evidence showing that the movement of populations is a key factor behind the spread. For example, a soccer match in Bergamo, Italy held in February 2020, before Italy recorded its first confirmed COVID-19 case, acted as an accelerant spreading the virus through Lombardy and beyond (Robinson, 2020). In the United States, COVID-19 also hit rural recreation counties such as Blain County, Idaho's ski slopes, early in the pandemic (Stafford and Irvine, 2020). Places with high degrees of natural amenities lure lots of tourists and turned out to be more susceptible to the virus than their

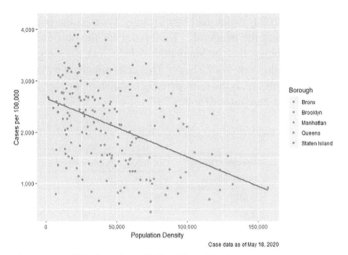

Note: A color version of this figure is available at the original source.
Source: Case data from New York City DOHMH as of May 18, 2020; population from U.S. Census Bureau.

Figure 4.2   Case rate vs. population density by Zip Code Tabulation Area (ZCTA)

less "touristy" counterparts, and even some urban areas. This is problematic because these rural areas generally have limited medical resources relative to the urban centers, which can lead to larger outbreaks and reduced access to care for non-COVID patients.

Connections also explain why New York City was among the hardest hit areas in the early stage of the pandemic. As one of the "superstar" cities, New York City is critically important to United States tourism and acts as a major point of entry for foreign travelers. As a destination, New York City accounted for over 6 percent of total United States travel in 2019 (foreign and domestic carriers). Regarding international tourism, Newark Liberty (EWR), LaGuardia (LGA), and John F. Kennedy (JFK) airports accounted for 9.7 percent of all U.S.-bound travel. Furthermore, two major epicenters for the outbreak, China and Italy, accounted for over 12 percent of all international visitations to New York City (based on 2018 data). Including France and Spain, which dealt with a large COVID-19 caseload early on, this figure jumps up to 22 percent of all visitations (NYC & Company, 2019).

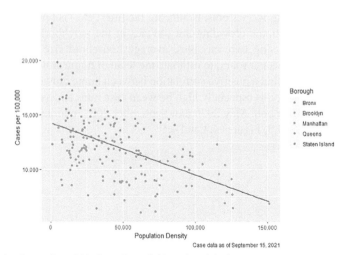

Note: A color version of this figure is available at the original source.
Source: Case data from New York City DOHMH as of September 15, 2021; population from U.S. Census Bureau.

Figure 4.3   *Case rate vs. population density by Zip Code Tabulation Area (ZCTA)*

Crowding, Not Density, Is a More Important Driver of Community Spread

Research highlights that crowding – measured as people per room or housing unit – better explains the ease of transmission of the virus. In that regard, it is not population density alone, but large gatherings and specific areas like dormitories, open-plan offices, churches, hospitals, public transport, planes, and cruise ships that are especially susceptible to the virus. We have seen that some rural counties that had high early infection rates being home to crowded facilities, such as prisons and meatpacking factories (OECD, 2021). Regarding the large gatherings, certain behaviors and circumstances also make these activities more dangerous (Pafka, 2020). For example, COVID-19 spread rapidly throughout Albany, Georgia in March 2020 following two large funerals – events with high levels of close physical contact, as well as high levels of aerosolizing activities such as singing (Barry, 2020).

Crowding and population density, while appearing similar, are very different concepts. Densely populated areas where people have the means to shelter in place, work remotely, and have all their food and other needs delivered to them differ greatly from places where remote work is not an option and the supply of essential services (grocery stores, healthcare facilities, etc.) is limited.

The impacts of home crowding are obvious at the neighborhood level in New York City. Using two variables, average household size and average number of occupants per room, to estimate the level of home crowding in each neighborhood, we find a positive correlation between home crowding and case rates. The correlation is especially high between case rates and average household size at 0.61 in both May 2020 and September 2021, and 0.69 in January 2021 (Tables 4.3–4.5, Figures 4.4 and 4.5).

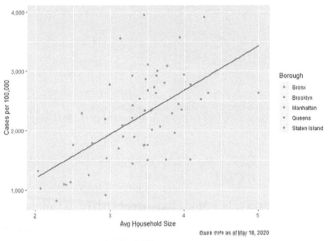

Note: A color version of this figure is available at the original source.
Source: Case data from New York City DOHMH as of May 18, 2020; demographics from U.S. Census Bureau 2015–19 ACS five-year PUMS.

Figure 4.4   *Case rate vs. average household size by PUMAs*

Table 4.3   *Correlation between case rates and crowding at home,
                  occupancy coefficient, and average household size*

	Average Household Size	Crowding (Average # of People per Room)	Occupancy Coefficient
5/18/2020	0.61	0.32	0.44
1/15/2021	0.69	0.24	0.37
9/15/2021	0.61	0.18	0.29

Source: Case data from New York City DOHMH as of May 18, 2020, January 15, 2021, and September 15, 2021; demographics from U.S. Census Bureau 2015–19 ACS five-year PUMS.

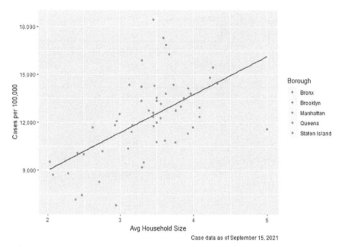

Case data as of September 15, 2021

Note: A color version of this figure is available at the original source.
Source: Case data from New York City DOHMH as of September 15, 2021; demographics from
U.S. Census Bureau 2015–19 ACS five-year PUMS.

Figure 4.5   *Case rate vs. average household size by PUMAs*

Table 4.4   *Top 10 neighborhoods with highest case rates as of
9/15/2021*

Neighborhood	Case rates 9/15/2021	Average household size		Crowding at home		Occupancy coefficient	
		Avg. household size	Ranking	People per room	Ranking	Occ. coefficient	Ranking
SI–Tottenville, Great Kills & Annadale PUMA	18,440	2.81	12	0.49	55	1.38	55
SI–New Springville & South Beach PUMA	17,305	2.89	11	0.55	53	1.49	49
SI–Port Richmond, Stapleton & Mariner's Harbor PUMA	16,845	2.75	17	0.57	50	1.51	46
Brooklyn–Sheepshead Bay, Gerritsen Beach & Homecrest PUMA	16,277	2.71	21	0.66	25	1.64	26
Brooklyn–Brighton Beach & Coney Island PUMA	15,887	2.41	36	0.70	16	1.68	17

Regional economic systems after COVID-19

Neighborhood	Case rates 9/15/2021	Average household size		Crowding at home		Occupancy coefficient	
		Avg. household size	Ranking	People per room	Ranking	Occ. coefficient	Ranking
QN–Jackson Heights & North Corona PUMA	15,426	2.99	7	0.82	5	1.92	2
QN–Howard Beach & Ozone Park PUMA	14,791	3.15	2	0.59	47	1.57	39
QN–Richmond Hill & Woodhaven PUMA	14,433	3.13	3	0.69	18	1.71	15
Bronx–Co-op City, Pelham Bay & Schuylerville PUMA	14,353	2.27	43	0.55	52	1.47	53
Bronx–Castle Hill, Clason Point & Parkchester PUMA	14,346	2.65	24	0.72	14	1.73	14

Source: Case data from New York City DOHMH as of September 15, 2021; demographics from U.S. Census Bureau 2015–19 ACS five-year PUMS.

Table 4.5   *Bottom 10 neighborhoods with highest case rates as of 9/15/2021*

Neighborhood	Case rates 9/15/2021	Average household size		Crowding at home		Occupancy coefficient	
		Avg. house-hold size	Ranking	People per room	Ranking	Occ. co-efficient	Ranking
MN–Hamilton Heights, MNville & West Harlem PUMA	10,016	2.30	41	0.64	34	1.59	33
MN–Chelsea, Clinton & Midtown Business District PUMA	9,549	1.61	55	0.66	23	1.56	42
Brooklyn–Crown Heights South, Prospect Lefferts & Wingate PUMA	9,500	2.40	37	0.65	29	1.64	25
QN–Bayside, Douglaston & Little Neck PUMA	9,191	2.56	33	0.52	54	1.43	54
MN–Battery Park City, Greenwich Village & Soho PUMA	8,813	1.83	53	0.67	19	1.59	35

Neighborhood	Case rates 9/15/2021	Average household size		Crowding at home		Occupancy coefficient	
		Avg. house-hold size	Ranking	People per room	Ranking	Occ. co-efficient	Ranking
MN–Murray Hill, Gramercy & Stuyvesant Town PUMA	8,733	1.69	54	0.61	42	1.48	51
Brooklyn–Brooklyn Heights & Fort Greene PUMA	8,302	2.10	48	0.65	26	1.59	30
MN–Upper East Side PUMA	7,470	1.88	51	0.59	48	1.49	50
MN–Upper West Side & West Side PUMA	7,167	1.87	52	0.59	46	1.48	52
Brooklyn–Park Slope, Carroll Gardens & Red Hook PUMA	6,827	2.34	40	0.60	45	1.54	44

Source: Case data from New York City DOHMH as of September 15, 2021; demographics from U.S. Census Bureau 2015–19 ACS five-year PUMS.

Studies on Social Vulnerability Highlight the Inequalities in the Pandemic

Research shows that certain social indicators like age, income, education, and the kinds of work people have are strongly correlated with infection and mortality rates (McPhearson et al., 2020). In the case of New York City, for example, hospitalization data shows a disproportionate risk for the elderly (age 65+) compared to others.[5] Studies also reveal the unequal burden of COVID-19 on low-income populations – often more likely to be people of color, living in crowded multi-generational households, heavily reliant on public transit, and less likely to work from home (Furman Center, 2020). These socioeconomic and demographic characteristics are the underlying forces that tend to deter-mine whether one can comfortably shelter in place, avoid close contact with an infected person, and have access to all basic needs and quality healthcare.

Such features help explain San Francisco's early success in containing COVID-19. The city has a higher share of workers in telework-capable indus-tries, fewer children per capita, and a higher overall educational attainment compared to other American cities. In that regard, it seems more resilient than Detroit, New Orleans, and even New York City, all far more diverse across socioeconomic and demographic lines.

Income and Education

Our analysis reveals a negative association between case rates and median income levels at −0.57 (May 2020), which is consistent with borough-level analysis where Manhattan stands out with higher level of income and lower case rates compared to the outer boroughs (Table 4.6, Figures 4.6 and 4.7). This is likely because higher-income populations are more likely to work from home and, in some cases, move to a secondary location during the crisis. These results showcase the importance of wealth and socioeconomic status in navigating the COVID-19 crisis, which is consistent with the literature reviewed above.

There is also a strong negative association between an area's case rate and its educational attainment regardless of the timeframe we observe, which is not surprising because income level and educational attainment are often highly correlated. Again, people with higher educational attainment tend to work in industries and occupations that are more telework-capable and can therefore avoid close contacts with the crowds, with a few exceptions such as the healthcare industry.

Table 4.6   Case rate by median income brackets

Median Income Bracket	ZCTA Count	Cumulative Cases	Cases per 100,000 people
Less than $50,000	34	266,240	12,964
$50,000–$74,999	62	438,884	12,859
$75,000–$99,999	47	234,273	12,537
$100,000–$149,999	26	80.602	8.687
$150,000 or higher	8	5,972	8,105

Note: ZCTA refers to Zip Code Tabulation Area which are put together by United States Bureau of Census and are the generalized areal representations of United States Postal Service (USPS) ZIP Code service areas.
Source: Income data from U.S. Census Bureau 2015–19 ACS five-year PUMS; case data from New York City DOHMH as of September 15, 2020.

Commuting Patterns

The association between case rates and commuting patterns yields some interesting and unexpected findings.[6] We find a strong negative association between the proportion of residents who bike to work (a solitary outdoor activity) and the case incidence, especially in the early stage (−0.68 in May 2020). On the other hand, as shown in Table 4.7, we find that regardless of timeframe, the proportion of residents who commute via the subway has a negative cor-

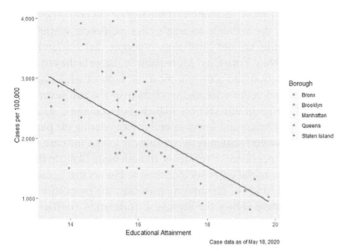

Note: A color version of this figure is available at the original source.
Source: Case data from New York City DOHMH as of May 18, 2020; demographics from U.S. Census Bureau 2015–19 ACS five-year PUMS.

Figure 4.6   Case rate vs. educational coefficient by PUMAs

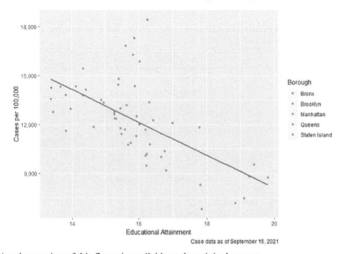

Note: A color version of this figure is available at the original source.
Source: Case data from New York City DOHMH as of September 15, 2020; demographics from U.S. Census Bureau 2015–19 ACS five-year PUMS.

Figure 4.7   Case rate vs. educational coefficient by PUMAs

relation with case incidence. Conversely, car usage appears to have a positive correlation with case rates, meaning that the higher the proportion of residents that drives to work, the higher is an area's case incidence. While this is coun- terintuitive, the results are not surprising to people that are familiar with the unique situation in New York City. More subway usage in the city often means better transit connection and a central location, both of which have appealed to higher-income and better-educated workers over the past several decades.

As discussed earlier in this section, higher socioeconomic status has trans- lated into better protection and lower infection rates during the pandemic. This explains the negative correlation between subway usage and case rates. For the same reasons, the outer borough residents, though more likely to drive, are also more vulnerable due to the other socioeconomic factors that come into play.

Among different kinds of commuting methods, the proportion of residents that works from home shows the strongest correlation coefficient at −0.72 (May 2020). Because this data was collected from 2015 to 2019 and does not reflect the working from home situation during the pandemic, our study equally examines the correlation between case rates and the proportion of residents in telework-capable occupations to confirm (Table 4.8, Figures 4.8 and 4.9). The result is similar at −0.75 (with May 2020 case rates) highlighting, again, the importance and effectiveness of social distancing, especially in the early stage.

Table 4.7   *Correlation between case rates and commuting patterns*

Commuting method	May 2020	Jan. 2021	Sept. 2021
Car/Truck/Van	0.48	0.63	0.60
Bus	0.63	0.67	0.59
Subway	−0.32	−0.48	−0.45
Long-distance Rail	0.00	−0.16	−0.23
Ferry	0.11	0.35	0.38
Taxi	−0.45	−0.56	−0.59
Bicycle	−0.68	−0.70	−0.63
Walk	−0.51	−0.52	−0.49
Work from home	−0.72	−0.72	−0.71
Telework-capable	*−0.75*	*−0.73*	*−0.70*

Source: Commuting data from U.S. Census Bureau 2015–19 ACS five-year PUMS; case data from New York City DOHMH as of May 18, 2020, January 15, 2021, and September 15, 2021.

Table 4.8   *Case rate by proportion of workers employed in telework-capable occupations*

Bracket	PUMA count	Case rate (confirmed + probable)		
		5/18/2020	1/15/2021	9/15/2021
Less than 20%	10	2,889	5,975	13,812
21–30%	29	2,411	5,633	13,131
31–40%	8	1,651	4,331	11,147
More than 40%	8	1,162	3,098	8,370

Source: Demographics from U.S. Census Bureau 2015–19 ACS five-year PUMS; case data from New York City DOHMH as of May 18, 2020, January 15, 2021, and September 15, 2021.

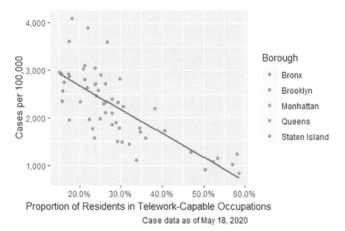

Note: A color version of this figure is available at the original source.
Source: Demographics from U.S. Census Bureau 2015–19 ACS five-year PUMS; case data from New York City DOHMH as of May 18, 2020.

Figure 4.8   *Case rate vs. proportion of residents employed in telework-capable occupations by PUMAs*

Timing and the Public Health Response Also Play a Critical Role

Beyond socioeconomic and demographic factors, research suggests timing also plays a critical role. While it might appear that density caused cities to become early hotspots, some argue that dense urban areas are also travel hubs that are more likely to attract the "first bolts of lightning" (Barr and Tassier, 2020). Furthermore, cities hit first by the virus have a steeper learning curve in responding, with fewer models and examples from which to learn and draw best practices. This, in turn, leads to slower and less effective initial responses

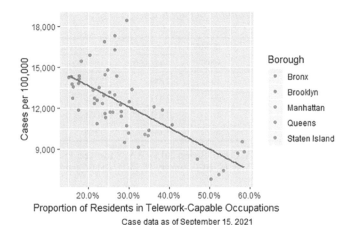

Source: Demographics from U.S. Census Bureau 2015–19 ACS five-year PUMS; case data from New York City DOHMH as of September 15, 2021.

Figure 4.9   Case rate vs. proportion of residents employed in telework-capable occupations by PUMAs

and a bigger outbreak. Simply put, places hit early by the virus have more cases, especially in the early stage.

There is a school of thought that suggests governments' responsiveness is more critical than a community's size or density (Wiener and Iton, 2020). For example, Chinazzi et al. (2020) estimate that the Wuhan lockdown reduced case importations by nearly 80 percent until mid-February on the international scale. In a county-level analysis of COVID-19 spread in the United States, Pei et al. (2020) find infection being significantly lower following social distancing and other control measures, with counterfactual simulations suggesting that cases and deaths would have been much lower had measures been implemented just 1–2 weeks earlier. California's first-in-the-nation stay-at-home order is an exemplar in the context of how a proactive public health measure explains, among other factors, why big cities in California stood out with early successes in dealing with COVID-19 relative to other metropolitan areas.

Even before COVID-19, the importance and effectiveness of the early control measures were already made clear based on observations from the 1918 influenza pandemic, as touched on at the beginning of this chapter. A 2007 study finds that the places that took quicker action on social distancing – closing schools and banning big public gatherings – had better outcomes. Cities in which multiple interventions were implemented at an early phase of the epidemic had peak death rates about 50 percent lower than those that did not. In addition, they exhibited less-steep epidemic curves, along with lower cumulative excess mortality (though the difference was smaller and less statistically significant than that for peak death rates) (Hatchett et al., 2007). The study points to the stark difference between Philadelphia, which was slow to act, and a more proactive St. Louis, as seen in Figure 4.10. Whereas St. Louis implemented social distancing measures two days after the first diagnosed case, Philadelphia officials understated the risk of disease transmission and did not take measures for over two weeks after the first case. For instance, the Philadelphia Liberty Loans Parade, a 200,000-attendee celebration, became one of the largest super-spreader events in the country's history (Roberts and Tehrani, 2020).

Quick response matters. But public health responses, even delayed, are still critical. Research on the stay-at-home order finds that these orders significantly reduced cases and fatalities, relative to counties that did not implement such measures (Fowler et al., 2021). Additional findings from the Centers for Disease Control and Prevention (CDC) also note the efficacy of social distancing measures in Arizona (Gallaway et al., 2020). The first of such measures to impact New York City was the statewide PAUSE order signed by Governor Andrew Cuomo on March 20, 2020. Shortly after, an analysis of the city's caseload indicated that the curve was flattening. The statewide mask mandate also proved to be effective in reducing transmission (Li et al., 2021).

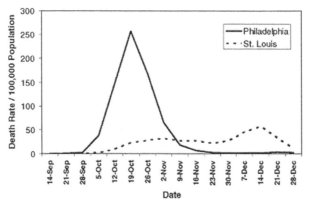

Source: Richard J. Hatchett, Carter E. Mecher, and Marc Lipsitch, "Public health interventions and epidemic intensity during the 1918 influenza pandemic," PNAS 104, no. 18 (May 2007): 7582–7, https://doi.org/10.1073/pnas.0610941104.

Figure 4.10   *Normalized death rate in Philadelphia and St. Louis during the 1918 pandemic*

4.5   DENSITY CAN ALSO BE A STRENGTH IN COPING WITH GLOBAL PANDEMICS

In certain aspects, there are benefits that also come with density, which are often overlooked by the public. Density can be advantageous for pandemic resilience in urban communities by supporting the provision of services due the interconnectivity and high-quality infrastructure. This, in turn, means faster emergency response times, better hospital staffing, and a greater concentration of intensive-care beds and other healthcare resources. This became evident in New York City hospitals' ability to absorb the large influx of new patients and sustain over 51,000 hospitalizations throughout the first wave while simultaneously developing and scaling up widespread testing and increasing supplies of personal protective equipment, supported by initiatives led by the city's economic development agency (Office of the Mayor, 2020a).[7]

Highly dense urban areas also have more robust innovation ecosystems and fiscal resources to cope with COVID-19 in general, meaning more effective interventions and a stronger safety net. As hinted earlier in this chapter, cities such as Seoul and Hong Kong were able to leverage their resources to develop robust test-and-trace programs early on to contain clusters rapidly, leading to lower case incidence than other urban areas. Several other cities, including Newcastle, Mexico City, and Budapest used technologies to assess social distancing measures, monitor mobility trends, and identify areas of crowding. In fact, the Organisation for Economic Co-operation and Development (OECD) notes that "digitalization has been a crucial lever in cities' response to the pandemic" (OECD, 2020).

The pandemic has also showcased cities' ability to smooth the transition to the temporary "new normal." For example, New York City's access to higher internet speeds has eased remote learning and working for residents. Initiatives such as New York City Department of Education's distribution of iPads to families without reliable access to technology have helped keep students up-to-date following school closures (Department of Education, 2020). In Massachusetts, Boston debuted a program early on to provide public school students with Chromebook computers for those without consistent access to technology (Department of Innovation and Technology, 2020). San Francisco installed Wi-Fi hotspots to bridge the digital divide and provide internet access to students lacking this critical infrastructure (Crowe, 2020). In Canada, Toronto partnered with private providers to provide temporary free Wi-Fi to low-income residents (Draaisma and Glover, 2020). Such solutions are more difficult to implement in smaller, rural communities without support from the state or federal government, forcing many of them to turn to smaller-scale interventions (Lai and Widmar, 2020). The implementation oftentimes is also less effective as free Wi-Fi hotspots struggle to reach the target population when students are spread too far apart.

Along with leveraging digital resources and partnerships, cities have demonstrated the ability to respond to the crisis through economic relief programs, which complement the national relief efforts. New York City launched a zero-interest loan program for small businesses through its Department of Small Business Services in April 2020 and invested a further $37 million in November 2020 through grants (Office of the Mayor, 2020b). Among other efforts, a public–private partnership between the Peter G. Foundation, New York City Economic Development Corporation (NYCEDC), and other partners, established Small Business Resource Network to provide guidance and resources to the city's affected businesses. Similar loan programs were established in Buenos Aires and Tokyo, with the latter also subsidizing business improvements aimed at supporting remote working implementation (OECD, 2020). Other cities established relief funds to protect economically vulnerable populations. For example, the city of Berlin acted promptly to distribute over $1 billion to self-employed individuals, such as freelancers and artists, and small businesses. In Italy, Milan's mutual aid fund paired €3 million from the city with private donations to support impacted populations. In the United Kingdom, private donors and investors organized the London Community Response, which gave out £57 million during the first year of its existence – an effort made possible by an active civil society in a highly dense area (London Community Response, 2021). Complementary to financial assistance, several cities, such as Bilbao, Yokohama, Seattle, and Lisbon also leveraged their resources to offer free consulting services to small businesses.

Urban areas also support the kind of redundancies that make communities more resilient during disasters (Badger, 2020). When travel becomes an issue, people are likely to find what they need within a walking distance or find alternative ways to get essentials through delivery services or bike couriers. As return to offices became more prevalent, many residents in urban areas changed commuting patterns by fully utilizing bike-sharing systems, so much so that demand for expansion of such amenities has significantly grown over the past year (Ley, 2021). When everyone is sheltering-in-place, it is easier for urban residents to create a public life with neighbors and friends while maintaining a physical distance, compared to less dense areas. Evidence abounds on how density has also helped to keep restaurants and other businesses afloat through easier takeout and delivery services in the urban communities (Loh et al., 2020).

4.6   CONCLUDING THOUGHTS

One unintended consequence of the density-transmission debate is that if governments and the public conclude that density itself is the problem, our society will encourage suburban sprawl rather than focusing on planning and investments that foster safe and sustainable urbanism (Weiner and Iton, 2020).

Many researchers advocate that society should use this crisis as an opportunity to rethink urban resilience from a broad and nuanced public health perspective, especially because density will be a critical component in addressing the climate crisis, which among many other things could easily lead to more frequent and deadly pandemics (Curseu et al., 2009; Liu et al., 2013). Several cities have already outlined plans for long-term recovery to address future shocks (OECD, 2020). Some are attempting to diversify their economies to be less reliant on tourism. Others, such as Paris and Nantes in France, are focusing on developing local food production to mitigate future supply chain disruptions and better feed vulnerable communities. In particular, the role of socioeconomic inequalities in the varying degrees of severity for different communities has spurred critical debates over the role of inclusivity and equity in urban development.

Density, certainly, is one of the solutions to the many social, urban, public health, and climate crises of this era.

NOTES

1.   Due to data availability, we conducted the correlation analysis at the Public Use Microdata Areas (PUMAs) level. PUMAs are geographic boundaries created by the United States Census Bureau. These are non-overlapping, statistical geographic areas that partition each state or equivalent entity into geographic areas containing no fewer than 100,000 people each.
2.   This analysis is conducted at the ZCTA (Zip Code Tabulation Area) level. ZCTAs are put together by United States Bureau of Census and are the generalized area representations of United States Postal Service (USPS) ZIP Code service areas.
3.   According to the *New York Times*, the estimated outflow in Manhattan ranges from 12.9 percent to 18.6 percent in May 2020. See Quealy, 2020.
4.   It is also likely that most of the population decline in the early stage had recovered as of September 2021. As such, it is probable that the actual case rate at that time is over-inflated.
5.   Data from New York City Department of Health and Mental Hygiene as of May 18, 2020.
6   Although it is difficult to draw significant insights due to the low volume of certain commuting methods such as motorcycles, ferryboats, or regional rails. If we look at the correlation coefficients for those commuting methods with somewhat sizable adherence, we confirm some expected trends.

7. Hospitalization data from New York City Department of Health and Mental Hygiene's github as of May 31, 2020.

REFERENCES

Abrams, E. M., & Szefler, S. J. (2020). COVID-19 and the impacts of social determinants of health. *The Lancet Respiratory Medicine*, 8(7), 659–61. https://doi.org/10.1016/S2213-2600(20)30234-4.

Aimone, F. (2010). The 1918 influenza epidemic in New York City: a review of the public health response. *Public Health Reports*, 125(3 Supp), 71–9. https://dx.doi.org/10.1177%2F00333549101250S310.

Badger, E. (2020, March 24). Density is normally good for us: that will be true after coronavirus, too. *The New York Times*. https://www.nytimes.com/2020/03/24/upshot/coronavirus-urban-density-risks.html.

Barr, J., & Tassier T. (2020, April 17). Are crowded cities the reason for the COVID-19 pandemic? *Scientific American*. https://blogs.scientificamerican.com/observations/are-crowded-cities-the-reason-for-the-covid-19-pandemic/.

Barry, E. (2020, March 30). Days after a funeral in a Georgia Town, Coronavirus 'hit like a bomb'. *The New York Times*. https://www.nytimes.com/2020/03/30/us/coronavirus-funeral-albany-georgia.html.

Bhardwaj, G., Esch, T., Lall, S., Marconcini M., Soppelsa, M. E., & Wahba, S. (2020, April 21). Cities, crowding, and the coronavirus: predicting contagion risk hotspots. *The World Bank*. https://documents1.worldbank.org/curated/en/206541587590439082/pdf/Cities-Crowding-and-the-Coronavirus-Predicting-Contagion-Risk-Hotspots.pdf.

Carozzi, F. (2020). Urban density and Covid-19. *SSRN*. https://dx.doi.org/10.2139/ssrn.3643204.

Chinazzi, M., Davis, J. T., Ajelli, M., Gioannini C., Litvinova, M., Merler, S., Pastore, Y., Piontti, A., Mu, K., Rossi, L., Sun, K., Viboud, C., Xiong, X., Yu, H., Halloran, M. E., Longini, I. M., & Vespignani, A. (2020). The effect of travel restrictions on the spread of the 2019 novel coronavirus (COVID-19) outbreak. *Science*, 368(6489), 395–400. https://doi.org/10.1126/science.aba9757.

Coryne, H. (2020, April 30). In Chicago, urban density may not be to blame for the spread of the Coronavirus. *ProPublica*. https://www.propublica.org/article/in-chicago-urban-density-may-not-be-to-blame-for-the-spread-of-the-coronavirus.

Crowe, C. (2020, April 9). San Francisco tackles digital divide with Wi-Fi SuperSpots. *SmartCities Dive*. https://www.smartcitiesdive.com/news/san-francisco-wifi-superspots-students-internet-access-digital-divide-coronavirus/575785/.

Curseu, D., Popa, M., Sirbu, D., & Stoian, I. (2009). Potential impact of climate change on pandemic influenza risk. In I. Dincer, A. Hepbasli, A. Midilli, & T. Karakoc (Eds.), *Global Warming* (pp. 643–57). Boston, MA: Springer. https://doi.org/10.1007/978-1-4419-1017-2_45.

De Jesus, M., Ramachandra, S. S., Jafflin, Z., Maliti, I., Daughtery, A., Shapiro, B., Howell, W. C., & Jackson, M. C. (2021). The environmental and social determinants of health matter in a pandemic: predictors of COVID-19 case and death rates in New York City. *International Journal of Environmental Research and Public Health*, 18(16), 8416. https://doi.org/10.3390/ijerph18168416.

Department of Education (2020). Your DOE-loaned iPad or laptop. *City of New York.* https://www.schools.nyc.gov/learning/digital-learning/ipads-and-laptops/your-doe-loaned-ipad-or-laptop.

Department of Innovation and Technology (2020, May 1). Internet connectivity and technology supports during COVID-19 response. *City of Boston.* https://www.boston.gov/news/internet-connectivity-and-technology-supports-during-covid-19-response.

Dingel, J. I., & Neiman, B. (2020). How many jobs can be done at home? *Journal of Public Economics*, 189, 104235. http://dx.doi.org/10.1016/j.jpubeco.2020.104235.

Draaisma, M., & Glover, C. (2020, September 10). Toronto joins forces with tech firm to provide free Wi-Fi to low-income families in 2 buildings. *CBC.* https://www.cbc.ca/news/canada/toronto/city-toronto-cisco-canada-free-wifi-two-buildings-digital-canopy-1.5718017.

Fang, W., & Wahba, S. (2020, April 20). Urban density is not an enemy in the Coronavirus fight: evidence from China. *The World Bank.* https://blogs.worldbank.org/sustainablecities/urban-density-not-enemy-coronavirus-fight-evidence-china.

Florida, R. (2020, April 3). The geography of Coronavirus. *Bloomberg CityLab.* https://www.bloomberg.com/news/articles/2020-04-03/what-we-know-about-density-and-covid-19-s-spread.

Fowler, J. H., Hill, S. J., Levin, R., & Obradovich, N. (2021). Stay-at-home orders associate with subsequent decreases in COVID-19 cases and fatalities in the United States. *PLOS One*, 16(6). https://doi.org/10.1371/journal.pone.0248849.

Furman Center (2020, April 10). COVID-19 cases in New York City, a neighborhood-level analysis. *New York University.* https://furmancenter.org/thestoop/entry/covid-19-cases-in-new-york-city-a-neighborhood-level-analysis.

Gallaway, M. S., Rigler, J., Robinson, S., Herrick, K., Livar, E., Komatsu, K., Brady, S., Cunico, J., & Christ, C. M. (2020). Trends in COVID-19 incidence after implementation of mitigation measures – Arizona, January 22–August 7, 2020. *Morbidity and Mortality Weekly Report*, 69(40), 1460–63. http://dx.doi.org/10.15585/mmwr.mm6940e3.

Gant, Z., Lomotey, M., Hall, H. I., Hu, X., Guo, X., & Song, R. (2012). A county-level examination of the relationship between HIV and social determinants of health: 40 states, 2006–2008. *The Open AIDS Journal*, 6, 1–7. http://dx.doi.org/10.2174/1874613601206010001.

Hatchett, R. J., Mecher, C. E., & Lipsitch, M. (2007). Public health interventions and epidemic intensity during the 1918 influenza pandemic. *PNAS*, 104(18), 7582–7. https://doi.org/10.1073/pnas.0610941104.

Kotkin, J. (2020, April 26). Op-ed: Angelenos like their single-family sprawl. The coronavirus proves them right. *Los Angeles Times.* https://www.latimes.com/opinion/story/2020-04-26/coronavirus-cities-density-los-angeles-transit.

Lai, J., & Widmar, N. (2020). Revisiting the digital divide in the COVID-19 era. *Applied Economics Perspective and Policy*, 43(1), 458–64. https://doi.org/10.1002/aepp.13104.

Le Bras, H. (2021, January 26). Population density: not a primary factor in Covid-19. *Polytechnique Insights.* https://www.polytechnique-insights.com/en/columns/health-and-biotech/geographic-not-social-factors-were-key-in-the-spread-of-covid-19/.

Ley, A. (2021, December 2). Citi Bike struggles to keep up with New Yorkers' love of cycling. *The New York Times.* https://www.nytimes.com/2021/12/02/nyregion/citi-bike-parking-docking-station.html?action=click&module=Well&pgtype=Homepage&section=New%20York.

Li, L., Liu, B., Liu, S. H., Ji, J., & Li, Y. (2021). Evaluating the impact of New York's executive order on face mask use on COVID-19 cases and mortality: a comparative interrupted times series study. *Journal of General Internal Medicine*, 36(4), 985–9. https://doi.org/10.1007/s11606-020-06476-9.

Liu, X., Rohr, J. R., & Li, Y. (2013). Climate, vegetation, introduced hosts and trade shape a global wildlife pandemic. *Proceedings of the Royal Society B*, 280(1753). https://doi.org/10.1098/rspb.2012.2506.

Loh, T. H., Love, H., & Vey, J. S. (2020, March 25). The qualities that imperil urban places during COVID-19 are also the keys to recovery. *Brookings*. https:// www.brookings.edu/blog/the-avenue/2020/03/25/the-qualities-that-imperil-urban -places-during-covid-19-are-also-the-keys-to-recovery/?utm_campaign=Bass %20Newsletter&utm_source=hs_email&utm_medium=email&utm_content= 86080579.

London Community Response (2021, March 26). Covid anniversary: over £57m distrib- uted by the London Community Response. https://londoncommunityresponsefund .org.uk/news/covid-anniversary-over-ps57m-distributed-london-community -response.

McPhearson, T., Grabowski, Z. J., Herreros-Cantis, P., Mustafa, A., Ortiz, L., Kennedy, C., Tomateo, C., Lopez, B., Olivotto, V., & Vantu, A. (2020). Pandemic injustice: spatial and social distributions of the first wave of COVID-19 in the US epicenter. *Advance*. https://doi.org/10.31124/advance.13256240.v2.

NYC & Company (2019). NYC & Company 2018–2019 Annual Report. https://indd .adobe.com/view/fcc4cd9f-7386-4b52-a39b-c401266a137f.

OECD (2021). The COVID-19 crisis in urban and rural areas. In *OECD Regional Outlook 2021: Addressing COVID-19 and Moving to Net Zero Greenhouse Gas Emissions*. OECD Publishing, Paris. https://doi.org/10.1787/c734c0fe-en.

OECD (2020, July 23). Cities policy responses. *OECD*. https://www.oecd.org/ coronavirus/policy-responses/cities-policy-responses-fd1053ff/.

Office of the Mayor (2020a, April 22). Mayor de Blasio announces new partnership to manufacture 400,000 hospital gowns. *City of New York*. https://www1.nyc.gov/ office-of-the-mayor/news/283-20/mayor-de-blasio-new-partnership-manufacture -400-000-hospital-gowns.

Office of the Mayor (2020b, November 25). Recovery agenda: city launches small business supports for hard-hit low and moderate income (LMI) communities. *City of New York*. https://www1.nyc.gov/office-of-the-mayor/news/812-20/recovery-agenda -city-launches-small-business-supports-hard-hit-low-moderate-income-lmi-.

Pafka, E. (2020, May 12). As coronavirus forces us to keep our distance, city density matters less than internal density. *The Conversation*. https://theconversation.com/as -coronavirus-forces-us-to-keep-our-distance-city-density-matters-less-than-internal -density-137790.

Pei, S., Kandula, S., & Shaman, J. (2020). Differential effects of intervention timing on COVID-19 spread in the United States. *Science Advances*, 6(49). https://doi.org/10 .1126/sciadv.abd6370.

Quealy, K. (2020, May 15). The richest neighborhoods emptied out most as Coronavirus hit New York City. *The New York Times*. https://www.nytimes.com/interactive/ 2020/05/15/upshot/who-left-new-york-coronavirus.html?action=click&module= Editors%20Picks&pgtype=Homepage.

Roberts, J. D., & Tehrani, S. O. (2020). Environments, behaviors, and inequalities: reflecting on the impacts of the influenza and Coronavirus pandemics in the United

States. *International Journal of Environmental Research and Public Health*, 17(12), 4484. https://doi.org/10.3390/ijerph17124484.

Robinson, J. (2020, April 1). The soccer match that kicked off Italy's Coronavirus disaster. *The Wall Street Journal*. https://www.wsj.com/articles/the-soccer-match -that-kicked-off-italys-coronavirus-disaster-11585752012.

Shoichet, C. E., & Jones, A. (2020, May 2). Coronavirus is making some people rethink where they want to live. *CNN*. https://www.cnn.com/2020/05/02/us/cities -population-coronavirus/index.html.

Singu, S., Acharya, A., Challagunda, K, & Byrareddy, S. N. (2020). Impacts of social determinants of health on the emerging COVID-19 pandemic in the United States. *Frontiers in Public Health*, 8, 406. https://doi.org/10.3389/fpubh.2020.00406.

Song, R., Hall, H. I., McDavid Harrison, K., Sharpe, T. T., Lin, L. S., & Dean, H. D. (2011). Identifying the impacts of social determinants of health on disease rates using correlation analysis of area-based summary information. *Public Health Reports*, 126(3 Supp), 70–80. https://doi.org/10.1177%2F00333549111260S312.

Stafford, K., & Irvine, M. (2020, March 28). 'Off the charts': virus hot spots grow in middle America. *AP*. https://apnews.com/article/health-ap-top-news-international -news-chicago-virus-outbreak-cb56e50250328b923776408386b3a82a.

Sun, Z., Zhang, H., Yang, Y., Wan, H., & Wang, Y. (2020). Impacts of geographic factors and population density on the COVID-19 spreading under the lockdown policies of China. *Science of the Total Environment*, 746, 141347. https://doi.org/10 .1016/j.scitotenv.2020.141347.

Turner-Musa, J., Ajayi, O., & Kemp, L. (2020). Examining social determinants of health, stigma, and COVID-19 disparities. *Healthcare*, 8(2), 168. https://doi.org/10 .3390/healthcare8020168.

Wiener, S., & Iton, A. (2020, May 17). A backlash against cities would be dangerous. *The Atlantic*. https://www.theatlantic.com/ideas/archive/2020/05/urban-density-not -problem/611752/.

PART III

Equitable and inclusive economic recovery and case studies

5. Gender equality as an economic imperative in a post-pandemic era

Bernadette Maria Antão Fernandes and Herb Emery

5.1 BACKGROUND

In 2021, why are we still talking about "gender equality as an economic imperative"? Over a century or more, the advance of economic inclusion of women has progressed but has not achieved full equality. The rise of female labour force participation, educational attainment and social and political leadership has driven economic growth. Economic advancement has been greatest when women not only participate in the workforce but find work that employs them to their full potential in higher paying jobs. However, the COVID-19 pandemic exposed hidden weaknesses and illuminated obvious problems that predated the pandemic, bringing intense focus on gender equality to the forefront.

Gender disparity has been more exposed and more widely discussed during the pandemic – perhaps because people, especially those that are most negatively impacted by disparities, have been more active on social media and other global platforms like WhatsApp that cross social and cultural boundaries, and there has been more discussion of opportunities globally through virtual platforms like Zoom.

And, how did we get here? Is it that we don't recognize the problem? We definitely do – that is evident from the fact that we are discussing it and have been for so long; we are comparing our situation to other regions, including developing countries, and we are collectively – across governments, academia, industry, and civic society – taking action along various lines to pursue gender equality to drive the ongoing economic recovery, "building back better".

COVID-19 laid bare the fragile base on which so many gains for female labour supply and earnings had been built. Sectors that had grown based on abundant, more educated female labour supply such as retail services and other customer-facing jobs were disproportionately impacted by pandemic lockdowns. With schools closed, and limited, if any, access to childcare services, working from home where many females found themselves proved challenging, compared to their male counterparts who were less encumbered because their blue-collar industries made working outside the home possible, if not required. This gender-based differential in COVID-19 labour market impacts is exacerbating existing stark inequalities, validating concerns in the immediate aftermath of the pandemic on the long-term implications of an unequal, "K-shape" recovery.

A 2021 analysis by the International Labour Organization (ILO) shows that while males are moving back to pre-pandemic labour market conditions, female employment levels and earnings are not, with 13 million fewer women expected to be in employment in 2021 compared to 2019, while men's employment will have recovered to 2019 levels. Compared to 68.6 per cent of working-age men, only 43.2 per cent of working-age women will be employed globally in 2021 (ILO, 2021).

COVID-19 raised a different problem for the gender earnings gap. Pre-pandemic, and carrying on since, most of the gender differences in earnings have been driven by the lower representation of females among the top earners in Canada. With COVID-19, the gendered dimensions across industry groups, occupational categories, and skill levels in Canada present varying levels of risks and opportunities even where average earnings have tended towards equality (OECD, 2022).

Crises often lay bare the social fault lines of society. Just like the Great Recession of 2007–09 widened socioeconomic inequities among historically marginalized groups, COVID-19 and its economic fallout are having a disproportionate impact on underrepresented communities – particularly women and people of colour.

In Canada, the 2008 recession impacted the goods-producing industries where men participated at a much higher rate, meaning males were much more impacted than females; the male population in Canada bore the brunt of these impacts due to manufacturing sector job losses, albeit other sectors were also hit (Gilmore & LaRochelle-Côté, 2019).

Jobs requiring little education and providing low wages declined, with a more disproportionate impact on females, immigrants, and youth. Therefore, an equitable recovery from the Great Recession did not happen before the pandemic struck since the income gap had continued to widen along with the labour market polarization.

COVID-19 and its economic impacts such as pay inequity, childcare issues, stress, and burnout run rampant in the service sector, retail and medical specifically, both of which are heavily populated by females. Considering that women face a higher likelihood of COVID-19-induced economic vulnerability, since they are more likely to report economic hardships due to second order impacts of adverse labour market outcomes, the importance of strategically deployed short-term relief and recovery efforts – specifically targeted at this demographic – along with longer-term policy interventions, cannot be overemphasized.

In supporting equality for all, we need to be intensely cognizant of the fact that in addition to gender equality as we know it (i.e. equality between men and women), it is important to make room for other non-binary gender nomenclatures and identities, and we need to address racial equality, Indigenous equality, migrant equality, and so on.

Women are more likely than men to be in vulnerable jobs, to be under-employed or without a job, to lack social protection, and to have limited access to and control over economic and financial resources (UN Women, 2018), making recovery from crises that much more difficult. Addressing the gender disparities in the COVID-19 labour market is an important issue that has been on the front burner of the public policy debate in Canada.

The federal government response was initially emergency payments to locked-down workers through the CERB (Canada Emergency Response Benefit) and other initiatives. This later shifted to a commitment to create universal $10 per day daycare to support females, and other marginalized groups with children, working for pay.

We are seeing a push for "new industrial policies" that would target projects, firms, and industries more likely to produce gender-equal gains and perhaps restraining the market-driven growth from traditional Canadian comparative advantages in male-dominated extractive resource industries for export, as corroborated by Mendelsohn and Zon:

> A well-designed industrial policy seeks to overcome collective action problems, address issues of scale and build ecosystems in which positive economic spillovers are more likely to occur. A well-designed inclusive industrial policy understands the additional positive good for society that stems from high quality jobs, broadly-shared economic security, community wealth and sustainable development. (Mendelsohn & Zon, 2021, p. 6)

Is it that in the absence of the global pandemic the problem was being resolved under business as usual and all we need is for the economy to return to its pre-COVID-19 "normal"? Clearly not. Achieving gender equality requires fundamental change in our society with a paradigm shift across the board – that means not only in how government behaves but in how society thinks, in how industry behaves towards equality and in making room for all, and in how education is geared towards attracting women to be educated in areas that are higher paying and go beyond entry-level jobs.

The remainder of the chapter is organized as follows. In Section 5.2, we highlight that gender progress and economic empowerment was sluggish pre-COVID-19 but potential solutions to this were known. Section 5.3 explains how the pandemic has created the awareness of the challenges to economic inclusion, the potential solutions to those challenges and hopefully, the political will to introduce solutions. The last section concludes with implications.

5.2   PROGRESS IN GENDER EQUALITY IS DIMINISHED WHEN PAY EQUALITY IS LACKING

After two centuries of progress in the global standard of living, despite world wars and global depressions, of late it feels like the economic gains are not inclusive and gains in well-being for some nations and leading segments of populations are stalled and perhaps reversing (World Economic Forum, 2020). Even more sobering and discouraging is the conclusion in the World Economic Forum's *Global Gender Gap Report 2020* that, "None of us will see gender parity in our lifetimes, and nor likely will many of our children." The report says further, "gender parity will not be attained for 99.5 years."

The *Global Gender Gap Report* echoes how the pandemic had added 36 years to the estimated time needed to close the gender pay gap, culminating in a total average of 135.5 years to reach absolute parity between men and women on four key dimensions: economic participation and opportunity, political empowerment, educational attainment, and health and survival. The analysis adds that although the "last mile" of progress is slow-moving with 14.2 years left to completely close the educational attainment gap, gender gaps in both educational attainment and health and survival are nearly closed, 95 per cent globally – with 37 countries already at parity in educational attainment, and 96 per cent in health and survival.

Even where gains have been noticeable over the past 150 years with respect to gender parity for economic and political participation in society, Canada has some tough "last miles" of the parity journey remaining, including addressing systemic problems like domestic violence, poverty, racism, homelessness, discrimination, and so on. Canada cannot rest on its "better" progress relative to many other nations as there are important future implications of disruptions due to the pandemic, as well as continued variations in quality across income, geography, race, and ethnicity.

Speaking or writing on gender equality has been an ongoing challenge, because a woman may also be a Black woman or an Indigenous woman or otherwise a person of colour. She may also be an immigrant and may therefore not even be accustomed to the same resources or opportunities as other women, let alone men. While there may be resources and opportunities to support her own qualifiers, she may just want to be treated the same as other women – she may want to be equal in opportunities, in rights, and in status, or she may just want to be treated the same as men. In that case, perhaps just the word equality is needed – not gender equality, not racial equality, just equality for all individuals, without the qualifier.

Perhaps the biggest challenge we are collectively feeling is attributed to the fact that in the 1960s and 1970s the women's liberation movement (WLM) was the only issue on the table on which economic and political progress has been made. Yet great and disturbing inequities remain 50 years on in our society. Now, we have other social movements globally like Black Lives Matter, Every Child Matters, LGBTIQ+, #MeToo, and so on, that are equally important yet create a new challenge with respect to balancing further progress on gender equality with growing gaps in progress on other social, economic, and political inequities.

Nonetheless, for those who refuse to be discouraged no matter how well-founded a projection is perceived to be, and are empowered to do so, we embrace it as a challenge and rise to the occasion, for ourselves and especially for those who will follow. After all, we have all been there before, if not in our generation, then certainly in that of those who came before us, and if not in a global pandemic like the 1918 influenza known as the "Spanish Flu", then certainly in any other global issue. In the time of the Spanish Flu, the vote for women was a prominent political cause that required change of legislation in Canada to recognize women as persons (Carter, 2020).

Thankfully, there were also those then who refused to be discouraged, who took risks for their children, and ultimately for generations to come. But today, even those heroes of female suffrage face judgement for the limitations of their view in extending the franchise only to white women to preserve Canada's white, settler society given great inequities remain in Canada along gender, race, and language divides.

The pandemic of 1918 was pivotal in advancing women's participation in the workforce and subsequently the right to vote. The right to vote was a permanent gain but advances in the workforce for women proved temporary. By 1918, men fighting in World War I, and dying from the flu (which seemingly still physically affects more men than women), left significant vacancies in the workforce, providing an opportunity for women to step into jobs previously held by men. It would not be until the 1960s and 1970s that political movements on par with the female suffrage movement would be seen again as one of the more successful multi-front political demands for greater equity and justice in society.

The successes of the feminist movement have been great, yet not complete, and increasingly contrast with the limited gains for First Nations. And yet COVID-19 has decreased women's participation in the workforce leading to what is called a "she-cession" and highlighting the fragility of perceived gains towards gender parity.

Women were hit harder by the pandemic than men as they worked in jobs that were disproportionately affected by COVID-related closures like hospitality and tourism, which have been pulled apart since the start of the pandemic, resulting in women earning less. When schools and daycares shut down, women's jobs were disproportionately affected because they are still the primary caregivers in the home – pre-COVID-19, women already spent about three times as many hours on unpaid domestic work and care work as men, and during the pandemic, one in four women became unemployed due to lack of childcare, double the rate of men, further overloading women with care work (Bateman & Ross, 2020).

Women are also more likely than men to work in low-wage jobs, and in two-income households where one partner must leave the workforce, it is typically the person with the lower income, the woman. What is interesting is that women were filling gaps left by men in science, research, laboratories, and manufacturing during World War I, yet 100 years later we still have a lower participation rate in STEM (Science, Technology, Engineering, and Mathematics) jobs. So, why has women's participation in STEM not increased at the same rate as in other industries? Is it that STEM jobs have less flexibility than women tend to need or want? If so, then perhaps the requirement for flexibility has inadvertently been met by the ability to work from home, the acceptance from employers, and, at least in Canada, by the federal government's election platform of reducing childcare costs to $10 per day per child.

Is the trend different for males? Or is it that male students are still more likely to enrol in courses like advanced mathematics, science, and engineering than female students, which then affects the percentage of women entering these professions? This suggests that enrolment by females in those fields needs to somehow be encouraged, and incentivized, and a STEM curriculum needs to be part of early education. Perhaps we need to look at what is driving the share of women employed in STEM fields in countries like Georgia, at 55.6 per cent.

As part of its feminist economic policy thrust to address the disproportionate impacts of the pandemic on women – considering their overrepresentation in frontline essential functions – the government of Canada aims to drive economic growth with this $10-a-day daycare plan by attracting more women back into the workforce and addressing gender disparity deepened by the pandemic. The Canadian Minister of International Trade, Export Promotion, Small Business and Economic Development, the Honourable Mary Ng, espouses this:

> Our government is supporting the success of women—from committing to a national early learning and child care system and income supports for parents, to targeted, inclusive investments to ensure their businesses can grow in Canada and around the

world. We will continue our efforts to ensure the gains women have made in recent years are not lost to the pandemic. (The Rosenzweig Report, 2021)

In Canada's Province of New Brunswick, Cathy Simpson started Up+Go (http://www.upandgo.ca), an organization dedicated to empowering girls and women to pursue opportunities in STEM, leadership, and entrepreneurship through experiential learning programmes and activities.

The underrepresentation of women in leadership extends beyond actual leadership positions to seats on corporate boards, with "women in Canada holding only 21.2 per cent of all board seats", while of the 629 Toronto Stock Exchange (TSX) companies reporting women board director data, the percentage of all-male boards decreased to 15.7 per cent in mid-2021, down from 18.3 per cent in mid-2020 (Catalyst, 2021).

The underrepresentation of women in decision-making roles constitutes an obstacle for them in terms of opportunities, better positions, better salaries, and the possibility of making a considerable impact on society. Simpson explains that by building up these girls, we're building a cohort of young scientists, engineers, entrepreneurs, computer scientists, and business leaders who bring a different type of competency, knowledge, and understanding to these fields (Canadian Broadcasting Corporation, 2017). More diverse voices mean better solutions and business results. And we know that diversity in organizations leads to an innovation mindset and stronger economic growth.

DEI and the Equity–Efficiency Argument

A common misconception about diversity, equity, and inclusion (DEI) and the economy is that DEI is a purely distributional concern that could represent a trade-off against economic (or Pareto) efficiency. As a distributional concern, economists see DEI as an issue that can be considered separately from economic efficiency. There is a long standing "economic orthodoxy" that has maintained that questions of efficiency and distribution can be considered separately in the context of economic growth. Associated with the seminal work of Kenneth Arrow and Gerard Debreu (1954), the separation of questions of market efficiency from distributional goals is appropriate when markets are competitive, when there is complete information and no market failures.

In addressing the question of whether continued economic growth was desirable, Robert Solow (1973) argued that "In principle, we can have growth with or without equity and we can have stagnation with or without equity." Often for economists, the focus is on ensuring that the economy is producing to its potential to maximize wealth creation but if society determines that the market's distributional outcomes are unacceptable then government can redistribute income, wealth, and opportunities using "lump sum", non-distortionary taxes and transfers to achieve society's distributional goals through competitive markets. The opportunity cost of redistribution, however, arises from the distortionary effects of taxes on labour and capital, regulations, and policies aimed at achieving equity which in practice creates losses of GDP. If this is the understanding of growth and redistribution, then DEI and its equity purposes are framed as an economic, if not social cost. The role of government in this case is to find the balance between efficiency and equity that best meets the values and goals of society.

DEI, properly understood, provides a different perspective on its impact on the economy which is growth-promoting. When market failures exist due to negative externalities (like pollution), or barriers to opportunities from discrimination or informational failures that limit a person's opportunity to participate fully in the economy, then the market outcomes generating growth are not efficient. Addressing market failures to ensure all persons face fair opportunities to contribute to their full potential creates GDP growth. In this context, the role of government is to address market failures like labour market discrimination to have the economy produce to its full potential and address fairness in society.

The perspective above supports the views of Mendelsohn and Zon (2021) who argue that inclusive growth is not only equitable, but also stronger growth. They report that between 20 and 40 per cent of economic growth in the past 50 years in the US resulted from reduced discrimination that allowed for women and racialized people participating in professions and roles from which they had been previously barred. They also highlight an IMF study for Canada that estimated that closing the labour force participation gap between men and women with high levels of education in Canada would result in a 4 percentage point increase in real GDP. To close the gender gaps in the labour market, more young girls and women need to be encouraged and given the same opportunities to pursue careers in male-dominated fields.

Simpson was passionate in sharing her thoughts:

> We need more digital talent. Period. We must look at our pipeline and it has to be more inclusive. We need girls and women to be not only a part of this digital transformation and economy but to be leading the way forward. Digital literacy and learning opens new educational paths for girls and careers for women. In the past 18 months, we have been using digital tools and the internet to learn, work, and live in new and exciting ways. Schools and post-secondary institutions were forced to teach online.
>
> Many companies have permanently embraced a hybrid (both in person and remote) working environment for many reasons including safety, flexibility, and openness to find talent that is located anywhere in the world. Our economy is transforming at an

accelerated pace because of necessity and through the use of technology and data. Now, more than ever, is the time for more diversity in the workplace.

To accelerate change we need to get more girls as makers and creators through the use of technology so we must support initiatives that will teach them digital skills, enable them to see incredible women working in STEM, leadership, and entrepreneurship positions, and find more avenues for post-secondary education in STEM. For women, we need to show them they belong in STEM careers, in boardrooms, and as founders of digital companies. We must invest in their companies, their education, and ensure the workplace culture evolves so they join, stay, and thrive in their workplace.

There are exciting opportunities ahead and the province or jurisdiction that leads in diversity and inclusion will drive great success in this digital transformation of their economy, and the companies that embrace diversity will attract incredible talent. (Canadian Broadcasting Corporation, 2017)

It's seemingly true that history repeats itself so we must be accustomed to findings like these where the gap is wide, and maybe even hopelessly wide. But, we are also accustomed to closing the gap, and not just minding the gap. It's not enough to mind the gap, to watch it widening and getting further away from us, or for that matter simply narrowing; we must close the gap and do it now, as the findings in the *Global Gender Gap Report* (discussed earlier) suggest the urgency for action on gender equality is only growing.

According to 2021 data from LinkedIn, female entrepreneurs now make up 34 per cent of small and medium-sized enterprises, up from 31 per cent in 2019. There is also a rise in younger entrepreneurs, with women aged 25–34 making up 41 per cent of all female founders in 2020–21 (LinkedIn, 2021). So, we absolutely need to look at the support mechanisms that are in place or missing, like funding, to continue to attract more women and more young entrepreneurs.

In 2015, a global community of generous women transforming the way we fund, support, and celebrate women-led ventures working on the World's To-Do List, launched SheEO. Since then, 4,000 activators – women and non-binary individuals who activate their buying power, networks and expertise to create a more equitable and sustainable world – in four countries have collectively loaned out $4 million to support 53 women-led ventures. Their goal is to reach one million women activators and a $1 billion perpetual fund which will support 10,000 women-led ventures each year for generations to come.

Without investment monies, growth is completely stagnated and then once again a great idea may be left on the shelf if for no other reason than lack of funds. While the $4 million to 53 companies is a wonderful start, that is just slightly over $75,000 per company; not very much seed capital when you need $2 million to get it off the ground while you have a competitive advantage.

When we can see the benefits of economic leverage of the "purse", political leverage and representation will follow much quicker.

In 2020, with only 15 per cent of Canadian partners in venture capital (VC) funds being female, and less in Atlantic Canada, a group of Atlantic Canadian businesswomen launched their first fund, Sandpiper Ventures, stepping up to invest in female-led businesses across Canada, as an underrepresented community. This was based on women representing 51 per cent of the world's population yet receiving just 2.8 per cent of VC funding available worldwide, and 4 per cent in Canada (The 51, 2021).

The founders of Sandpiper Ventures know that investing in women, and women's innovation, brings big returns. In fact, they provide a platform where women investors and founders can radically disrupt the VC environment. Cathy Bennett is the founding and co-managing director of Sandpiper Ventures, and a board member of SheEO. Her insights on gender equality in entrepreneurship are succinctly captured below:

> The ability to access capital is a significant barrier for women entrepreneurs. Financial feminists need to disrupt or create new systems to get capital to women entrepreneurs. As entrepreneurs, I believe women are more capital efficient – we pay back loans at high rates and we make better profits in companies with strong purposes. Watching SheEO's team, under the inspiring leadership of Vicki Saunders, change the landscape for women in numerous countries by connecting capital with entrepreneurs who need it and repay it back to the pool has been an inspiration for me in my work with Sandpiper Ventures and the Atlantic Women's Venture Foundation.
>
> We created and launched Sandpiper Ventures to invest in women and women's innovation as a proactive and profitable business decision. Sandpiper was one of the first venture funds in Canada investing in women-led companies at the seed stage, and the first on the East Coast. Sandpiper's team of global C-suite executives have access to national and global networks, deep experience in building and scaling large companies, executing new market entry, M&A, and multi-billion-dollar transactions. Each company in the Sandpiper portfolio has active access to these opportunities, enabling rapid growth.
>
> Investing in female founders is simply good business. Sandpiper Fund 1 has the largest number of private investors in an Atlantic Canadian venture fund. Sandpiper investors include numerous entrepreneurs and leaders from the community and ecosystem across the region and country. Statistics show that female founders experience greater successes than their male counterparts, but traditional VC doesn't yet reflect this fact. Sandpiper is disrupting this so we can accelerate innovation and entrepreneurism by adding more capital, diversity, investors, and entrepreneurs to the ecosystem.
>
> So why are we called Sandpiper? The Sandpiper – and if you've ever seen Sandpipers, they fly in tremendous precision – they takeoff with a highly orchestrated pattern done together. At Sandpiper, we're proud to be bringing our experience, expertise, and networks to entrepreneurs as they take their market-changing ideas out into the world. And we believe this is best done together. (The Huddle Podcast, 2021)

Gender equality has been shown time and time again to be essential for economic prosperity, which is important in both developed and developing countries, and especially in jurisdictions with higher unemployment rates and less economic opportunity. Before there was "gender equality", there were women's rights – rights that were made part of the International Human Rights by the Universal Declaration of Human Rights in 1948.

> Gender equality is more than a goal in itself. It is a precondition for meeting the challenge of reducing poverty, promoting sustainable development and building good governance. (Kofi Annan Foundation, n.d.)

It's fair to say that the importance of gender equality really came to global limelight in 2015 when the United Nations adopted the 17 Sustainable Development Goals (SDGs), with SDG 5's mission statement being to "Achieve gender equality and empower all women and girls". While women have a critical role to play in all of the SDGs – with many targets around women's equality and empowerment as the objective and solution – regions, businesses, and even individuals around the world began mainstreaming the values and indicators in their strategic and programmatic endeavours.

It's also fair to say that we saw a downturn – or a halt –in progress during 2020 to 2021 as the world focused on mitigating the impact of the pandemic on all people, with a focus on vulnerable populations, particularly women and economically disadvantaged racial and ethnic minorities. The *Sustainable Development Goals Report 2021* highlights the impacts of COVID-19 on SDGs implementation and identifies areas that require urgent and coordinated action (United Nations, 2021).

Specific to SDG 5: On women's equal participation in decision-making, the percentage of national female parliamentarians has seen a slow rise from 11.3 per cent in 1995 to the current 28.2 per cent of managerial positions occupied by women. While there has been some progress in disarming gender disparities in both economic and political realms over the decades, women in the global labour market still earn on average 20 per cent less than men.

Even while programmes continue to advance gender equality, additional programmes are emerging to provide similar resources and opportunities in response to barriers faced by other vulnerable groups like Black, Indigenous, and People of Colour (BIPOC) business owners. For example, in Canada, Ryerson University's startup incubator, DMZ, is powering a mentorship and grant programme for BIPOC business owners across Canada. Through this programme, 100 qualifying business owners receive tools, resources, and community to help them thrive, in addition to a $10,000 grant from American Express Canada to help them grow their business.

While government does not appear to be involved in this programme, it still fits a helix innovation model by engaging industry, academia, and community – through consultation with BIPOC-focused community organizations across Canada. According to a survey of small business owners commissioned by American Express, BIPOC entrepreneurs cited a lack of access to mentorship and financing at a rate higher than their white counterparts (American Express, 2021).

Also, 48 per cent of BIPOC entrepreneurs reported that they lacked mentors to help solve business challenges, compared to just 32 per cent of white entrepreneurs. Interestingly, of the seven companies in Atlantic Canada that are among the 100 winners of the Amex Blueprint programme, five of them (70 per cent) are owned by women. One of the seven is Sankara, an online multicultural marketplace representing around 25 different countries where the majority of their vendors are BIPOC women. The company is co-founded and co-owned by a Black, Indigenous woman, Lily Lynch, and a Black, Immigrant man, Chinweotito Atansi. Lily was also one of 18 women recognized nationally by the BMO Celebrating Women Grant, which recognizes a company's contributions to social, environmental and/or economic sustainability.

Black women entrepreneurs in Canada were found to have particular difficulty accessing funding, according to market research firm Pitch Better Canada's FoundHERS survey. Having surveyed 1,545 Black women, according to the survey, 65 per cent reported to have either not secured funding or to have secured less than $50,000 in external funding, even though 59 per cent of Black women entrepreneurs earn a bachelor's degree or higher; 53 per cent have generated less than $50,000; while 51 per cent profited less than $25,000 (Pitch Better Canada, 2021).

> The COVID-19 pandemic has disproportionately affected women, amplified long-standing inequalities they face, and threatens their hard-fought progress worldwide. The Generation Equality Forum is a critical opportunity for bold and collective action to align our global efforts, renew our momentum, and accelerate progress to achieve gender equality, so all women and girls can reach their full potential. (The Rt. Hon. Justin Trudeau, Prime Minister of Canada, Government of Canada, 2021)

According to the *Global Gender Gap Report 2021*, the gap in politics remains the largest of the four categories tracked, with only 22 per cent closed to date, having further widened since 2020 by 2.4 percentage points. Although there are more women in parliaments overall since the last report, they still only occupy 26.1 per cent of some 35,500 parliament seats and represent just 22.6 per cent of over 3,400 ministers worldwide (World Economic Forum, 2021). If women are not seated at the table, they are not contributing their perspective and experience towards the development of policies, and therefore, we are all at risk of their needs being neglected or not being met.

As of January 2021, there were 81 countries of the 156 countries assessed where there has never been a female head of state, including countries considered relatively progressive with respect to gender parity such as Sweden, Spain, the Netherlands, and the United States. In an additional 17 countries, women have been in power collectively for less than one year in the last 50 years, which is the case with Canada at 0.36 years. Canada's one female prime minister, Kim Campbell, did not win election in October 1993 after her brief time as leader of the Progressive Conservative Party of Canada from June 1993. In Canada, female premiers of provinces face challenges with re-election. Still, at the current rate, it is estimated to take 145.5 years to attain gender parity in politics globally; in Canada (averaged with the US), this will take 61.5 years (World Economic Forum, 2021).

Canada is at 30 per cent female Members of Parliament after its most recent election of 2021. That's a 1.3 per cent increase over the federal election in 2019 and higher than the worldwide benchmark as well as the United States' highest share in history at 27 per cent. Signalling some progress for Canada, since 2015, the federal Liberal government has prioritized gender parity in cabinet (Equal Voice, 2021).

In New Brunswick, a diverse group of strong and committed women from different backgrounds – former cabinet ministers, industry leaders, academics – employed their own triple helix of innovation towards non-partisan, gender-balanced politics, to ensure political representatives better reflect the people they represent. Named "Women for 50 per cent", it was as much about the female voice being heard and respected as it was about inclusion. In 2017, there was no other organization in New Brunswick, or even in Canada, that was laser-focused on getting to gender equality in their provincial legislature. The benefits of gender equality, including the perspective and experience of women in policymaking, had become increasingly evident – we needed pioneers to see the way forward as we had in the 1960s, and we need them still.

While women had increasingly gained space in the Legislature since the WLM in the 1960s, by the 1990s they had begun losing ground in terms of percentage of seats in the Legislature and appeared to be stalling, leaving the political infrastructure dominated by men. The Women for 50 per cent group felt the need to continue to build networks for women, educate them on what is essential in an election campaign, and build a strong foundation for the province.

5.3   NARROWING THE GENDER GAP THROUGH FEMALE WORKFORCE PARTICIPATION

As in any other era, there will be both challenges and opportunities post-pandemic – we say "will be" as, with all the variations of COVID-19 surfacing, we really do not have a line of sight to post-pandemic life. Some will have existed pre-pandemic, some will have ceased to exist during the pandemic, and some will be new challenges that we never imagined. The important thing as always is to first mitigate the challenges that are here to stay – unless we take action – and to then leverage the opportunities that will cease to exist.

It is also important to not lose vision – the ability to see what is coming down the pipeline. One thing is certain, the pandemic has affected, and is continuing to affect, the economy (and society) in such an unanticipated way that we will need to do things very differently. But, there is no going back to normal; there is only building back better.

There is no doubt that employers were quick to respond to COVID-19, especially in terms of supporting their employees, but what no one, neither employer nor employee, could have anticipated was the impact COVID-19 would have on women. A higher proportion of female employees either had to, or chose to, stay at home with their young children.

As discussed in the earlier sections, in the immediate aftermath of the pandemic in Canada, women exited the workforce in far higher numbers than their male counterparts. As unpaid "housework" increased for women at home, so did the pressure and stress from searching for paid work, putting food on the table, the loss of health benefits, and in some cases having to educate their children. In addition to the pressures of unemployment where women make up a larger share of the employee base of businesses most impacted by COVID-19, women also make up a larger share of frontline healthcare providers, witnessing for the first time hospitals at capacity, and death tolls like they had never imagined. The pandemic also disproportionately affected women as it pertains to mental health, and it exposed women to domestic violence as tensions intensified in confined living spaces during lockdowns.

The pandemic has forced many businesses across many industries, especially those businesses with brick and mortar providing retail or other customer-facing services, to close. The industries most impacted have been tourism and hospitality, two industries that are disproportionately populated by women.

Even before the pandemic, the digital revolution was already shifting the composition of Canada's trade with the rest of the world, as witnessed by rapidly proliferating supply chains and waning interests in traditional sectors like resource extraction and manufacturing, where Canada's technology and innovation expertise is globally acclaimed. One of the industries expected to see a shift in representation is the blue-collar industry. For instance, in Canada, women make up 51 per cent of the population but less than 10 per cent of the national transportation, construction, and skilled trades sectors workforce –

with an even lower female representation in New Brunswick at 4 per cent (MAP Strategic Workforce Services, n.d.).

So, the New Boots resource hub started as a pilot project to promote, support, and mentor women in non-traditional skilled trades sectors such as construction, maintenance, manufacturing, automotive, truck and transport, and forestry. With the displacement of restaurant workers during the pandemic and with resource hubs like New Boots and the Women's Trucking Federation of Canada supporting a career change, it is expected that women will experience a much smoother transition to well-paying jobs with great benefits, and rewarding careers. For example, truckers earn at least $20,000 per year more than retail and other service jobs, yet they are vastly underrepresented by women, with women filling only 3.5 per cent of Canada's 300,000 truck driver seats. By generating awareness, along with advancements made, and support from men as the dominant players, employment voids can be filled and pay gaps closed quicker and easier.

Basically, if we cannot effect change quickly enough in terms of the pay gap, then perhaps women need to invoke the old adage "if you can't beat 'em, join 'em" by stepping into higher paying jobs traditionally held by men, like manufacturing, the trades, and trucking.

Depending on the industry, many businesses were able to pivot or introduce new products or processes while waiting for the economy to pick up steam. Some industries were forced to innovate, reimagine every facet of their operations, or transform their businesses digitally just to survive. Now some businesses, like manufacturing, are actually poised to thrive in the post-pandemic era under a new sector, Advanced Manufacturing. This presents an opportunity for women to also pivot their career paths to higher-paying jobs from newly automated processes or digitalized sectors while businesses adjust to the new way of working remotely and interacting virtually.

In Atlantic Canada, both government and academia have stepped up to support traditional industry by collaborating on innovation. By the second quarter of 2021, the government of Canada had provided $3.7 million through their Regional Relief and Recovery Fund for Atlantic Canadian businesses affected by the pandemic to undergo a digital transformation. The fund was meant to help businesses accelerate the adoption of digital technologies to remain, and become more, resilient and competitive through this period of recovery.

In September 2021, the University of New Brunswick launched The McKenna Institute, a connector and catalyst, aimed at fostering collaboration between industry, government, and academia to design a technology-enabled future that improves life for every resident. Because digital transformation requires diverse skill sets and mindsets, it is focused on a robust talent pipeline that can support the growth of a digital economy, reskilling underrepresented groups and minorities in the workforce, such as women.

5.4 CONCLUDING REMARKS AND IMPLICATIONS

Gender equality is a human right. As a result, it is also every human's obligation to ensure it is applied. It is not only a woman's issue, it is everyone's issue. It was an issue before the pandemic, it was an issue during the pandemic, and it will be an issue after the pandemic. But it does not have to be, nor should it be.

The thought-provoking thing about issues is that if we are not able to resolve an issue of human rights then what does that say about our ability to resolve any issue, any conflict? What else could be more important to humanity than human rights, to treat everyone fairly and equitably? The other thing to consider is, if we were not able to tackle pressing issues before the pandemic, then perhaps we need to do things differently. So, let us throw out old solutions around the issue of gender equality, let us gather around the table, and let us focus on the right to equality ... collectively.

But, how do we do that? What have we learned through even writing this chapter? It means nothing unless we start effecting change, unless we do as Nelson Mandela said almost 20 years ago – now is the time to double down, to not only talk the talk but walk the walk. It's time to change attitudes and actions, build foundations that don't allow backslides, develop policies and programmes that support and generate forward motion. It's time to learn from those who have fought the fight and made headway in resolving disparities like pay equality, even if that headway was in sport versus economics, and to build on it.

It's time to share the "power of the purse" by not allowing a minority of 49 per cent to control a majority of 51 per cent through withholding funding or stipulating who gets paid how much or who has access to a seat at the table. Let us not look back; let us look forward so that change can evolve much faster and stronger; let us build back better.

As we come out of the pandemic, we need to help build a stronger and unrelenting voice for women and equality. Even with other voices/movements rising and getting due attention, and we cannot lose sight of other marginalized groups, we cannot let up or lose momentum or women face taking a back seat to men once again.

In closing, in terms of interventions that can address the long-term gendered adverse impacts of the pandemic, based on the analysis so far, work-based and digital learning priorities that will enable women to rapidly acquire new skills that can allow them to pivot to new opportunities as the economy recovers amidst the ongoing digital transformation will be appropriate. In addition to the manufacturing sector, referenced above, replicating this across other traditional sectors (e.g. agriculture, mining, and renewable energy) will go a long way in ensuring regional economic systems are more resilient, equitable, and sustainable, post-COVID-19.

REFERENCES

American Express (2021). 'Blueprint' mentorship and grant program from American Express is fueling the next stage of growth for 100 BIPOC-owned businesses in Canada. Retrieved from https://about.americanexpress.com/newsroom/press -releases/news-details/2021/Blueprint-Mentorship-and-Grant-Program-From -American-Express-is-Fueling-the-Next-Stage-of-Growth-for-100-BIPOC-Owned -Businesses-in-Canada-09-29-2021/default.aspx.

Arrow, K. and G. Debreu (1954). Existence of a competitive equilibrium for a competitive economy. *Econometrica* Vol. 22, No. 3.

Bateman, N. and M. Ross (2020). Why has COVID-19 been especially harmful for working women? Brookings. Retrieved from https://www.brookings.edu/essay/why -has-covid-19-been-especially-harmful-for-working-women/.

Canadian Broadcasting Corporation (2017). IT exec launches social enterprise to empower girls in science, technology. Retrieved from https://www.cbc.ca/news/ canada/new-brunswick/women-science-technology-up-and-go-cathy-simpson-1 .4138426.

Carter, S. (2020). *Ours by Every Law of Right and Justice: Women and the Vote in the Prairie Provinces*. Vancouver: UBC Press.

Catalyst (2021). Women on corporate boards. Retrieved from https://www.catalyst.org/ research/women-on-corporate-boards/.

Equal Voice (2021). 2021 federal election. Retrieved from https://www.equalvoice.ca/ final_press_release_federal_elections.

Gilmore, J. and S. LaRochelle-Côté (2019). Canada's employment downturn. Perspectives on Labour and Income Vol. 10, No. 12. Statistics Canada Catalogue no. 75-001-X.

Government of Canada (2021). https://pm.gc.ca/en/news/news-releases/2021/06/30/ prime-minister-announces-measures-advance-gender-equality-worldwide.

ILO (2021). Fewer women than men will regain employment during the COVID-19 recovery. Retrieved from https://www.ilo.org/global/about-the-ilo/newsroom/news/ WCMS_813449/lang--en/index.htm.

Kofi Annan Foundation (n.d). Gender, equality and inclusion. Retrieved from https:// www.kofiannanfoundation.org/our-work/gender-equality-and-inclusion/.

LinkedIn (2021). How entrepreneurship is changing. Retrieved from https://www .linkedin.com/news/story/how-entrepreneurship-is-changing-4567417/.

MAP Strategic Workforce Services (n.d.). About new boots. Retrieved from https://nb -map.ca/new-boots/about-new-boots/.

Mendelsohn, M. and N. Zon (2021). No country of San Franciscos: an inclusive industrial policy for Canada. Canadian Inclusive Economy Initiative.

OECD (2022). Gender wage gap (indicator). https://doi.org/10.1787/7cee77aa-en.

Pitch Better Canada (2021). Canadian Black women founders report. Retrieved from https://foundhers.ca.

Solow, R. (1973). Is the end of the world at hand? In Andrew Weintraub, Eli Schwartz, and J. Richard Aronson (eds), *The Economic Growth Controversy*. White Plains, NY: International Arts and Science Press.

The Huddle Podcast (2021). https://huddle.today/2021/03/07/podcast-cathy-bennett -and-rhiannon-davies-of-sandpiper-ventures/.

The Rosenzweig Report (2021). The 16th Annual Rosenzweig Report. Retrieved from https://static1.squarespace.com/static/5512c694e4b0dc3ba767febe/t/60537 88734a5e93dae71a7ae/1616083084692/16th-Annual-Rosenzweig-Report-2021 .pdf.

The 51 (2021). The 51 and Atlantic Women's Venture Fund announce national part-nership to power future-fit female entrepreneurship. Retrieved from https://the51 .com/news/he51-and-atlantic-womens-venture-fund-announce-national-partnership -to-power-future-fit-female-entrepreneurship.

UN Women (2018). Facts and figures: economic empowerment. Retrieved from https:// www.unwomen.org/en/what-we-do/economic-empowerment/facts-and-figures.

United Nations (2021). The Sustainable Development Goals report. Retrieved from https://unstats.un.org/sdgs/report/2021/The-Sustainable-Development-Goals -Report-2021.pdf.

World Economic Forum (2020). COVID-19: how women are bearing the burden of unpaid work. Retrieved from https://www.weforum.org/agenda/2020/12/covid -women-workload-domestic-caring/.

World Economic Forum (2021). Global gender gap report. Retrieved from https:// www3.weforum.org/docs/WEF_GGGR_2021.pdf.

6. The imperative of childcare provision as critical infrastructure

Melissa Pumphrey and Poorvi Goel

6.1 INTRODUCTION

Since the early days of the COVID-19 pandemic, many labor market statistics and news headlines have highlighted the disproportionate impact that COVID-19 has had on women's labor market participation. A study by McKinsey and Lean In (2021a) found that while men left jobs more frequently than women before the pandemic, the trend reserved in 2020: one in four women considered leaving the workforce or downshifting their careers versus one in five men. Working parents, particularly working mothers of young children, were considering downshifting their career or leaving the workforce altogether at higher rates than non-parents; for example, 10 percent of men and women without children were considering leaving the labor force, compared to 23 percent of mothers with children under 10 (McKinsey & Lean In, 2021b). In September 2020, over 1.1 million U.S. workers left the labor force, with women making up 80 percent (or 865,000) of those exiting (Ewing-Nelson, 2020).

But the pandemic did not create the childcare crisis – it merely exacerbated it. Pre-pandemic, working mothers already faced lower average wages than working fathers and non-parents, and already shouldered the burden of family caregiving responsibilities (Bateman & Ross, 2020). Across the country, childcare was unaffordable for many families even before the pandemic: in 2019, families spent an average of $9,400 per child on childcare, representing about 10 percent of household income for the average married household and 34 percent of household income for the average single parent household (Leonhardt, 2021). And the childcare workforce earned depressingly low wages: in 2019, childcare workers earned a median wage ($24,230) less than half that of the median wage of kindergarten teachers ($56,850) (Schilder & Sandstrom, 2021). Our analysis of American Community Survey 2015–19 five-year estimates show that among the 309 occupation codes in New York City (NYC), childcare worker pay ranks 308th (U.S. Census Bureau, 2021a).

Social distancing measures and shutdown orders disrupted normal daycare arrangements. Childcare businesses faced pandemic-related staffing shortages, unpredictable demand for care from families, and increased operating costs (mostly related to enhanced cleaning protocols). Many families who previously relied on daycare arrangements for their children had to grapple with providing childcare at home while working remotely, while other parents who were not able to shift to remote work had to balance working outside the home while providing increased caregiving within the home. Many parents left the labor force to provide care for children who were not able to attend their normal daycare arrangements. In the NYC metro area, about 519,000 people were not working because they were taking care of a child at home in late January 2021 (U.S. Census Bureau, 2021b). Based on the magnitude of workers impacted, the childcare crisis presents a risk to the economic recovery, in both NYC and across the U.S.

In this chapter, we dive deeper into the childcare supply and demand factors that contribute to industry challenges and discuss how the pandemic exacerbated these factors. Then, we discuss how the dual impacts of COVID-19 and caretaking responsibilities are impacting families and pushing parents out of the workforce, with associated impacts on businesses, tax revenues, and the economic recovery path. Finally, we discuss international childcare policy and innovative public and private sector solutions.

6.2   WHAT IS WRONG WITH THE CHILDCARE MARKET?

The neoclassical market model is based on a default assumption of efficiency; that is, in perfectly competitive markets, self-interested agents behave in ways that produce equilibrium outcomes that maximize benefit and minimize waste. If that were the case, government intervention would be rendered unnecessary. In fact, real world markets often do not reflect this theoretical ideal. Market failures result from inefficiencies arising from excess or insufficient supply or demand, noncompetitive markets, externalities, and information asymmetries. The childcare market is one such salient example of a market failure, manifesting multiple aspects of the sources of inefficiencies.

In NYC, the total value of the childcare services industry is estimated to be $2 billion in 2020, employing approximately 57,000 childcare workers (EMSI, 2021; U.S. Census Bureau, 2021a).Of these workers, almost 51,400 are female, and 46,000 are minorities. Even before the COVID-19 crisis in 2020, the childcare market was strained by multiple challenges: parents confronted with limited and unaffordable options, and suppliers unable to provide sufficient childcare spots – constrained by liquidity and plagued by poor working conditions for its workforce. On the other hand, long-lasting benefits from early childhood education and investment are well documented. This implies that the insufficient investment and provisioning in childcare has failed to account for its positive externalities. And since provision of public goods is often associated with market failures due to externalities, there is a case to be made for treating childcare as a public good, by ensuring that it meets the conditions of "basic availability" and "open access" (Kallhoff, 2014).

In this section, we analyze the forces behind the demand and supply of childcare in NYC, and the sources of market failures within this landscape.

Demand for Childcare

In the absence of full-time at-home parents, childcare is not a private or family matter. A well-functioning childcare market would balance supply and demand, while considering the positive externalities associated with early childhood education and care. Previous research shows abundant evidence of benefits of high-quality early childhood education programs. Children who attend these programs perform better on school tests (Cascio & Schanzenbach, 2013), have higher rates of graduation (Reynolds et al., 2018), experience better mental and physical health (Ludwig & Miller, 2007), and have higher lifetime earnings (Thompson, 2018). These benefits far outweigh the costs of investment, taking just eight years for the societal benefits of investment in high-quality prekindergarten to exceed costs (Garcia et al., 2020). Despite the long-term benefits of early childhood care, parents are confronted with choices varying along dimensions of cost, proximity, quality, hours of operation, provisions for special needs, and cultural fit, among many other considerations.

There were about 545,000 children under five living in NYC in 2019. Of these, 325,000 were children under three (U.S. Census Bureau, 2021a). Who provides the care for all these children and what does it cost? Before the pandemic, 86 percent of parents in dual-income households availed of some kind of nonparental childcare arrangements in the U.S., although less than 50 percent of those whose highest degree was High School or less availed of such arrangements (Cui & Natzke, 2019). Almost 60 percent benefitted from center-based care, with many others relying on relatives or nannies. The remainder of the childcare burden automatically falls on the parents, but data shows that this burden is disproportionately borne by mothers. By time spent on caring for children under six, women in the U.S. were spending an average of 7.5 hours more each week than men in 2019 (U.S. Bureau of Labor Statistics, 2021a). And despite childcare being shared between parents and nonparental providers, many working families struggle to afford the ever-rising associated costs. In NYC, childcare is considered affordable if it costs families no more than 8 percent of their income (New York City Comptroller, 2019). Yet, average family daycares in the city cost over $10,000, and center-based care costs an average of $19,000. To afford these arrangements, a family would need to earn more than $130,000 for family daycare and more than $230,000 for center-based care. These are staggering costs for most working families: 75 percent of families make less than $130,000 and 91 percent make less than $230,000 in NYC. In New York State (NYS), infant care for one child can take up 22 percent of a median family's income (Economic Policy Institute, 2021).

Lack of access to affordable childcare also negatively impacts women's labor force participation. Studies show that working mothers often make work-related accommodations to take care of young children, including measures like switching from full-time to part-time, taking a pay cut, or dropping out of the labor force entirely. These accommodations exacerbate negative labor market outcomes, a manifestation of which is the "motherhood penalty" and "fatherhood premium" in wages. Our calculations reveal that in NYC, while the wage gap for mothers (relative to non-mothers) is 88 cents to a dollar, the wage premium for fathers (relative to non-fathers) is $1.04 to a dollar (U.S. Census Bureau, 2021a). However, increasing access to subsidized childcare and preschool increases the chance that mothers, particularly low-income women, remain in the workforce (Olivetti & Petrongolo, 2017).

Blau (2001) found that decreasing childcare costs by 1 percent increases mother's labor force participation by 0.2 percent. Another study found that the resulting increase in labor force participation from capping childcare costs at 10 percent of family income could translate to a GDP increase of 1.2 percent, equivalent to $210 billion (Bivens et al., 2016). Another study examined the impact of the introduction of highly subsidized, universally accessible childcare in Quebec, and found that in response, married mothers increased their employment rate by 7.7 percentage points, while single mothers increased their employment by 4 percentage points relative to the rest of Canada (Baker et al., 2008).

A final demand consideration is quality of care and its impact on achievement in later life. Ever-widening income gaps correlate with differential investments in children's productive potential, contributing to a widening achievement gap, even as early as kindergarten. Previous research shows that children are less likely to have formal childcare if they belong to a lower socioeconomic status, are Hispanic, or have parents who are not college graduates (Wang et al., 2021). Non-parental care for children with higher-income parents is more likely to be in childcare centers, where average quality is higher, and less likely to be provided by relatives where average quality is lower (Flood et al., 2021). It follows that in the face of existing limitations on affordable childcare, low-income families are especially vulnerable to the vicissitudes of their childcare needs.

Supply of Childcare

Childcare is a basic need, but the cost of care is a serious impediment for low-income families. With cost of care being largely unaffordable as described in the previous section, the question arises about what factors influence the supply of childcare.

Data from Upfront shows that there are about 1,400 center-based and 5,600 home-based daycares in NYC, with a total capacity of 96,000 in centers and 61,000 in home-based daycares (Upfront, 2021). Figure 6.1 shows the capacity distribution of these daycares in the city.

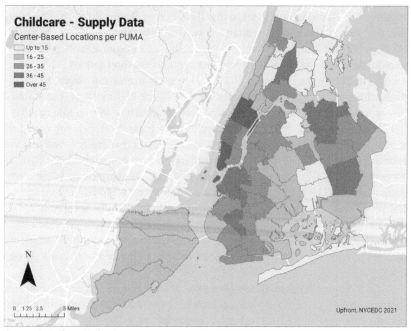

Source: Data from Upfront.

Figure 6.1   Supply of center-based capacity in NYC

What immediately jumps out is that where center-based care is in short supply, home-based care abounds. The supply of home-based care varies substantially by neighborhood and tends to be more concentrated in lower income neighborhoods in the Bronx, Brooklyn, and Queens, rather than higher income neighborhoods in Manhattan. This is seen most starkly in neighborhoods such as Morris Heights, Fordham South, and Mount Hope; Bedford Park,

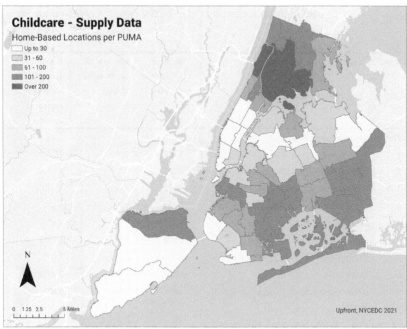

Source: Data from Upfront.

Figure 6.2   Supply of home-based capacity in NYC

Fordham North, and Norwood; Pelham Parkway, Castle Hill, Clason Point, and Parkchester; and Morris Park and Laconia. The median family income in these neighborhoods is $37,536; $42,123; $50,507; and $67,097, respectively. The opposite is true in Manhattan, where in the neighborhoods of Upper West Side and West Side; Battery Park City, Greenwich Village, and Soho; and Upper East Side, home-based care is largely missing. The corresponding median family incomes in these neighborhoods are $209,086; $246,411; and $237,727, respectively (U.S. Census Bureau, 2021a). This disparity is attributable to the fact that home-based care is generally more affordable than center-based care.

Further, in response to the expensive and exclusive center-based options available to parents of children in higher income neighborhoods, communities may respond by providing more affordable childcare businesses out of their homes. Overall, the ratio of the number of spots available for children under five (whether home- or center-based) to the number of children under five is 0.25. Put another way, there is one spot for every four children in the city.

*Table 6.1   Top 10 Public Use Microdata Areas (PUMAs) with lowest
                  and highest access to center-based care for children under
                  three*

Rank	Neighborhood	Number of children aged 0–2	Capacity of center-based childcare	Ratio of center-based capacity to number of children
Top 10 highest access PUMAs				
1	Battery Park City, Greenwich Village & Soho	5401	819	15.20%
2	Chelsea, Clinton & Midtown Business District	3248	470	14.50%
3	Greenpoint & Williamsburg	8495	934	11.00%
4	Murray Hill, Gramercy & Stuyvesant Town	3199	299	9.30%
5	Brooklyn Heights & Fort Greene	6010	517	8.60%
6	Chinatown & Lower East Side	2889	233	8.10%
7	Crown Heights North & Prospect Heights	4760	361	7.60%
8	Upper West Side & West Side	6289	474	7.50%
9	Crown Heights South, Prospect Lefferts & Wingate	3811	259	6.80%
10	Port Richmond, Stapleton & Mariners Harbor	5581	366	6.60%
Top 10 lowest access PUMAs				
1	Flatbush & Midwood	6967	10	0.10%
2	Richmond Hill & Woodhaven	5230	8	0.20%
3	Howard Beach & Ozone Park	3994	10	0.30%
4	Jamaica, Hollis & St. Albans	8594	28	0.30%
5	Elmhurst & South Corona	4804	18	0.40%
6	Jackson Heights & North Corona	7123	28	0.40%
7	Bedford Park, Fordham North & Norwood	6382	35	0.50%
8	Far Rockaway, Breezy Point & Broad Channel	6371	36	0.60%
9	Concourse, Highbridge & Mount Eden	5303	38	0.70%
10	Pelham Parkway, Morris Park & Laconia	4933	38	0.80%

Source: Author calculations using data from U.S. Census Bureau American Community Survey 2015–19, five-year estimates and Upfront.

The disparities of access in center-based care are reflected more starkly with regard to the youngest children in the city. When we further drill down the aggregate capacity numbers by neighborhood to relative supply of center-based care for children under three, we find that lower income neighborhoods have serious supply constraints compared to wealthier neighborhoods (Table 6.1).

It is important to note the caveat that it is not necessary to provide a licensed center-based spot for every child under three in the city. Some parents of young children prefer to care for them at home, hire nannies, or enlist the help of grandparents or other relatives, even if there is adequate supply of daycares (New York City Comptroller, 2019). However, the stark relative undersupply in a majority of the lower income neighborhoods compared to the higher income neighborhoods suggests that parents in the former category do not have the kind of daycare options that are more forthcoming to those in the latter category. In NYC, the ratio of the number of spots in childcare centers to the number of children under three is 3.2 percent, and in 22 of 55 PUMAs, the ratio is less than 1.5 percent. Battery Park City, Greenwich Village and Soho, Chelsea, Clinton and Midtown, and Greenpoint and Williamsburg, with an average median family income of approximately $159,000, have the highest availability of childcare centers. On the other hand, Flatbush and Midwood, Richmond Hill and Woodhaven, and Howard Beach and Ozone Park, with an average family income of about $83,000 have the lowest availability of centers relative to demand (U.S. Census Bureau, 2021a).

One reason for the lack of availability of licensed facilities is that the U.S. grossly underinvests in early childhood education and care, compared to other developed countries. According to the Organisation for Economic Co-operation and Development (OECD), the U.S. spends 0.2 percent of its GDP on public expenditure for children under three, translating to about $500 annual public spending per child (Organisation for Economic Co-operation and Development, 2021a). This is compared to 1 percent of GDP in France and the Nordic countries – with spending as high as 1.6 percent in Sweden and 1.8 percent in Iceland, mainly through heavily subsidized childcare (Organisation for Economic Co-operation and Development, 2021b). Even within the U.S., spending on children under three is much less than children in other age groups: about $2,800 per child for three- and four-year-olds, and $12,800 per child for children ages 5–18 (U.S. Department of the Treasury, 2021a). Most public spending on children under three is for low-income children with programs such as Head Start, Child Care and Development Fund (CCDF), Social Services Block Grant, and Temporary Assistance for Needy Families. However, these programs remain underfunded and underutilized; for example, only 14 percent of eligible children (under federal rules) received public childcare assistance in 2017 (U.S. Government Accountability Office, 2021). Giannarelli et al. (2019) modeled the effects of providing CCDF childcare subsidies for all eligible families with incomes below 150 percent of the federal poverty level and found that the increase in CCDF subsidies would allow about 270,000 mothers to join the labor force, increase the number of children under the age of 13 receiving assistance to two million, and reduce the number of children living in poverty by 3 percent.

Sources of Market Failures

As we previewed earlier, market failures result from inefficiencies in the market, and the previous section showed that parents of young children, especially those under three are confronted with very limited and unaffordable childcare options. Why is the supply side of the childcare market so constrained? There are multiple inefficiencies that contribute to supply distortions in NYC.

Firstly, there are strikingly few center-based options for children under three. In NYC, the ratio of the number of spots in childcare spots to the number of children under three is 3.2 percent, and in 22 of 55 PUMAs, the ratio is less than 1.5 percent. Put another way, there is one spot in a center-based care for every 33 children in the city. This is compared to a ratio of 27.5 percent center capacity to the number of children for those in the age bracket three to five, roughly equivalent to one spot for every four children. One reason for the sparse center-based supply for children under three is that most for-profit childcare facilities operate on razor-thin margins that are usually less than 1 percent (Davies & Grunewald, 2011).

Many childcare facilities are relatively small (a center in NYC has an average capacity of 30, and a home-based care has 10), meaning that even minor fluctuations in enrollment can impact revenue. As a result, many facilities are non-profit or affiliated with religious/community organizations, dependent on subsidies and government assistance (U.S. Department of the Treasury, 2021a).With such tight margins and fluctuating revenue, there are few incentives for entrepreneurs to launch their small businesses in this sector. The narrow margins also preclude the policy option of enacting price ceilings to make the childcare centers more affordable, because a binding price ceiling would make many existing centers unviable.

Secondly, this market that is simultaneously unaffordable for most families and financially unattractive for most small businesses is also persistently low-paying to its predominantly female labor force. In the U.S., the median hourly wage for a childcare worker is under $12 (McLean et al., 2021). Based on these low wages, nearly 18 percent of childcare workers are below the poverty line in NYS, nearly three times more than K-8 teachers. Demographically, in NYC, the childcare workforce is 90 percent female and 80 percent persons of color (U.S. Census Bureau, 2021a). The industry also experiences high rates of worker burnout and turnover. Surveys have shown that early childhood educators report high levels of burnout and stress, although this is mediated when workers have more job control (Schaaka et al., 2020). Because of this, there is also high turnover in this sector: national estimates suggest that 26–40 percent of the childcare workforce leaves their job every year, even though there is demonstrated evidence of the positive effects of consistency and routine to children's development (Roberts et al., 2018).

Bassok et al. (2021) studied the link between pay and childcare worker retention, offering teachers at a randomly selected set of sites $1,500 if they stayed in their positions. Nearly a quarter of teachers who were not selected to receive payments were no longer at their positions after eight months, while departures for those who did receive these modest payments were cut nearly in half, illustrating that increasing economic security for such workers will lead to significant impacts on worker retention. In addition, most early childhood care workers lack collective bargaining rights, increasing obstacles for them to advocate for better working conditions (Bivens et al., 2016). In contrast, unionization rates are much higher among K-12 teachers. Without incentives to attract and retain workers with good-paying jobs, the childcare industry will continue to be plagued with capacity constraints.

6.3   HOW DID COVID-19 CHANGE THE DYNAMIC?

The economic downturn associated with COVID-19 differed from recent economic crises in NYC, distinguishing itself along three primary features (New York State Department of Labor, 2021):

1. *Greater loss of private sector employment.* From February to December 2020, NYC private employment declined by 642,000, or 16 percent. For context, during the global financial crisis (GFC), NYC private employment fell by roughly 140,000, or 4 percent.
2. *The speed at which employment loss occurred.* During the GFC, private employment in NYC never fell by more than roughly 25,000 jobs in any given month and job loss occurred over a period of about a year (August 2008 through August 2009). This is in stark contrast to the COVID-19 downturn: between February and April 2020, NYC private employment declined by 922,000.
3. *The sectors in which employment loss occurred.* During the GFC, employment loss in NYC was concentrated in the finance and insurance industries, as well as pro-cyclical sectors like construction and manufacturing. The economic downturn associated with COVID-19 is unique among recent downturns in that it deeply impacted the in-person service sectors of the economy, because of the nature of shutdown and social distancing measures. The restaurant and hotel industry shed 197,000 jobs in 2020 (−52 percent), and half of the jobs in the arts, entertainment, and recreation industry were lost (−48,000). Retail and personal services businesses like barber shops, salons, and dry cleaners also experienced significant job losses.

With this context, it is important to note that the COVID-19 downturn had outsize impacts on U.S. female employment and labor force participation. In one year since February 2020, female employment had fallen 6.1 percent compared to 5 percent for men, and 2.5 million women had left the labor force compared to 1.8 million men. Because women left the labor force at higher rates than men, the female versus male unemployment rates understated the impacts that the downturn had on women. In NYC, almost twice as many women as men had dropped out of the labor force by May 2020.

There were a few reasons behind these trends. Firstly, industries that were hardest hit like accommodation and food services, arts and entertainment, and retail and personal services employ relatively more women and minorities. Overall, minority women, and women with lower levels of education experienced greater unemployment compared to men with similar characteristics (U.S. Census Bureau, 2021c). Secondly, the burden of caregiving disproportionately fell on women as childcare centers around the country shut down following lockdown orders. Pre-pandemic, women in the U.S. were spending an average of two hours more each day cooking, cleaning, taking care of children and doing other unpaid work than men, equivalent to 37 percent more time (Hess et al., 2020). This gap was even larger for younger women (51 percent more) and persisted for full time working women (22 percent).

With the pandemic, a survey by Krentz et al. (2020) found that U.S. parents had nearly doubled the time spent on education and household tasks, from 30 to 59 hours, and women were taking on a greater share of this additional time. Another survey showed that 70 percent of women said they were fully or mostly responsible for housework during lockdown, and 66 percent said so for childcare (Miller, 2020). The unpaid work performed by women for household and childcare responsibilities before the pandemic is valued at $1.48 trillion per year, or 7 percent of U.S. GDP (Wezerek & Ghodsee, 2020; U.S. Bureau of Economic Analysis, 2021). The pandemic not only increased the time spent on caregiving and other responsibilities, but also the lost value of their labor doing unpaid work. In the NYC metro area, about 519,000 people were not working because they were taking care of a child at home in late January 2021 (U.S. Census Bureau, 2021b). Household provision of childcare was keeping a larger share of workers out of the labor force in NYC (about 19 percent of workers who could potentially rejoin the labor force), compared with 10 percent for Los Angeles and Houston.

While parents were struggling to find and afford childcare to meet their needs, childcare businesses were struggling to provide quality care while operating on razor-thin margins. The pandemic made a bad situation worse as many childcare providers closed and employment in the childcare industry fell to an historically low level. Using data from Quarterly Census of Employment and Wages (2020:Q2 – 2021:Q1), we estimate that employment in the NYC childcare industry fell from roughly 37,000 workers in February 2020 to 23,500 in July 2020 (a 37 percent decline).

During the first year of the pandemic, roughly one-third of New York City childcare businesses closed at least temporarily (for at least three months), and one in eight childcare businesses closed permanently. Nearly 400 childcare businesses permanently closed during the first four quarters of the pandemic in the city, while just 120 new childcare businesses started over that same time period (U.S. Bureau of Labor Statistics, 2021b). Many providers were forced to shut down, and even though some have reopened, they are operating with even lower enrollment and more instability due to uncertainties associated with the pandemic (National Association for the Education of Young Children, 2020). Analysis by the Center for American Progress (2020) found that operating costs for childcare providers (center- and family-based care) in NYS increased about 39 percent, mainly to meet pandemic-related state guidelines. While childcare centers were eligible for the Paycheck Protection Program under the CARES Act, only 6 percent of 670,000 childcare businesses in the U.S. were able to access the program and received less than 5 percent of the total funds distributed (U.S. Department of the Treasury, 2021b; Smith et al., 2021). The vast majority of loans (about 90 percent) to childcare businesses were under $150,000, and NYS received about 6 percent of such loans. However, the data on increased costs for childcare businesses shows that much more funding is needed since the impact of the pandemic is likely to be felt long beyond when these funds are utilized by the few that received them.

6.4 HOW LACK OF ACCESS TO CHILDCARE PRESENTS RISKS FOR BUSINESSES, GOVERNMENTS, AND THE ECONOMIC RECOVERY

For over 75 years, businesses and the government have largely treated the provision of childcare as a private family matter. Families cover about 60 percent of childcare costs in the U.S., while the government pays about 39 percent of costs, and businesses pay just 1 percent (Schulte, 2018).

As outlined in prior sections, the downturn associated with COVID-19 hit the economy swiftly and deeply, separating millions of parents from their jobs. And for those workers who were able to shift to remote work, many now had to juggle the dual burdens of work and providing childcare. In October 2020, 65 percent of teleworking parents were balancing childcare duties while working from home (Igielnik, 2021). Unsurprisingly, many parents reported feelings of burnout. In March 2020, about 58 percent of teleworking mothers and 67 percent of teleworking fathers said handling childcare responsibilities while working was either "easy" or "somewhat easy". Six months later, morale had deteriorated: 47 percent of teleworking fathers and 57 percent of teleworking mothers report that balancing working and childcare was "difficult" or "somewhat difficult".

Many economists predicted a V-shaped recovery once shutdown orders and social distancing guidelines were relaxed. However, the recovery to date in 2021 has been a bit slower and more uneven. While the U.S. unemployment rate hit 4.2 percent in November 2021 (compared to a pre-crisis level of 3.5 percent and a peak of 14.8 percent in April 2020), there are about 2.4 million fewer U.S. workers compared to February 2020 (U.S. Bureau of Labor Statistics, 2021c). This is because of two factors: (1) some workers who were laid off either have not found new employment or have decided not to re-enter the labor force, and (2) the number of workers who are quitting their jobs is increasing.

In November 2021, nearly 4.5 million U.S. workers (or nearly 3 percent) quit their jobs – the highest number of workers since the Bureau of Labor Statistics began measuring this in 2000 (U.S. Bureau of Labor Statistics, 2021d). Quits rates in certain sectors have surged even higher – about 6.9 percent of all hotel and restaurant workers in the U.S. quit their job in November 2021 alone. This surge in the number of people leaving their jobs has been dubbed "the Great Resignation," a term coined by Texas A&M University professor, Anthony Klotz. This is partially linked to increased worker burnout in service-oriented industries, and unresolved caretaking duties, particularly childcare (Prasad et al., 2021; Stevenson, 2021). In NYS, about 63 percent of service sector firms and 71 percent of manufacturing firms reported having difficulty hiring workers in August 2021. Moreover, about one-third of firms reported seeing fewer job applications per listing compared to three months prior (Federal Reserve Bank of New York, 2021). And, with 10.6 million job openings in the U.S. as of November 2021, this is a widespread problem which impacts individual businesses and the overall economic recovery (U.S. Bureau of Labor Statistics, 2021d).

Increased turnover creates huge costs for businesses – even pre-COVID-19, one estimate by McFeely and Wigert (2019) finds that voluntary turnover cost businesses $1 trillion per year. The cost of replacing an employee ranges anywhere from $10,000 to twice their annual salary in terms of costs associated with the hiring process, direct employment costs like signing bonuses or relocation expenses, onboarding and training, decreased productivity while a new employee is brought up to speed, and potentially decreased morale among coworkers (especially if an existing employee has to cover additional tasks until a position is filled). The Great Resignation has tax impacts at the city, state, and federal levels as well. In financial year 2019, NYS collected $54 billion in personal income tax revenues (with average employment of about 9.8 million) (New York State Department of Taxation and Finance, 2021).

As of August 2021, employment in NYS is just 91 percent of pre-COVID-19 levels (New York State Department of Labor, 2021). To better understand why some New Yorkers are not seeking employment, we look at data from the U.S. Census Bureau Household Pulse Survey. The Census Bureau has been asking households since the early days of the pandemic how it is impacting them – their employment arrangements, their household finances, and so on. They also survey people who are not seeking a job and ask them why. Some survey respondents may be retired, but many of these workers could plausibly rejoin the labor force in the future.

For each of the large metro areas in the survey, we constructed an estimate of the number of unemployed persons who could plausibly rejoin the labor force or gain employment by taking the total number of adults not working at the time of the survey (who may or may not be actively seeking work, and thus may or may not be counted in the labor force) and subtracted those who are retired, those who are sick or disabled, and those who did not report a reason. We then grouped reasons into categories. For example, COVID-19 reasons include being sick with the coronavirus, caring for someone with COVID-19, or being concerned about getting or spreading the coronavirus.

Cyclical reasons are those related directly to the economic downturn. For example, your employer downsized, or temporarily or permanently closed. Providing care for one's children has emerged as a top reason for not seeking employment across several metro areas, and generally is a larger factor than COVID-19 itself for people not seeking employment. As shown in Table 6.2, nearly eight million U.S. adults were not seeking employment in June 2021 because they were providing childcare. In the NYC metro area, more than half a million people were not working because of childcare issues.

Table 6.2   *Household provision of childcare is keeping millions of people out of the labor force*

	U.S.	NYC	Los Angeles	Chicago	Phoenix
Workers who could rejoin labor force (in millions)	27.2	1.8	1.8	0.625	0.502
Cyclical reasons %	42	39	47	47	37
COVID-19 reasons %	18	25	20	12	18
Childcare %	29	30	27	28	29
Eldercare %	8	4	6	8	9
Transportation %	4	3	1	5	6

Source: U.S. Census Bureau Household Pulse Survey Data, Week 32 (June 9–21, 2021). Data refers to metro areas of cities.

Even as NYC schools re-opened to fully in-person schooling in September 2021, there are still hundreds of thousands of families reporting childcare disruptions. About 330,000 NYC metro area children were unable to attend normal daycare arrangements in September 2021 due to the pandemic. And, for these families providing alternative childcare arrangements, many are making drastic career decisions: about 40 percent of these NYC parents either left or lost a job, about 30 percent of parents cut their work hours, and nearly one-fifth did not look for a job.

Fiscal Analysis of Childcare Impacts

To put a finer point on how the dual impacts of COVID-19 and parents providing childcare at home are impacting the NYC economy, we construct a fiscal model based on pre-COVID-19 NYC employment levels by industry from the NYS Department of Labor (2021). This is augmented with American Community Survey 2015–19 five-year estimates on the share of workers by industry who are parents, to estimate the following fiscal impact scenario based on McKinsey & Lean In (2021b).

We assume:

1. 7 percent of mothers and 4 percent of fathers leave the workforce entirely (assume 0 percent of salary)
2. 8 percent of mothers and 2 percent of fathers shift to part time (assume 50 percent of salary)
3. 16 percent of mothers and 10 percent of fathers reduce their hours, take a less demanding FT job, or take a leave of absence (assume 75 percent of salary).

Based on the scenario outlined, we estimate that NYC parents leaving the workforce or downshifting their careers due to the dual impacts of COVID-19 and lack of access to childcare would cost NYC $2.2 billion per year in City tax revenues, or roughly 3.7 percent of financial year 2021 estimated City tax revenues. This could impact roughly 124,000 working fathers and 248,000 working mothers in NYC.

Beyond tax impacts, a change of this magnitude could impact the economy as a whole. To better understand the economic impact of NYC parents downshifting or leaving the labor force due to COVID-19 and the lack of access to childcare, we use Regional Economic Modeling, Inc. (REMI), a dynamic econometric forecasting model, to generate five-year projections of output and employment changes using a 70-sector model of the NYC economy. This analysis compares the REMI PI+ version 2.5.0 using data filtered for the NYC region. We assume any downshifting persists for three years before returning to pre-COVID-19 levels. Overall, our results show that private employment would be 250,000 person-years lower, the NYC economy would be about $67 billion smaller, growth would be 1 percent slower per year, and there would be about $18.6 billion less in disposable personal income for residents to spend on services like restaurants and retail, including $5.4 billion in 2021 alone.

Finally, there could be long-term impacts on women as a result of the Great Resignation. First, individual families may suffer significant setbacks in wealth accumulation. It's not just about the lost salary; there are long-term wage growth impacts and foregone retirement benefits associated with leaving the labor force. For example, a woman making the median income in NYC, about $57,000 a year, who leaves the workforce when she becomes a mother to provide care for her child until they turn three, will lose over $480,000 in wages, wage growth, and retirement assets over her lifetime (U.S. Census Bureau, 2021a). This could impact her ability to buy a house, start a business, or send a child to college.

Next, the gender wage gap could stagnate or widen. In the 1970s and 1980s, the gender wage gap closed in America; in 1973, women earned just 57 cents to a man's dollar and by 1990, just 17 years later, women earned 72 cents to a man's dollar (Leisenring, 2020). Over the past 30 years, the pace of improvement on the gender wage gap has slowed, as women's labor force participation rate flattened (Schanzenbach & Nunn, 2017). This could also impact women's ability to achieve gender parity in the C-suite. In 2019, just 85 women were promoted to manager in the U.S. per 100 men (McKinsey & Lean in, 2021b). Ensuring gender parity in promotion to the most junior management levels is key to eventually achieving gender parity at upper levels of management.

6.5   WHAT CAN BE DONE?

We outlined in Section 6.2 that childcare programs increase women's employment and labor force participation, and at the same time, have positive development impacts on children and their later-life outcomes. Yet, the U.S. has among the lowest public spending on early childhood education and care within OECD countries. According to the OECD, the U.S. spends 0.2 percent of its GDP on public expenditure for children under three, compared to the OECD average spend of 0.7 percent of GDP on toddlers, mainly through heavily subsidized childcare. In Europe, it is common for new parents to have paid leave of 14 months on average. Nordic countries have the most generous childcare subsidies which includes free care for low-income families. In Denmark, parents of toddlers receive a quarterly child benefit of $700.

While the Biden administration has made childcare a priority policy issue as part of its Build Back Better agenda, it is unlikely that comprehensive universal childcare will be enacted any time soon. However, businesses and city governments cannot necessarily afford to wait to act. Businesses rely on workers to be productive, but working parents need childcare in order to be productive. The onus is now on businesses: they have historically paid a miniscule share of childcare costs, and we believe now is the time for innovative public–private sector solutions.

For example, in January 2021, policymakers in Michigan introduced an innovative tri-share pilot model which was originally funded with $1 million to set up three childcare hubs. Each hub recruits local employers, who identify and recruit eligible employees. Employees must have income levels between 150 and 250 percent of the federal poverty level, and not be eligible for other childcare subsidies available to low-income families. Childcare costs are split evenly between the individual employee, his or her employer, and the State of Michigan. In October 2021, the pilot program was awarded an additional $2.2 million to expand as part of Michigan's financial year 2022 state budget.

As another example, Executives Partnering to Invest in Children (EPIC) is a Colorado-based business executives' network, which is partnering to invest in childcare. They do this via (i) outreach efforts to educate the business community on the importance of childcare; (ii) developing childcare infrastructure by promoting access to affordable real estate and fostering public–private partnerships in childcare infrastructure; and (iii) policy advocacy.

In NYC, we're confronting childcare as an economic development issue with the creation of the Childcare Innovation Lab, part of the New York City Economic Development Corporation (NYCEDC) women.nyc initiative. Women.nyc's Childcare Innovation Lab positions childcare as a key driver of inclusive economic development. It leads research on the effects of access to childcare, or lack thereof, on NYC's economy and families and takes a data-driven approach to defining future interventions. In addition, it works to catalyze innovations that can disrupt the childcare sector to expand accessible, affordable quality childcare for New Yorkers.

To solve a crisis of this magnitude, we believe both the public and private sector will need to influence and shape policy; cooperation between government and business will be critical.

REFERENCES

Baker, M., Gruber, J., & Milligan, K. (2008). Universal childcare, maternal labor supply, and family well-being. *Journal of Political Economy*, 116(4): 709–45. Retrieved from https://doi.org/10.1086/591908.

Bassok, D., Doromal, J., Michie, M., & Wong, V. (2021). Reducing teacher turnover in early childhood settings: findings from Virginia's PDG B-5 recognition program. University of Virginia. Retrieved from http://www.see-partnerships.com/uploads/1/3/2/8/132824390/pdg_teacher_turnover_study_summary.pdf.

Bateman, N., & Ross, M. (2020). Why has COVID-19 been especially harmful for working women? The Brookings Gender Equality Series 19A. The Brookings Institution. https://www.brookings.edu/essay/why-has-covid-19-been-especially-harmful-for-working-women/.

Bivens, J., García, E., Gould, E., Weiss, E., & Wilson, V. (2016). It's time for an ambitious national investment in American's children. Economic Policy Institute. Retrieved from https://files.epi.org/uploads/EPI-Its-time-for-an-ambitious-national-investment-in-Americas-children.pdf.

Blau, D. (2001). *The child care problem: an economic analysis*. New York: Russell Sage Foundation. Retrieved from https://www.jstor.org/stable/10.7758/9781610440592.

Cascio, E., & Schanzenbach, D. (2013). The impacts of expanding access to high-quality preschool education. Brookings Papers on Economic Activity, Economic Studies Program. The Brookings Institution, 47(2): 127–92. Retrieved from https://www.brookings.edu/bpea-articles/the-impacts-of-expanding-access-to-high-quality-preschool-education/.

Center for American Progress (2020). The cost of child care during the coronavirus pandemic [interactive webpage]. Retrieved from https://www.americanprogress.org/article/cost-child-care-coronavirus-pandemic/.

Cui, J., & Natzke, L. (2021). Early childhood program participation: 2019 (NCES 2020-075REV). National Center for Education Statistics, Institute of Education Sciences, U.S. Department of Education. Retrieved from http://nces.ed.gov/pubsearch/pubsinfo.asp?pubid=2020075REV.

Davies, P., & Grunewald, R. (2011). Hardly child's play. Federal Reserve Bank of Minneapolis, July 1. Retrieved from https://www.minneapolisfed.org/article/2011/%20hardly-childs-play.

Economic Policy Institute (2021). The cost of child care in New York [interactive webpage]. Retrieved from https://www.epi.org/child-care-costs-in-the-united-states/#/NY.

EMSI (2021). Childcare industry in NYC [dataset]. Retrieved from https://www.economicmodeling.com/.

Ewing-Nelson, C. (2020). Four times more women than men dropped out of the labor force in September. National Women's Law Center, October 2020 fact sheet. https://nwlc.org/wp-content/uploads/2020/10/september-jobs-fs1.pdf.

Federal Reserve Bank of New York (2021). Empire State Manufacturing Survey, supplemental survey report. Retrieved from https://www.newyorkfed.org/medialibrary/media/survey/business_leaders/2021/2021_08supplemental.pdf?la=en.

Flood, S., McMurry, J., Sojourner, A., & Wiswall, M. (2021). Inequality in early care experienced by US children. NBER Working Paper 29429. Retrieved from https://www.nber.org/papers/w29249.

García, J., Heckman, J., Leaf, D., & Prados, M. (2020). Quantifying the life-cycle benefits of an influential early-childhood program. *Journal of Political Economy*, 128(7): 2502–41. Retrieved from https://econpapers.repec.org/paper/nbrnberwo/22993.htm.

Giannarelli, L., Adams, G., Minton, S., & Dwyer, K. (2019). What if we expanded child care subsidies? Urban Institute, June. Retrieved from https://www.urban.org/sites/default/files/publication/100284/what_if_we_expanded_child_care_subsidies_6.pdf.

Hess, C., Ahmed, T., & Hayes, J. (2020). Providing unpaid household and care work in the United States: uncovering inequality. Institute for Women's Policy Research, January. Retrieved from https://iwpr.org/wp-content/uploads/2020/01/IWPR

-Providing-Unpaid-Household-and-Care-Work-in-the-United-States-Uncovering
-Inequality.pdf.

Igielnik, R. (2021). A rising share of working parents in the US say it's been difficult to handle childcare during the pandemic. Pew Research Center, January 26. Retrieved from https://www.pewresearch.org/fact-tank/2021/01/26/a-rising-share -of-working-parents-in-the-u-s-say-its-been-difficult-to-handle-child-care-during -the-pandemic/.

Kallhoff, A. (2014). Why societies need public goods. *Critical Review of International Social and Political Philosophy*, 17(6): 635–51. Retrieved from https://www .tandfonline.com/doi/abs/10.1080/13698230.2014.904539.

Krentz, M., Kos, E., Green, A., & Garcia-Alonso, J. (2020). Easing the COVID-19 burden on working parents. Boston Consulting Group, May 21. Retrieved from https://www.bcg.com/publications/2020/helping-working-parents-ease-the-burden -of-covid-19.

Leisenring, M. (2020). Women still have to work three months longer to equal what men earned in a year. US Census Bureau, March 31. Retrieved from https://www .census.gov/library/stories/2020/03/equal-pay-day-is-march-31-earliest-since-1996 .html.

Leonhardt, M. (2021). Parents spend an average of $8,355 per child to secure year-round child care. CNBC News, May 19. https://www.cnbc.com/2021/05/19/ what-parents-spend-annually-on-child-care-costs-in-2021.html.

Ludwig, J., & Miller, D. L. (2007). Does Head Start improve children's life chances? Evidence from a regression discontinuity design. *Quarterly Journal of Economics*, 122(1): 159–208. Retrieved from https://doi.org/10.1162/qjec.122.1.159.

McFeely, S., & Wigert, B. (2019). This fixable problem costs US businesses $1 trillion. Gallup, March 13. Retrieved from https://www.gallup.com/workplace/247391/ fixable-problem-costs-businesses-trillion.aspx.

McKinsey & Lean In (2021a). Seven charts that show COVID-19's impact on women's employment. McKinsey and Company Article, March 8. https://www.mckinsey .com/featured-insights/diversity-and-inclusion/seven-charts-that-show-covid-19s -impact-on-womens-employment.

McKinsey & Lean In (2021b). Women in the workplace 2021. McKinsey and Company Article, September 27. https://www.mckinsey.com/featured-insights/diversity-and -inclusion/women-in-the-workplace.

McLean, C., Austin, L., Whitebook, M., & Olson, K. (2021). Early childhood workforce index – 2020. Center for the Study of Child Care Employment, University of California, Berkeley. Retrieved from https://cscce.berkeley.edu/workforce-index -2020/report-pdf/.

Miller, C. (2020). Nearly half of men say they do most of the home schooling. 3 percent of women agree. *New York Times*, May 8. Retrieved from https://www.nytimes.com/ 2020/05/06/upshot/pandemic-chores-homeschooling-gender.html.

National Association for the Education of Young Children (2020). Holding on until help comes: a survey reveals child care's fight to survive. Retrieved from https:// www.naeyc.org/sites/default/files/globally-shared/downloads/PDFs/our-work/ public-policy-advocacy/holding_on_until_help_comes.survey_analysis_july_2020 .pdf.

New York City Comptroller (2019). NYC under three: a plan to make child care affordable for New York City families. Bureau of Policy and Research. Retrieved from https://comptroller.nyc.gov/wp-content/uploads/documents/Child-Care-Report.pdf.

New York State Department of Labor (2021). Labor data [dataset]. Retrieved from https://dol.ny.gov/labor-data.

New York State Department of Taxation and Finance (2021). Fiscal year tax collections: 2019–2020 [dataset]. Retrieved from https://www.tax.ny.gov/research/collections/fy_collections_stat_report/2019_2020_annual_statistical_report_of_ny_state_tax_collections.htm.

Olivetti, C., & Petrongolo, B. (2017). The economic consequences of family policies: lessons from a century of legislation in high-income countries. *Journal of Economic Perspectives*, 31(1): 205–30. Retrieved from https://www.aeaweb.org/articles?id=10.1257/jep.31.1.205.

Organisation for Economic Co-operation and Development (2021a). Family database [dataset]. Retrieved from https://www.oecd.org/els/family/database.htm.

Organisation for Economic Co-operation and Development (2021b). Indicator B2. How do early childhood education systems differ around the world? OECD iLibrary, Education at a Glance 2021. Retrieved from https://www.oecd.org/education/education-at-a-glance/EAG2021_Annex3_ChapterB.pdf.

Prasad, K., McLoughlin, C., Stillman, M., Poplau, S., Goelz, E., Taylor, S., Nankivil, N., Brown, R., Linzer, M., Cappelucci, K., Barbouche, M., & Sinsky, C. (2021). Prevalence and correlates of stress and burnout among US healthcare workers during the COVID-19 pandemic: a national cross-sectional survey study. *EClinicalMedicine*, 35, 100879, ISSN 2589-5370. Retrieved from https://doi.org/10.1016/j.eclinm.2021.100879.

Roberts, A., Gallagher, K., Sarver, S., & Daro, A. (2018). Early childhood teacher turnover in Nebraska. Bufett Early Childhood Institute. Retrieved from https://bufettinstitute.nebraska.edu/-/media/beci/docs/early-childhood-teacher-turnover-in-nebraska-new.pdf?la=en.

Reynolds, A. J., Ou, S., & Temple, J. A. (2018). A multicomponent, preschool to third grade preventive intervention and educational attainment at 35 years of age. *JAMA Pediatr.*, 172(3): 247–56. Retrieved from https://jamanetwork.com/journals/jamapediatrics/fullarticle/2668645.

Schaacka, D., Leb, V., & Stedronc, J. (2020). When fulfillment is not enough: early childhood teacher occupational burnout and turnover intentions from a job demands and resources perspective. *Early Education and Development*, 31(7): 1011–30. Retrieved from https://doi.org/10.1080/10409289.2020.1791648.

Schanzenbach, D., & Nunn, R. (2017). The 51%: driving growth through women's economic participation. The Hamilton Project, The Brookings Institution. Retrieved from https://www.hamiltonproject.org/papers/the_51_driving_growth_through_womens_economic_participation.

Schilder, D., & Sandstrom, H. (2021). The pandemic exacerbated the child care crisis. How can states reverse the trend? *Urban Wire: Children*, October 28. Urban Institute. Retrieved from https://www.urban.org/urban-wire/pandemic-exacerbated-child-care-crisis-how-can-states-reverse-trend.

Schulte, B. (2018). The corporate case for child care. *Slate*, February 8. Retrieved from https://slate.com/human-interest/2018/02/the-corporate-case-for-childcare.html.

Smith, L., Mchenry, K., Suenaga, M., & Thornton, C. (2021). Child care, essential to economic recovery, received just $2.3 billion in PPP funds during 2020. Bipartisan Policy Center Briefing, March 9. Retrieved from https://bipartisanpolicy.org/blog/child-care-essential-to-economic-recovery-received-just-2-3-billion-in-ppp-funds/.

Stevenson, B. (2021). Women, work, and families: recovering from the pandemic-induced recession. The Hamilton Project, The Brookings Institution.

Retrieved from https://www.brookings.edu/wp-content/uploads/2021/09/20210929 _Hamilton_stevenson_womenWorkFamilies.pdf.

Thompson, O. (2018). Head Start's long-run impact: evidence from the program's introduction. *Journal of Human Resources*, 53(4): 1100–1139. Retrieved from https://doi.org/10.3368/jhr.53.4.0216-7735R1.

Upfront (2021). Home and center based capacity for children under five in New York City [dataset]. Retrieved from https://www.allupfront.com/.

U.S. Bureau of Economic Analysis (2021). Gross domestic product [GDPA] [dataset]. Retrieved February 23, 2021 from FRED, Federal Reserve Bank of St. Louis, https:// fred.stlouisfed.org/series/GDPA.

U.S. Bureau of Labor Statistics (2021a). American time use survey summary Table 7 – time adults spent caring for household children as a primary activity, by sex of childcare provider and age of youngest child, averages for May to December, 2019 and 2020 [dataset]. Retrieved from https://www.bls.gov/news.release/atus.nr0.htm.

U.S. Bureau of Labor Statistics (2021b). Quarterly census of employment and wages [dataset]. Retrieved from https://www.bls.gov/cew/.

U.S. Bureau of Labor Statistics (2021c). Current employment statistics [dataset]. Retrieved from https://www.bls.gov/ces/.

U.S. Bureau of Labor Statistics (2021d). Job openings and labor turnover survey [dataset]. Retrieved from https://www.bls.gov/jlt/.

U.S. Census Bureau (2021a). 2015–2019 American Community Survey 5-year Public Use Microdata Samples [dataset]. Retrieved from https://www.census.gov/programs -surveys/acs/data.html.

U.S. Census Bureau (2021b). Household Pulse Survey Data [dataset]. Retrieved from https://www.census.gov/programs-surveys/household-pulse-survey/data.html.

U.S. Census Bureau (2021c). Current Population Survey [dataset]. Retrieved from https://census.gov/programs-surveys/cps.html.

U.S. Department of the Treasury (2021a). The economics of child care supply in the United States. September. Retrieved from https://home.treasury.gov/system/files/ 136/The-Economics-of-Childcare-Supply-09-14-final.pdf.

U.S. Department of the Treasury (2021b). Paycheck Protection Program. Policy Issues. Retrieved from https://home.treasury.gov/policy-issues/coronavirus/assistance-for -small-businesses/paycheck-protection-program.

U.S. Government Accountability Office (2021). Child care: subsidy eligibility and receipt, and wait lists. GAO-21-245R. Retrieved from https://www.gao.gov/ products/gao-21-245r.

Wang, W., Suarez, M., & Brown, P. (2021). Familia sí, guardería no: Hispanics least likely to prefer and use paid child care. Institute for Family Studies blog, May 26. Retrieved from https://ifstudies.org/blog/familia-si-guarderia-no-hispanics-least -likely-to-prefer-and-use-paid-child-care.

Wezerek, G., & Ghodsee, K. (2020). Women's unpaid labor is worth $10,900,000,000,000. *New York Times*, March 5. Retrieved from https://www .nytimes.com/interactive/2020/03/04/opinion/women-unpaid-labor.html.

7. The future of work and inclusion: case studies and takeaways for economic developers

Swati Ghosh and Louise Anderson

7.1 INTRODUCTION

Prior to the COVID-19 pandemic, automation, robotics, artificial intelligence, and other such technologies were already projected to impact the future of work significantly. Their adoption skyrocketed in 2020, in part so businesses could continue to operate with minimal disruption during the pandemic. A survey of 800 companies conducted by McKinsey and Company in 2020 found that 85 percent of respondents had accelerated digitization efforts, and 67 percent had accelerated automation and artificial intelligence efforts (Lund et al., 2020).

Data through May 2021 shows that women and Black, Indigenous and People of Color (BIPOC) have been disproportionately impacted during the pandemic. Women accounted for 53 percent of the labor force exits during the first 12 months of the pandemic and have been slower to return to the labor market as the recession abates (Ellingrud, 2021). Job losses for BIPOC, especially Black workers, were slightly higher at the peak of the pandemic, and unemployment rates have not decreased as sharply as they have for white workers (Congressional Research Service, 2021). Some of the overlapping challenges that historically excluded populations have faced during the pandemic include:

1. Higher concentration in industries that were disproportionately impacted by the pandemic – including hospitality and accommodations, tourism, and food services, among others – leading to higher job losses.
2. Women and BIPOC also predominantly work in low-wage occupations, most of which required workers to work in-person during the pandemic, leading to higher exposure to COVID-19 (Brown, 2020). Even though Black workers make up roughly 12 percent of the workforce, they represent 17 percent of frontline workers (Gould & Wilson, 2021).[1] As schools

and daycare centers closed and childcare options shrank during the pandemic, many were pushed out of the labor force when forced to choose between caring for their children and low-wage jobs.

Experts worry that trends in automation and digitalization will have additional negative impacts on historically excluded workers because they are more likely to occupy highly automatable jobs across all industries. A 2019 McKinsey Global Institute report found that African American and Latinx workers are overrepresented in low-wage occupations such as cooks, food preparation workers, stock clerks and order fillers, and cashiers (Lund et al., 2019). These jobs are expected to experience high rates of job displacement by 2030 due to automation: 47 percent of cooks, 46 percent of stock clerks and order fillers, 28 percent of food preparation workers, and 24 percent of cashiers (Lund et al., 2019).

Jobs least susceptible to automation require high degrees of technological and inter-personal skills. Even before the pandemic, decades of inequitable education systems had produced a wide racial skills gap, leaving Black and Latinx students less technologically skilled and less equipped with other skills important for jobs of the future. In 2012, OECD found that among adults between the ages of 16 and 65, Latinx and Black workers were over three times and two times, respectively, more likely to lack technological skills than white workers (Mamedova & Pawlowski, 2018). Research further indicates that as many as one-third of U.S. workers lack adequate digital skills, and digitally under-skilled workers are more likely to be low-income earners (Bergson-Shilcock, 2020). The education and skills divide, specifically the digital skills divide, leaves BIPOC workers behind in a labor force challenged by heightened automation and technology dependency rates.

The pandemic also led to increased use of remote learning, starting as early as pre-K. But inequitable school funding mechanisms and unequal access to broadband internet, known as the digital divide, made it more difficult for BIPOC students to continue attending school remotely. The longer-term impacts on learning (and, potentially, future job opportunities) of this unequal access to remote education are yet to be seen.

The interplay of the above factors has led to significant inequities in the labor market. *A large segment of the working population not only lacks the skills that employers demand (such as digital skills) but often also lacks the ability to acquire those skills (such as through access to training for reskilling and upskilling).*

Economic development organizations (EDOs), in partnership with workforce development organizations, education institutions, community-based organizations, and local and state governments, have a responsibility to ensure broad prosperity for all workers in their communities. That responsibility –

coupled with a heightened awareness of the impact of structural racism on opportunities for minority populations in the United States – underscores the need for economic development leaders to examine their strategies and practices through an equity lens.

Diversity, equity, and inclusion (DEI) initiatives are not only a moral imperative, but they also make good economic sense for both businesses and communities. Companies with a diverse workforce "out-innovate and out-perform" their counterparts by significant margins (Hewlett, Marshall, & Sherbin, 2013). Such benefits translate to the broader community level. Estimates from a 2020 Citigroup report found that closing racial gaps in wages, education, housing, and business investment for the Black community in the United States 20 years ago would have:

- generated an additional $16 trillion in GDP,
- provided an additional $2.7 trillion in income available for Black consumption and investment,
- resulted in 770,000 additional Black homeowners (with combined housing sales and expenditures generating an additional $213 billion),
- bolstered lifetime earnings by $90 billion to $113 billion for Black students,
- produced $13 trillion in Black-owned business revenue, and
- created 6.1 million jobs per year (Peterson & Mann, 2020).

Closing those same racial gaps for Black people today would generate an additional $5 trillion in GDP over the next five years (Peterson & Mann, 2020).

EDOs must work with the relevant public and private sector partners to ensure that BIPOC workers have access to safe, well-paying employment opportunities in the post-COVID-19 world through intentional strategies that address the root causes of inequities.

This chapter explores how EDOs can support efforts at the local and regional levels that prepare current and prospective BIPOC employees for the future. It starts by outlining past, current, and expected trends in automation and employment, followed by case studies and recommendations.

7.2 EMPLOYMENT TRENDS AND IMPACTS ON COMMUNITIES OF COLOR

To understand the long-term impacts of COVID-19 on communities of color, an examination of trends in the labor market following the Great Recession (which began in 2007 and ended in 2009) may be helpful.

BIPOC workers fared poorly on nearly every indicator during the Great Recession and the following decade. Black and Latinx workers had higher unemployment rates than other population groups prior to the Great Recession, a gap that only grew during the economic crisis (U.S. Bureau of Labor Statistics, 2010, 2021) (Figure 7.1). Employees in jobs at high risk of automation experienced greater job loss than low-risk employees, and most of the jobs lost to automation around that time, mainly in manufacturing, did not come back (Ding & Molina, 2020). Unemployment rates for Black and Latinx workers stayed higher than other population groups in the pandemic recession as well.

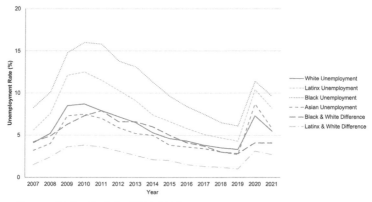

Source: Bureau of Labor Statistics (2010, 2021).

Figure 7.1   *Unemployment rate by race (2007–21)*

The disparities between BIPOC and white workers can be seen in other broader indicators of prosperity too. The Black–white wage gap grew to 26.5 percent in 2019 from 23.5 percent in 2007 (Gould, 2020), and the Black–white home-ownership gap had grown by three percent 10 years after the Great Recession started (Famighetti & Hamilton, 2019). Median net worth of Black families declined by 44.3 percent from 2007 to 2013, compared to a 26.1 percent decline for white families, widening the wealth gap that already existed prior to the Great Recession.

The racial wealth gap has held through recessions and expansions over the last 30 years. In fact, the ratio of white family wealth to Black family wealth is higher today than at the start of the century (Brookings, 2020).

Job loss and automation during the COVID-19 recession have been concentrated in the services sector, particularly those occupations that required in-person engagements (Ding & Molina, 2020). As noted above, minorities are overrepresented in highly automatable service sector jobs such as food preparation workers, stock clerks, and cashiers (Lund et al., 2019). As of August 2020, minority workers in automatable jobs had experienced "5.1

more job losses per 100 jobs" than white people in automatable jobs (Ding & Molina, 2020, p. 4). It is unclear whether service sector jobs automated during the pandemic will remain fully or partially automated, but it seems likely based on historic trends (Ding & Molina, 2020).

While automation displaces jobs, it also creates job opportunities. Findings from the World Economic Forum (WEF) 2020 Future of Jobs Survey estimate that by 2025, 87 million jobs worldwide will be displaced by automation, but 97 million new roles will be created (Zahidi et al., 2020). The challenge lies in bridging the skills and knowledge gaps that exist between jobs lost and those expected to be created as a result of automation. Table 7.1 identifies the top 10 jobs and skills expected to increase in demand by 2025, according to the WEF's 2020 survey (Zahidi et al., 2020). The skills projected to be most in demand are digital/technological skills and interpersonal skills. It will be important that such skills are promoted from elementary school through post-secondary education and beyond.

Table 7.1   *Top 10 jobs and skills expected to increase by 2025*

Jobs	Skills
Data analysts and scientists	Analytical thinking and innovation
AI and machine learning specialists	Active learning and learning strategies
Big data specialists	Complex problem-solving
Digital marketing and strategy specialists	Critical thinking and analysis
Process automation specialists	Creativity, originality, and initiative
Business development professionals	Leadership and social influence
Digital transformation specialists	Technology use, monitoring and control
Information security analysts	Technology design and programming
Software and applications developers	Resilience, stress tolerance, and flexibility
Internet of Things specialists	Reasoning, problem-solving, and ideation

Source: Zahidi et al. (2020).

Given the connections between digital literacy, income, and race, promoting the development of digital and other in-demand skills within communities of color is a promising strategy for EDOs, educational institutions, and local governments to pursue.

7.3   CASE STUDIES

EDOs around the country recognize that lack of progress for some sections of the population hampers growth for the entire region. Prior to the pandemic when unemployment rates were at historic lows, businesses were struggling to find talented workers, leading to concerns about reduced productivity in the economy. EDOs were already starting to address worker shortages by intentionally targeting growth and development opportunities towards under-represented segments including women and people of color. Many focused on upskilling BIPOC workers for jobs of the future as a way to improve their access to well-paying jobs and ability to build wealth while also addressing worker shortages for local and regional businesses.

The following section features two programs: Dallas Independent School District's (ISD) Pathways in Technology Early College High School (P-TECH) initiative and Minneapolis Saint Paul Economic Development Partnership's (GREATER MSP) ConnextMSP program. Both programs started before the pandemic out of a desire to help BIPOC workers and address racial disparities, but offer insights for promoting racially inclusive job growth as labor demands shift rapidly in response to the pandemic, recession, and technological advancements.

Dallas P-TECH

Dallas ISD, which serves predominantly Latinx and Black students, recognized that many students were not able to finish high school or take advantage of post-secondary education due to a mix of economic and societal barriers. In 2015, before Dallas launched the P-TECH initiative, 8.6 percent of high school students dropped out before graduation (Texas Education Agency (TEA), 2016), a substantially higher number than the national dropout rate of 5.9 percent (National Center for Education Statistics (NCES), 2019). BIPOC students also were more likely to drop out than white students. The 2015 dropout rates amongst Black, Latinx, and multiracial students were 10.3 percent, 8.1 percent, and 12.1 percent, respectively, while white students dropped out at a rate of 6.5 percent (TEA, 2016).

Economic opportunities for those without a post-secondary education are limited in a knowledge and technology-based economy. Even in 2019 when unemployment was at historic lows, the national unemployment rates amongst workers with no high school diploma (5.4 percent) or just a high school diploma (3.7 percent) were higher than the overall national average (3 percent). Median weekly earnings for workers with no high school diploma ($592) or only a high school diploma ($746) were also substantially lower than the national average ($969) (BLS, 2019).

In 2010, 27 percent of Dallas County high school graduates earned a degree within six years; yet among Dallas County high school students of color, less than 15 percent earned a certificate or degree within six years (11 percent for Latinx and 13 percent for African Americans), according to Dallas ISD Assistant Superintendent Dr. Usamah Rodgers.[2] In 2016, Dallas ISD partnered its high schools with seven local community college campuses under the

Dallas College network and 82 local employers (dubbed industry partners) to provide economic mobility and opportunity to disadvantaged students through its P-TECH education model. The partnership is aligned with one of the strategic priorities for the Dallas College board, which is to meet the needs of the community and employers through a teaching and learning environment that exceeds learner expectations.

Dallas ISD adopted the P-TECH model at eight of its high schools to prepare students who are less likely to attend college (primarily minority students) for career-track jobs after graduating high school. Through Dallas's current 18 P-TECH campuses, participating public high school students can obtain a certification or an associate degree by earning up to 60 hours of tuition-free college credit and free college textbooks from a partnering community college. Training is offered in 23 "pathways," such as healthcare, communications, STEM (Science, Technology, Engineering, and Mathematics), education, business, and hospitality. Industry partners are paired with P-TECH campuses based on the pathways offered at the school. For example, those that offer pathways in healthcare are paired with hospitals; others offering pathways in hospitality are partnered with hotels.

Evidence shows that early college programs like P-TECH make academic success in high school and college more attainable:

- Early college students are 12 percent more likely to graduate high school than other students,
- Students at four public Texas universities with early college credit were 30 percent more likely to earn their bachelor's degrees within six years than other students,
- Early college students also were 42 percent more likely to complete bachelor's degrees within four years (College in High School Alliance, 2020).

Up to 125 students are admitted to each campus's P-TECH cohort every academic year. Participants are admitted as high school freshmen, taking courses for two years at the high school before taking college courses at the partnering community college for their junior and senior years.

The Dallas P-TECH program helps participating students gain meaningful workplace experience and develop skills through mentorships and internships, while ensuring they are trained for jobs that are in demand in the region. As freshmen, students participate in job interviews and receive feedback on their resumes. As juniors, students shadow employees from industry partners and participate in internships the following summer.

Industry partners play an important role in structuring curricula for P-TECH participants. They offer guidance on what skills are projected to be in demand when students are ready to graduate high school, information on relevant certifications that are valued by employers, and practical experience through internships. Since many industry partners are tech companies, lessons on digital skills (such as the use of standard business applications such as Word, Excel, and PowerPoint) are a key component of all P-TECH certificate and degree pathways. (Google's Career Certificates are a similar example of training in high-demand growth sectors, developed with input from an employer network that also provides job opportunities to program graduates.)

For example, Pinnacle Group, an IT workforce solutions group, partnered with P-TECH to offer students career pathways in business administration, visual communication, and computer and information technology. According to Erin Stewart, general counsel for Pinnacle Group, they wanted to provide students, mainly Latinas from the surrounding neighborhoods, with opportunities in STEM and business. They were one of first industry partners of P-TECH and continue to support its growth.

> Dallas Independent School District and the Dallas College network created a partnership between eight high schools and seven community colleges with the aim to improve graduation rates for BIPOC students. Using the P-TECH education model, college-level courses are offered to high school students in high-demand industries. The partnership includes 82 employers that offer guidance on projected skill demand for curriculum and certification development, while also offering internships and mentorships to program participants. Courses are offered in 23 different "pathways" such as healthcare, communication, STEM, business, and hospitality. Research from similar programs is promising; participants have higher graduation rates from high school and higher chances of enrolling and completing four-year college degrees.
>
> More than 70 percent of the first cohort of 700 students of the Dallas P-TECH program – the vast majority of them BIPOC – graduated with an associate degree during the height of the pandemic. Many enrolled for four-year college programs even before they graduated from high school. Enrollment for the 2020–21 academic year was also higher than in the past with more than 800 students expected to graduate in 2021.
>
> The Dallas P-TECH program organizers also realized that it takes more than academic desire for students to excel. BIPOC students many times also need additional support such as access to transportation, scholarships to cover tuition and other expenses, etc., which the program provides. It also provided students with Wi-Fi enabled laptops to continue their education remotely during the pandemic.
>
> The economic development department of the City of Dallas has been a strong partner. They include this program as part of their incentive negotiations and help recruit more employers to offer internships and mentorships to program participants.[3]

Dallas ISD and their partners, through funding from the JP Morgan Chase Foundation, built a toolkit for virtual internships when the global pandemic forced significant shutdowns in the summer 2020. The toolkit guided employers on structuring internships with remote interns so students could continue gaining workplace experience. Many graduates from 2020 and 2021 found full time employment with industry partners as a result of relationships built during these internships.

Early results show that the program is having a significant impact. In total, roughly 6,500 students currently are participating in Dallas P-TECH. According to Dallas College Vice Provost for Educational Partnerships Anna Mays, the first cohort of nearly 700 students graduated high school in spring 2020, of which 72 percent earned an associate degree or certificate along with their high school diploma. The 2020–21 cohort was composed of 2,028 freshmen across all the schools. Over 800 students are expected to graduate from the class of 2021. In comparison, Dr. Rodgers noted that prior to Dallas P-TECH's adoption, only 21 percent of the district's 2015 high school graduates obtained a post-secondary degree six years after high school, which is typical for the school district.[4] Although data is scarce during these initial years, the early success of the program is remarkable, in spite of the additional challenges posed by a global pandemic.

To reduce barriers to participation, P-TECH's admission process is not based on a student's academic achievement. However, due to the limited number of spaces in each campus's cohort, the application process is very competitive. Interested students fill out an application form that requires parental buy-in, participate in an interview, and must demonstrate a strong commitment to their education by pledging not to take on significant childcare or job-related responsibilities. Although that might be difficult for some low-income students who rely on part-time jobs to supplement family income or provide childcare to younger siblings while parents are at work, the program is rigorous enough to require such commitment.

The program is also structured to provide students with additional support and services needed to succeed. As mentioned before, tuition-free credits and free college textbooks remove barriers that often exclude the most economically disadvantaged students. Free transportation to community college campuses during participants' junior and senior years further increases accessibility. During the pandemic, students received Wi-Fi enabled laptops so they could continue participating in remote learning. However, the intensity of the workload does push a small proportion of students to abandon the program midway, according to Dr. Rodgers. Despite barriers, the average course success rate of these dual credit students has exceeded that of non-dual credit students at Dallas College.

Although Dallas P-TECH is a school district and community college initiative, the city's economic development department has been a dedicated partner by helping to connect it with local and regional employers as industry partners. When a major employer relocates to Dallas, the economic development department encourages it to become a P-TECH industry partner. EDOs, serving as an intermediary between private companies, local government, and other community stakeholders, are well positioned to attract industry partners, provide curriculum guidance based on regional business needs, and even participate as industry partners themselves.

Greater MSP's ConnextMSP

Racially inequitable levels of employment and earnings have been problems for the Minneapolis St. Paul (MSP) region for a long time. Average yearly earnings for Black households in 2019 was about $46,000 less than white households – one of the worst racial income gaps in the country (Rosalsky, 2020). According to data from November 2020, the Black unemployment rate in MSP was 15.4 percent, more than double the white unemployment rate of 7.1 percent (Minnesota Department of Employment and Economic Development, 2020). As a result of these disparities, the Black poverty rate in MSP (25.4 percent) is over four times that of white poverty (5.9 percent) (Rosalsky, 2020).

To address these persistent inequities, employers in the region invested in a variety of career readiness programs and organizations aimed at minority high school students from low-income backgrounds over the years. BIPOC students comprised 80–90 percent of enrollment in these programs in the region. Such programs typically helped students with degree attainment and demonstration of competencies while preparing them for life after high school – either in college or career or both – through additional training and social support services. Yet outcomes of these programs had been mixed in the region. GREATER MSP – the regional EDO – learned that program alumni were continuing to struggle to find good, local jobs, and employers who had invested in these programs were missing out on opportunities to hire local talent, according to Matt Lewis, Vice President of Strategic Initiatives. They stepped in to serve as matchmaker.

GREATER MSP staff identified a lack of capacity in existing career readiness programs to provide ongoing support to alumni, especially after graduating from high school (or college) but before a student's first job. As a result, many BIPOC young professionals lost connections to local employers built during the career readiness programs, struggled to showcase their skills, and failed to secure meaningful employment.

A new program, ConnextMSP, launched in late summer 2021 as a partnership between GREATER MSP and 13 career readiness programs to ensure that young BIPOC professionals are recruited, hired, and supported by local employers as they enter the workforce. By using GREATER MSP's regional employer network and facilitating connections between career readiness alumni and employers, ConnextMSP is designed to serve as an online networking platform for BIPOC young professionals and regional employers. The initiative will facilitate opportunities for thousands of career readiness program alumni to network with employers, search for jobs, and learn about career fairs and professional development opportunities in the MSP metro area.

ConnextMSP is not offering new skill-building or career readiness programming; instead, its goal is to fill an existing gap in the community. Currently, there are roughly 2,500 career readiness alumni registered on the ConnextMSP network, 80–90 percent of whom are estimated to be BIPOC (the platform does not require registrants to share race and ethnicity).

Lewis hopes to "restructure the early career exploration process for BIPOC students" through this program, substantially improving meaningful employment opportunities through access to exclusive job boards, networking opportunities, and career fairs. Research suggests that white workers and workers of color end up in vastly different types of industries and occupations as a result of labor market segregation based on race. Such segregated job search and referral networks are one of the reasons preventing BIPOC students from accessing many useful resources (Brown, 2020).

ConnextMSP's programming and network-building focus on the skills most in-demand by employers and jobs offered by the fastest-growing employers in the region. GREATER MSP has organized cohort meetings between career readiness alumni and employers to identify critical skills and job opportunities. For example, the program has developed a cohort of alumni and employers focused on the future of work, skills and education needs in the agriculture and food industry, a target industry sector in the region. Because the tech sector in Minneapolis is among the largest and fastest growing in the country, ConnextMSP has another cohort focused on digital skills. The pandemic also emphasized the need for flexibility and adaptability in remote and hybrid work environments for all types of businesses, and the need for digital skills irrespective of industry.

Building partnerships for pipeline development is also part of the puzzle (i.e., identifying future alumni of career readiness programs in the region). At the time of publication, it has more than 15 career pathway partners, including college and career readiness non-profits, community colleges, and universities, and additional partners are joining on a monthly basis.

Research shows that BIPOC students don't have strong networks to connect them to good jobs, especially after graduating high school or college. ConnextMSP takes career readiness programs one step further by providing ongoing support to alumni, especially in the period between graduating high school (or college) and a student's first job. GREATER MSP, the regional economic development organization, connects career readiness alumni to its regional employer network through an online platform for jobs, networking, and professional development opportunities.

Although not designed specifically for BIPOC students, almost 90 percent of alumni currently registered on the platform are BIPOC.

GREATER MSP is also building a link to skills that will be in high demand in the future by engaging employers to highlight those skills and job offerings on the platform. Skills and education in the agriculture and food industry, and digital skills for the growing tech sector are examples of sector-specific strategies that would help MSP employers while also providing pathways for BIPOC students.[5]

ConnextMSP's design does limit participation for many individuals who would likely benefit from joining the network. For example, GREATER MSP has decided to avoid partnerships with career readiness programs that do not offer internships or work experience for alumni, potentially excluding many economically disadvantaged young professionals who need help accessing well-paying job opportunities.

On the other hand, GREATER MSP is seeing much interest from local and regional employers in this initiative and is signing up new employers on a weekly basis, indicating that they see the value of such efforts. However, GREATER MSP is also cognizant of the fact that just signing employers up for the initiative is not sufficient.

7.4   TAKEAWAYS FOR ECONOMIC DEVELOPERS

As technological advancements in automation, artificial intelligence, and digitalization accelerate, businesses will continue to struggle to find talent that will satisfy their labor needs. Ensuring that an adequate talent pool is available for employers – now and in the future – is critical for EDOs to attract, retain, and grow businesses in their communities. Historically low unemployment rates and a shortage of talented workers before the global pandemic gave EDOs a taste of how talent shortages affect their local and regional competitiveness.

Yet, the most sobering finding from this research is that EDOs aren't sufficiently focused on this issue. Cross-sector partnerships between economic development, workforce development, and education partners aimed at addressing not just employer but also workers' needs remain episodic and transactional.

Businesses are becoming ready partners in solving the BIPOC talent puzzle, as a result of demand from customers as well as employees. In response to the Black Lives Matter protests nationwide in summer 2020, corporations pledged to undertake DEI initiatives internally. They collectively promised $50 billion in investments. Local and regional leaders have an opportunity to leverage this passion and momentum to address systemic issues. EDOs can support such businesses that commit to long-term investment and align with the community's DEI vision. Developing metrics, gathering data, and analyzing the data to understand short- and long-term impacts will be crucial.

EDOs will need to devise strategies that address the future of work and inclusion for a multitude of workers and settings. Both the Dallas P-TECH and ConnextMSP examples shared in this chapter are geared towards high school and college students (i.e., they are longer-term strategies). Incumbent workers will need support with re-skilling and up-skilling and should not be ignored, as they are the ones who will face the impacts of automation much earlier, and businesses will need these workers to drive that change. Work-based learning models, such as apprenticeships and internships, are promising approaches and becoming increasingly popular. EDOs would be well served to align themselves and support broader adoption of these tools.

Racism and racial inequity are deep, longstanding problems. EDOs alone cannot solve these problems, but they understand that they can contribute to meaningful solutions by *connecting* students and workers to better opportunities and jobs of the future. Intentionally focusing these approaches on historically excluded populations promises to have an even more significant impact on the community's overall economic outcomes. For as devastating as the pandemic has been, its exacerbation of long-standing racial inequities and highlighting of an under-equipped workforce have enabled EDOs and other related organizations to reflect on how they can help create future economic opportunity and sustainability for everyone in their communities.

NOTES

1. The definition of frontline workers used by Gould & Wilson (2020) is from the NYC Comptroller's report on frontline workers in NYC: "Frontline workers consists of direct-service, mostly non-governmental employees in the grocery, pharmacy, transit, delivery & storage, cleaning, healthcare, and social services industries."
2. P-Tech and Early College Programs: https://www.dallasisd.org/collegiateacademies.
3. Dual Credit Brings Dual Degrees: https://www.dallascollege.edu/news/pages/newsitem.aspx?ArticleId=64.
4. P-Tech and Early College Programs: https://www.dallasisd.org/collegiateacademies.
5. Greater MSP Partnership: https://www.connextmsp.org/.

REFERENCES

Bergson-Shilcock, A. (2020, May). *The New Landscape of Digital Literacy*. National Skills Coalition. Retrieved from https://www.nationalskillscoalition.org/wp-content/uploads/2020/12/05-20-2020-NSC-New-Landscape-of-Digital-Literacy.pdf.

BLS (2018). Median weekly earnings $606 for high school dropouts, $1,559 for advanced degree holders. Retrieved from https://www.bls.gov/opub/ted/2019/median-weekly-earnings-606-for-high-school-dropouts-1559-for-advanced-degree-holders.htm.

Brookings (2020). Examining the black–white wealth gap. Retrieved from https://www.brookings.edu/blog/up-front/2020/02/27/examining-the-black-white-wealth-gap/.

Brown, Steven K. (2020, September). *Racial Inequality in the Labor Market and Employment Opportunities*. WorkRiseNetwork. Retrieved from https://www.workrisenetwork.org/sites/default/files/2020-09/racial-inequality-labor-market-and-employment-opportunities.pdf.

College in High School Alliance (2020). *Evidence of Success*. Retrieved from https://www.collegeinhighschool.org/evidence-of-success.

Congressional Research Service (2021). *Unemployment rates during the COVID-19 pandemic*. Retrieved from https://crsreports.congress.gov/product/pdf/R/R46554.

Dallas Independent School District (n.d.). *P-TECH and Early College Programs*. Retrieved from https://www.dallasisd.org/Page/41736.

Ding, L., & Molina, J. S. (2020, September 1). *"Forced Automation" by COVID-19? Early trends from current population survey data*. Federal Reserve Bank of Philadelphia. Retrieved from https://www.philadelphiafed.org/community-development/workforce-and-economic-development/forced-automation-by-covid-19.

Ellingrud, K. (2021, June 11). *What we lose when we lose women in the workforce*. McKinsey & Company. Retrieved from https://www.mckinsey.com/about-us/covid-response-center/inclusive-economy/what-we-lose-when-we-lose-women-in-the-workforce.

Famighetti, C., & Hamilton, D. (2019, May 15). *The Great Recession, education, race, and homeownership*. Economic Policy Institute. Retrieved from https://www.epi.org/blog/the-great-recession-education-race-and-homeownership/.

Gould, E. (2020, February 27). *Black–white wage gaps are worse today than in 2000*. Economic Policy Institute. Retrieved from https://www.epi.org/blog/black-white-wage-gaps-are-worse-today-than-in-2000/.

Gould, E., & Wilson, V. (2021, June 1). *Black workers face two of the most lethal preexisting conditions for coronavirus – racism and economic inequality*. Economic Policy Institute. Retrieved from https://files.epi.org/pdf/193246.pdf.

Hewlett, S. A., Marshall, M., & Sherbin, L. (2013, December 1). How diversity can drive innovation. *Harvard Business Review*. Retrieved from https://hbr.org/2013/12/how-diversity-can-drive-innovation.

Lund, S., Manyika, J., Segel, L. H., Dua, A., Hancock, B., Rutherford, S., & Macon, B. (2019, July). *The future of work in America: people and places, today and tomorrow*. McKinsey & Company. Retrieved from https://www.mckinsey.com/~/media/mckinsey/industries/public%20and%20social%20sector/our%20insights/future%20of%20organizations/the%20future%20of%20work%20in%20america%20people%20and%20places%20today%20and%20tomorrow/the-future-of-work-in-america-full-report.pdf.

Lund, S., Sanghvi, S., Robinson, O., De Smet, A., Dua, A., & Cheng, W.-L. (2020, November 17). *What 800 executives envision for the postpandemic workforce*. McKinsey & Company. Retrieved from https://www.mckinsey.com/featured-insights/future-of-work/what-800-executives-envision-for-the-postpandemic-workforce.

Mamedova, S., & Pawlawski, E. (2018, May). *A description of U.S. adults who are not digitally literate*. National Center for Education Statistics. Retrieved from https://nces.ed.gov/pubs2018/2018161.pdf.

Minnesota Department of Employment and Economic Development (2020). *Alternative measures of unemployment*. Retrieved from https://mn.gov/deed/data/current-econ-highlights/alternative-unemployment.jsp.

National Center for Education Statistics (2019). Table 219.75: *Percentage of high school dropouts among persons 16 to 24 years old (status dropout rate) and per-*

centage distribution of status dropouts, by labor force status and years of school completed: Selected years, 1970 through 2018. Retrieved from https://nces.ed.gov/programs/digest/d19/tables/dt19_219.75.asp.

Peterson, D. M., & Mann, C. L. (2020, September). *Closing the racial inequality gaps*. Citi GPS. Retrieved from https://ir.citi.com/%2FPRxPvgNWu319AU1ajGf%2BsKbjJjBJSaTOSdw2DF4xynPwFB8a2jV1FaA3Idy7vY59bOtN2lxVQM%3D.

Rosalsky, G. (2020, June 2). Minneapolis ranks near the bottom for racial equality. MRP News. Retrieved from https://www.mprnews.org/story/2020/06/02/npr-minneapolis-ranks-near-the-bottom-for-racial-equality.

Texas Education Agency (August 2016). *Four-year graduation and dropout data, class of 2015.* Retrieved from https://tea.texas.gov/reports-and-data/school-performance/accountability-research/completion-graduation-and-dropout/four-year-graduation-and-dropout-data-class-of-2015.

U.S. Bureau of Labor Statistics (2010, February 5). *Labor force statistics from current population survey.* U.S. Bureau of Labor Statistics. Retrieved from https://www.bls.gov/cps/cpsatabs.htm.

U.S. Bureau of Labor Statistics (2021, April 21). *Earnings and employment rates by educational attainment, 2020.* Retrieved from https://www.bls.gov/emp/chart-unemployment-earnings-education.htm.

Zahidi, S., Ratcheva, V., Hingel, G., & Brown, S. (2020, October). *The Future of Jobs report 2020.* World Economic Forum. Retrieved from https://www.weforum.org/reports/the-future-of-jobs-report-2020.

PART IV

Factor reallocation and regional innovation
ecosystems

8. Modeling decreased labor access after the COVID-19 pandemic: economic, social, and demographic implications

Jeffrey Dykes, Billy Leung and Fred Olayele

8.1 BACKGROUND

The U.S. economy has evolved significantly in the last few decades, with technology driving remarkable gains in productivity, economic growth, and employment across a wide range of industries. In March 2020, the COVID-19 pandemic brought the longest economic expansion in U.S. history to an abrupt halt. At the end of February 2020, economic expansion in the country had spanned 128 months.[1] Also, before the COVID-19-induced recession, the U.S. economy was close to full employment, with unemployment rate at a historic low of 3.5 percent. Although the downturn happened, in principle, during the nationwide lockdowns in March and April 2020, the impact of the pandemic continues to play out.

The unprecedented magnitude of the decline in employment and production heralded by COVID-19 has laid bare many flaws in existing economic and social structures. Unlike in previous recessions, job losses during the pandemic recession were more significant for workers with low wages. Apart from exacerbating existing inequalities, its impacts and remedies are atypical.

Typically, a recession is triggered by a demand shock, a supply shock, or a financial shock. When demand outstrips supply, this causes overheating, as the economy reaches the limits of its capacity. When not caused by overheating, then, random external shocks to the economy can puncture an expansion. COVID-19 is in this category; the trigger of the present crisis is an exogenous shock.

COVID-19 represents an unprecedented shock to labor markets. The pandemic disproportionately affected marginalized populations and a wide array of small businesses, particularly those in sectors involving person-to-person engagements (e.g., restaurants, retail, tourism, and travel). COVID-19 also accelerated economic trends that were related to the "future of work," with major implications for sectors and jobs already projected to decline with the rise of new technologies and task automation.

The cyclicality of the labor share[2] of output, especially following a recession, has received considerable attention in the literature.[3] Among others, uncertainty and structural factors perpetuate wage depression in the aftermath of a recession. Contemporary evidence on the labor market effects of the pandemic, based on changes in labor costs, shows that low-wage, essential workers are worse off.[4][5][6]

Clearly, COVID-19 has perpetuated and deepened existing inequalities. As such, policies, programs, and practices that favor economic activity reallocation with asymmetric, distortionary impact on labor's share of output can only exacerbate existing gaps. To ensure the post-pandemic economy is more equitable and resilient, interventions must prevent a further erosion of labor's share of GDP, and the concomitant increase in inequality.

Tackling the dual public health and economic crises heralded by the pandemic will involve looking at both demand and supply sides, with emphasis on hard hit sectors. As such, rethinking the issue of labor access in the post-COVID-19 economy cannot be overemphasized. Labor access, among other key factors, will determine how strong the recovery will be and what scars the recession leave on the economy, long after COVID-19 stops dominating the headlines. Strategic policy interventions for increased labor access, particularly in industries better positioned to thrive in the "new normal," cannot be overemphasized. These, and related issues, are examined in this chapter.

The remainder of the chapter is organized as follows. In Section 8.2, we discuss the labor market puzzle, in the context of why the post-COVID-19 job market is defying the odds. Section 8.3 examines labor access and its implications for long-term social distance requirements and transit capacity. Methodological details and results are unpacked in Section 8.4, while the fifth section highlights the distributional implications.

8.2   THE LABOR MARKET PUZZLE

At the onset of the COVID-19 pandemic, a significant decline in economic activity was visible. This was observed through the usual indicators of a recession (e.g., real GDP, real income, employment, industrial production, and wholesale-retail sales). However, as the ongoing economic recovery peaks up momentum, a rather unusual trend is unfolding: workers are quitting in record numbers – in what has been called the "Great Resignation." In September 2021 alone, a record 4.4 million U.S. workers quit their jobs.

Texas A&M University professor, Anthony Klotz, coined[7] the term "Great Resignation" to predict a mass, voluntary exodus from the workforce. Klotz's theory is based on four underlying trends: a backlog of resignations, height-ened levels of burnout (burnout is a predictor of turnover), a shift in identity, and remote workers not willing to return to the office.

Obviously, workers now have leverage in the post-COVID-19 economy, partly because the pandemic has, somehow, jolted their understanding of work and life dynamics. As a quick reminder, the current wave of resignations was preceded by almost a decade of wage and benefits stagnation – especially in lower-end jobs.

In many ways, the pandemic has flipped the employment market. While conventional economic theory suggests that during downturns, employers have the upper hand (because employees need work and would typically hold on to their jobs), the current trend is refuting this theory. From childcare needs and personal safety to two-income household economics and lifelong passion, other critical factors – beyond market incentives and demand-supply dynamics – explain why the post-COVID-19 labor market is defying the odds.

Earlier in the pandemic, there was a consensus[8] among economists that once pandemic unemployment aid (e.g., unemployment benefits, pandemic-relief checks, and eviction moratoriums) expired, lower-income workers would return. However, the expiry of these emergency financial relief measures has yet to translate to an increase in returning workers. More so, contrary to the notion that quit rates are higher in dense urban centers (because jobs in the services sector tend to be more concentrated here), a recent *Washington Post* article[9] shows higher quit rates in the more-rural states.

These mixed signals, in a way, underscore the need to examine impor-tant underlying trends. One potential way to resolve the puzzle that has beset the U.S. labor market is to take a critical look at the issue of labor access. Behavioral changes are difficult to predict in the face of many uncertainties. Because this crisis stems from a pandemic, understanding its impact on the economy and healthcare system remains critical for any mean-ingful policy action. Long-term economic impacts are difficult to measure in the face of many unknowns. While supply is gradually returning to satisfy pent-up demand, what is not certain is what the new equilibrium levels of economic activity and demand patterns will be. Nonetheless, simulations, along with dynamic adjustments as more information becomes available, will continue to be helpful.

8.3   LABOR ACCESS AND THE POST-PANDEMIC ECONOMY

The labor theory of value has deep roots in both classical, free-market econom-ics and traditional Marxism. Karl Marx in his 1867 work, *Capital*, explains the distinction between labor and "labor power" through the labor theory of value – which explains labor power in the context of the capacity of workers to produce goods and services. Marxian economics faults the foundations of capitalist profits on the basis that workers are exploited by capitalists. However, mainstream neoclassical economics has since advanced entrepreneurial capitalism as the source of profits.

In the neoclassical tradition, labor's marginal productivity and the price of its output are the key determinants of the demand for labor. In other words, the demand for labor as an input in the production process is a derived demand. This is simple and straightforward: a firm demands labor because it values its marginal productivity. In a perfectly competitive output market, this is computed as the value of the marginal product of labor (VMPL), where VMPL is interpreted as the price firms are willing to pay the last worker hired. Under non-perfectly competitive market settings, the equivalent paradigm is the marginal revenue product of labor (MRPL). The MRPL is the additional revenue generated when one additional employee is employed, and under this construct, firms will employ labor until the MRPL and the wage rate are equal. Though largely theoretical, this has implications for labor access. This is discussed further below.

Labor access is a measure of the labor pool available for employers when hiring and retaining workers. Having a greater labor access benefits employers by allowing them to select from a wider pool of potential workers. For example, a large city has a strong labor access because the large population includes a larger labor force that employers can choose from, compared to a limited pool from a small town. Similar to how a large city provides companies located there increased labor access because of the large population, the pandemic has created awareness on the availability of a much larger labor pool than previously thought as a result of the ability of employees to work remotely while maintaining at least the same level of productivity.

While it is expected that decreased labor access would be detrimental to the economy, based partly on the above analysis, our objective is to determine to what degree a decrease in labor access would affect the economy, both at the local and national level. We therefore compare one-year shocks to labor access in several cities across the U.S.: New York City, Atlanta, Chicago, Houston, Seattle, San Francisco, Los Angeles, and Miami. Following this, the magnitude of the shock between cities, the duration of the economic impact, and how the shock affects the rest of the U.S. are compared.

If a particular city loses its competitiveness in the labor market by having a decreased access to labor, it is expected to suffer long-term negative economic consequences – whether from other regions attracting workers more effectively, another shutdown resulting from an additional COVID wave, or the transportation system not efficient enough to support the economy to its best potential.

Table 8.1   Expected growth of employment, GDP, and population for the eight selected cities, the rest of the U.S., and the U.S. as a whole

Region	Category	Units	Average 2021–30
All Regions	Employment	Thousands (Jobs)	206,518
	Gross Domestic Product (GDP)	Billions of Fixed (2012) Dollars	21,555
	Population – All Races – Total	Thousands	341,634
New York City Area	Employment	Thousands (Jobs)	6,147
	Gross Domestic Product (GDP)	Billions of Fixed (2012) Dollars	880
	Population – All Races – Total	Thousands	8,335
Fulton County, GA (Atlanta)	Employment	Thousands (Jobs)	1,226
	Gross Domestic Product (GDP)	Billions of Fixed (2012) Dollars	169
	Population – All Races – Total	Thousands	1,149
Cook, IL (Chicago)	Employment	Thousands (Jobs)	3,591
	Gross Domestic Product (GDP)	Billions of Fixed (2012) Dollars	406
	Population – All Races – Total	Thousands	5,152
Harris County, TX (Houston)	Employment	Thousands (Jobs)	3,283
	Gross Domestic Product (GDP)	Billions of Fixed (2012) Dollars	435
	Population – All Races – Total	Thousands	4,841
King County, WA (Seattle)	Employment	Thousands (Jobs)	1,948
	Gross Domestic Product (GDP)	Billions of Fixed (2012) Dollars	308
	Population – All Races – Total	Thousands	2,489

Region	Category	Units	Average 2021–30
San Francisco County, CA	Employment	Thousands (Jobs)	1,020
	Gross Domestic Product (GDP)	Billions of Fixed (2012) Dollars	177
	Population – All Races – Total	Thousands	916
Los Angeles County, CA	Employment	Thousands (Jobs)	6,684
	Gross Domestic Product (GDP)	Billions of Fixed (2012) Dollars	750
	Population – All Races – Total	Thousands	10,073
Miami-Dade County, FL	Employment	Thousands (Jobs)	1,893
	Gross Domestic Product (GDP)	Billions of Fixed (2012) Dollars	176
	Population – All Races – Total	Thousands	2,846
Rest of U.S.	Employment	Thousands (Jobs)	180,726
	Gross Domestic Product (GDF)	Billions of Fixed (2012) Dollars	18,254
	Population – All Races – Total	Thousands	305,833

Source: REMI baseline data: 8 major cities and rest of U.S. 70-sector PI+ model version 2.5.

Table 8.2   *Baseline employment, GDP, and population projections through 2030*

Region	Category	Units	2021	2022	2023	2024	2025	2030
All Regions	Employment	Thousands (Jobs)	198,857	202,604	204,097	205,769	207,388	209,906
	Gross Domestic Product (GDP)	Billions of Fixed (2012) Dollars	19,580	20,308	20,669	21,050	21,472	23,171
	Population – All Races – Total	Thousands	332,463	334,545	336,589	338,647	340,701	350,543
New York City Area	Employment	Thousands (Jobs)	5,845	5,972	6,048	6,146	6,208	6,261
	Gross Domestic Product (GDP)	Billions of Fixed (2012) Dollars	796	825	843	864	882	943
	Population – All Races – Total	Thousands	8,248	8,241	8,253	8,284	8,320	8,450
Fulton County, GA (Atlanta)	Employment	Thousands (Jobs)	1,161	1,196	1,210	1,223	1,233	1,251
	Gross Domestic Product (GDP)	Billions of Fixed (2012) Dollars	152	159	162	165	169	183
	Population – All Races – Total	Thousands	1,091	1,105	1,119	1,133	1,145	1,200
Cook, IL (Chicago)	Employment	Thousands (Jobs)	3,439	3,505	3,537	3,579	3,613	3,653
	Gross Domestic Product (GDP)	Billions of Fixed (2012) Dollars	367	380	388	396	405	437
	Population – All Races – Total	Thousands	5,110	5,108	5,113	5,124	5,139	5,214

Regional economic systems after COVID-19

Region	Category	Units	2021	2022	2023	2024	2025	2030
Harris County, TX (Houston)	Employment	Thousands (Jobs)	3,132	3,197	3,234	3,278	3,310	3,328
	Gross Domestic Product (GDP)	Billions of Fixed (2012) Dollars	386	403	413	424	435	472
	Population – All Races – Total	Thousands	4,742	4,758	4,780	4,805	4,831	4,932
King County, WA (Seattle)	Employment	Thousands (Jobs)	1,803	1,873	1,903	1,938	1,960	2,016
	Gross Domestic Product (GDP)	Billions of Fixed (2012) Dollars	266	281	289	298	306	341
	Population – All Races – Total	Thousands	2,320	2,361	2,401	2,441	2,478	2,639
San Francisco County, CA	Employment	Thousands (Jobs)	946	980	1,000	1,022	1,032	1,049
	Gross Domestic Product (GDP)	Billions of Fixed (2012) Dollars	155	163	168	173	177	192
	Population – All Races – Total	Thousands	872	877	886	899	911	960
Los Angeles County, CA	Employment	Thousands (Jobs)	6,395	6,509	6,594	6,688	6,747	6,786
	Gross Domestic Product (GDP)	Billions of Fixed (2012) Dollars	682	705	720	736	751	802
	Population – All Races – Total	Thousands	9,964	9,954	9,972	10,009	10,051	10,225

Region	Category	Units	2021	2022	2023	2024	2025	2030
Miami-Dade County, FL	Employment	Thousands (Jobs)	1,808	1,823	1,851	1,878	1,902	1,942
	Gross Domestic Product (GDP)	Billions of Fixed (2012) Dollars	159	163	167	171	175	192
	Population – All Races – Total	Thousands	2,761	2,775	2,795	2,816	2,838	2,926
Rest of U.S.	Employment	Thousands (Jobs)	174,327	177,549	178,719	180,017	181,382	183,621
	Gross Domestic Product (GDP)	Billions of Fixed (2012) Dollars	16,618	17,229	17,520	17,823	18,173	19,609
	Population – All Races – Total	Thousands	297,355	299,365	301,271	303,134	304,989	313,997

Source: REMI baseline data: 8 major cities and rest of U.S. 70-sector PI+ model version 2.5.

The potential for long-term social distance requirements could translate to a decreased capacity on the transit system. Long-term social distance requirements may arise because of the potential for COVID variants not covered under the latest vaccines or the potential for unvaccinated people being present on public transit. In addition to the potential of social distance requirements being incorporated for the long term, projected population growth could also cause increased strain on public transit if no plan is in place to expand public transit capacity at a sustainable pace.

These eight cities are projected to grow an average of 21.2 percent in GDP from 2021 to 2030, surpassing the expected growth of the U.S. as a whole at 18 percent over the same time period (Table 8.1). The levels of these projections are detailed in Table 8.2.

8.4   METHODOLOGY AND RESULTS

The simulations in this study are based on the REMI diversity, equity, and inclusion (DEI) module. This contains data on employment by quintile, price changes by income level, an inequality coefficient, and other data that combines economic and demographic data in order to determine if the economic impacts affect different racial or income groups disproportionately. The REMI model linkages provide a summary of how these economic and demographic concepts are interrelated (Figure 8.1).

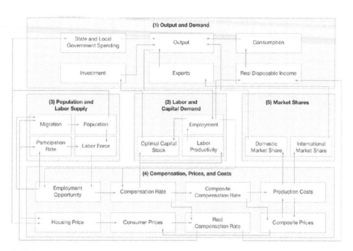

Source: REMI.

Figure 8.1   REMI model linkages (excluding economic geography linkages)

The simulations involve a scenario where no in-person work occurs during the entire year of 2021 for eight selected cities across the U.S.: New York City, Atlanta, Chicago, Houston, Seattle, San Francisco, Los Angeles, and Miami. This simulation provides an idea of what types of economic consequences can be expected after being required to work completely remotely. The effect on each city of decreased labor access resulting from fewer employees being able to attend work in-person depends on each industry's ability to work remotely and the unique industry makeup of each city.

Each industry has a different set of job functions that define its ability to work remotely, so we first determine each industry's ability to work remotely. Industries such as finance, management, professional services, and telecommunications contain tasks that can mostly be performed remotely, whereas industries such as construction, transportation, and manufacturing are largely unable to operate remotely. Therefore, the simulation involves large decreases for industries that largely require workers to be present in-person, and smaller decreases for industries where work can more easily be performed remotely (Table 8.3).

Each industry is assigned an Effective Potential, a score which ranks how well the industry can perform tasks remotely on a 0–100 scale (0 being nothing can be done remotely and 100 being all tasks can be performed remotely). "Labor Access" is calculated by subtracting the Effective Potential from 100 and multiplying the result by −0.01 to equal the input to the simulation. The Finance and Insurance industry experiences the smallest decrease in labor access (24 percent) since it has the greatest ability for workers to perform functions remotely, whereas the Accommodation and Food Services industry experiences the largest decrease at 92 percent.

Table 8.3 *Simulation inputs: by industry, effective potential, and labor access change within the simulation*

Industry	Effective potential (national average)	Labor access (100%)
Finance and insurance	76	−0.24
Management	68	−0.32
Professional, scientific, and technical services	62	−0.38
IT and telecommunications	58	−0.42
Education	33	−0.67
Wholesale trade	41	−0.59
Real estate	32	−0.68
Government and administrative support	31	−0.69
Utilities	31	−0.69

Industry	Effective potential (national average)	Labor access (100%)
Arts, entertainment, and recreation	19	−0.81
Healthcare and social assistance	20	−0.8
Retail trade	18	−0.82
Mining	19	−0.81
Manufacturing	19	−0.81
Transportation and warehousing	18	−0.82
Construction	15	−0.85
Accommodation and food services	8	−0.92

Source: McKinsey & Company (2020).

Labor Access Index Equation

The Labor Access Index policy variable operates in the model by estimating the effect of access to labor choice and individual characteristics by occupation and industry on labor productivity.

$$FL_{i,t}^k = \left[\left(\frac{\left(\frac{\left(\sum_{j=1}^{nocc} d_{j,i} * FLO_{j,t}^k \right) + RCW_{i,t}^k}{2} \right)}{FL_{i,T}^k} \right) \right] * FLPRMPV_{i,t}^k$$

$FL_{i,t}^k$ = Labor productivity due to labor access to industry and relevant occupations by industry i, in region k, time t, normalized by $FL_{i,T}^k$.

$d_{j,i}$ = Occupation j's proportion of industry i's employment.

$FLO_{i,t}^k$ = Labor productivity for occupation type j that depends on the relative access to labor in occupation j in region k, time t.

$nocc$ = The number of occupations in industry I.

$FL_{i,T}^k$ = Labor productivity due to access by industry i in region k in the last year of history.

$RCW_{i,t}^k$ = Relative labor productivity due to industry concentration of labor.

$FLPRMPV_{i,t}^k$ = The policy variable for Labor Access Index.

The default labor access index policy variable affects labor productivity without having any effect on labor intensity; but in this simulation, we assume that labor intensity is also affected. An increase in labor productivity also increases labor intensity when the increase in labor productivity is assumed to add to output instead of the firm keeping the level of output constant, and cutting employment to maintain a constant level of production

Results

The following results describe the impact of decreased labor access in 2021 and the effect on employment and GDP. A one-year decrease in labor access has profound impacts on each city in the long term. Even though the direct shock to labor access does not extend beyond 2021, the negative effects extend all the way to 2060. The results demonstrate that while decreases in labor access may be temporary, they cause a permanent drain on the economy.

Table 8.4 compares the employment and GDP impacts from each scenario, where the region indicated in each row corresponds to the city with the decrease in labor access in the model. The results for each scenario are shown for the specific region within the scenario (for example, the "New York City" row shows the impact on New York City of the decrease in labor access within New York City). In order to compare how labor access shocks affect the same cities in which they occur, impacts from particular cities on other regions are excluded, allowing a comparison of the resilience of each city to a given labor access shock.

By percentage change from baseline, the largest decreases in employment occur in Houston (−37.4 percent), Los Angeles (−34.9 percent), and Chicago (−35.4 percent), so these three cities are the ones most susceptible to a decrease in labor access. These three cities also experience the largest decreases in GDP. Houston, Los Angeles, and Chicago are most susceptible to a given decrease in labor access because of the prevalent industries in these three cities, compared to the other cities tested in the model.

The largest decrease in employment for each scenario occurs in the construction industry, ranging from a 76.7 percent decrease in Miami to 99.8 percent in Chicago. The other industries with large employment decreases are manufacturing, retail trade, accommodation and food services, and real estate.

Discussion

The decrease in labor access leads to a corresponding decline in labor productivity, which causes a decrease in employment since the labor intensity effect is enabled. As a result, real disposable income, consumption, and output also decrease (Figure 8.2).

Table 8.4   *Employment and GDP by simulation*

Employment by simulation (units: thousands of jobs; differences from baseline)

Region	2021	2025	2030	2035	2040	2045	2050	2055	2060
New York City	-1,637	-1,270	-1,185	-1,159	-1,106	-1,035	-966	-907	-865
Atlanta	-305	-285	-292	-299	-293	-279	-261	-242	-226
Chicago	-1,216	-999	-995	-1,001	-982	-938	-888	-843	-814
Houston	-1,172	-1,172	-1,242	-1,236	-1,234	-1,192	-1,127	-1,049	-983
Seattle	-614	-556	-520	-527	-527	-511	-491	-471	-459
San Francisco	-261	-233	-225	-224	-217	-205	-191	-177	-164
Los Angeles	-2,232	-1,372	-1,187	-1,135	-1,098	-1,065	-1,043	-1,038	-1,054
Miami	-593	-470	-452	-450	-432	-401	-371	-348	-335

GDP by simulation (units: thousands of jobs; differences from baseline)

Region	2021	2025	2030	2035	2040	2045	2050	2055	2060
New York City	-195	-170	-170	-182	-195	-208	-223	-240	-260
Atlanta	-35	-36	-38	-41	-45	-48	-52	-56	-60
Chicago	-125	-111	-114	-122	-131	-140	-150	-162	-176
Houston	-130	-145	-159	-169	-182	-195	-209	-224	-242
Seattle	-80	-76	-75	-82	-93	-105	-119	-136	-156
San Francisco	-39	-37	-36	-38	-41	-44	-49	-54	-59
Los Angeles	-226	-159	-149	-156	-168	-181	-198	-218	-242
Miami	-52	-44	-43	-46	-50	-52	-56	-59	-65

Employment by simulation (units: thousands of jobs; percentage change from baseline)

Region	2021	2025	2030	2035	2040	2045	2050	2055	2060
New York City	–28.0%	–20.5%	–18.9%	–18.4%	–17.5%	–16.1%	–14.6%	–13.3%	–12.4%
Atlanta	–26.3%	–23.1%	–23.3%	–23.5%	–22.6%	–21.1%	–19.2%	–17.5%	–16.1%
Chicago	–35.4%	–27.6%	–27.2%	–27.2%	–26.4%	–24.8%	–22.9%	–21.2%	–20.1%
Houston	–37.4%	–35.4%	–37.3%	–37.1%	–36.6%	–34.8%	–32.2%	–29.4%	–27.3%
Seattle	–34.0%	–28.4%	–25.8%	–25.3%	–24.2%	–22.2%	–20.0%	–18.0%	–16.6%
San Francisco	–27.6%	–22.6%	–21.5%	–21.1%	–20.1%	–18.5%	–16.6%	–14.7%	–13.2%
Los Angeles	–34.9%	–20.3%	–17.5%	–16.5%	–15.7%	–14.8%	–14.1%	–13.6%	–13.5%
Miami	–32.8%	–24.7%	–23.3%	–22.9%	–21.7%	–19.9%	–18.3%	–17.0%	–16.3%
Alberta	–34.4%	–6.9%	–2.8%	–2.2%	–2.2%	–2.2%	–2.3%		

GDP by simulation (units: thousands of jobs; percentage change from baseline)

Region	2021	2025	2030	2035	2040	2045	2050	2055	2060
New York City	–24.6%	–19.3%	–18.0%	–18.1%	–18.2%	–18.0%	–17.9%	–17.8%	–17.8%
Atlanta	–23.3%	–21.5%	–20.8%	–20.9%	–20.9%	–20.7%	–20.5%	–20.2%	–20.0%
Chicago	–34.1%	–27.4%	–26.0%	–25.9%	–26.0%	–25.7%	–25.4%	–25.3%	–25.4%
Houston	–33.8%	–33.2%	–33.7%	–33.1%	–33.0%	–32.4%	–31.8%	–31.2%	–30.9%
Seattle	–30.0%	–25.0%	–22.0%	–21.3%	–21.0%	–20.5%	–20.0%	–19.6%	–19.3%
San Francisco	–25.1%	–21.0%	–18.8%	–18.2%	–18.0%	–17.7%	–17.5%	–17.3%	–17.2%
Los Angeles	–33.1%	–21.1%	–18.6%	–18.1%	–17.9%	–17.9%	–17.8%	–18.0%	–18.3%
Miami	–32.6%	–25.2%	–22.6%	–22.4%	–22.2%	–21.8%	–21.6%	–21.6%	–21.8%
Alberta	–31.3%	–7.9%	–3.4%	–2.4%	–2.2%	–2.2%	–2.2%		

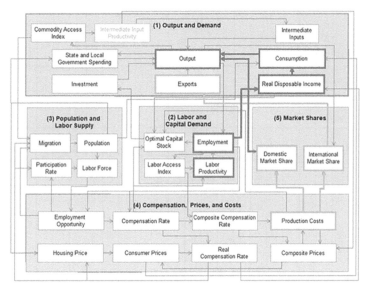

Source: REMI.

Figure 8.2   REMI model linkages with the economic impact of decreasing labor access highlighted

For the Los Angeles scenario in 2021, there is a loss of 2.2 million jobs, and from 2022 to 2060, there is an average decrease of 1.2 million jobs from the baseline, indicating that the economy never fully recovers from the shock to labor access in 2021. The cost of production also increases in 2021 by 76.2 percent in Los Angeles, which makes the region to become less competitive, thereby compounding the negative effects of the decrease in labor access.

The discrepancy between the percentage decrease in the simulation inputs for labor access for Los Angeles, New York City, and Chicago versus the percentage change in employment and GDP in the results for Houston, Chicago, and Los Angeles could suggest that certain cities are better prepared for a decrease in access to labor than others. In order to quantify the magnitude of the labor access change for each region (since the Labor Access policy variable is entered as the same percentage change from the baseline for each city), Table 8.5 provides a means of comparing the magnitude of the labor access shock between each city.

The values in the table include the following calculation: first, the labor access percentage change for each industry is multiplied by the baseline employment for that particular industry (for example, the labor access shock for the Finance and Insurance industry is −24 percent, so for New York City,

−24 percent is multiplied by the region's baseline employment for Finance and Insurance, which is 536,069 jobs, which equals −128,660. After doing this same calculation for all the other industries within New York City, the sum is calculated, which equals the value shown in the table: −3,568. This same calculation is done for the other regions, allowing a comparison of the magnitude of the input for each region with the Labor Access Index policy variable.

New York City's weight as a percentage of the sum of weights for all regions is 23 percent (−3,568 divided by the total, −15,446, equals 23 percent), representing the second largest shock to labor access index as a percentage basis out of the simulations for the eight cities (Table 8.5, second column).

Table 8.5   Weighted labor access index inputs

Labor access index inputs weighted by baseline employment	Sum of weights	Percentage of total (excluding Rest of U.S. region)
New York City Area	−3,568	23%
Fulton County, GA (Atlanta)	−672	4%
Cook, IL (Chicago)	−2,165	14%
Harris County, TX (Houston)	−2,085	13%
King County, WA (Seattle)	−1,106	7%
San Francisco County, CA	−539	3%
Los Angeles County, CA	−4,140	27%
Miami-Dade County, FL	−1,171	8%

Source: REMI baseline data: 8 major cities and rest of U.S. 70-sector PI+ model version 2.5; McKinsey & Company (2020).

8.5   DISTRIBUTIONAL IMPLICATIONS

Multiple factors have influenced the recent social movements, which, in turn, have pushed issues related to DEI to the front burner of the policy debate. Combined with the way the COVID-19 pandemic exacerbated the impacts of systemic inequities, the argument for rethinking social policymaking is compelling – particularly in the context of addressing the adverse, inequitable outcomes of unfair economic designs that have perpetuated extreme inequality and poverty for too long.

From complex infrastructure projects and social justice to public health and climate change, the increasingly complex nature of society means policy questions are becoming more difficult to address. In addition to analyzing the impact of decreased labor access on core macroeconomic indicators such as employment, GDP, and population, it is also important to consider important socioeconomic and demographic factors, which we collectively call DEI indicators in this analysis. The more inequality that exists in a society, the less likely it is for economic growth alone to lead to mobility for those at the bottom of the socioeconomic ladder.

Due to limited equality of educational and economic opportunities in the U.S., the income and wealth gap remains pervasive, resulting in the unequal distribution of income that persists across generations. As seen by the various populist and social movements of the last two decades, particularly in the aftermath of the Great Recession, the lack of social mobility has economic, societal, and political consequences. To address the issues and create a more equitable economic system, opportunities need to be created for more segments of society, especially those facing the greatest barriers. This underscores the importance of DEI considerations in the policy design process.

Labor market trends both before and after the Great Recession show persistent income gaps, particularly along racial and gender lines. Before the COVID-19 pandemic, the recovery from the Great Recession took significantly longer for people of color, resulting in increased inequality. To ensure policy and programmatic interventions are effective at correcting the inequities in the current economic and social systems, DEI indicators, if tracked over a reasonably long period of time and across key variable, can offer useful insights.

In addition to providing equal opportunity for all socioeconomic groups, equity and inclusion are key for maximizing economic growth. First, having a more diverse and inclusive workforce can foster innovation due to the advantages that accrue from varying perspectives. Also, companies that are more diverse tend to perform better on key metrics than those that lack such diversity (Herring, 2009; Slater et al., 2008).

The economic impact of a decrease in labor access would differ based on the location of the shock to labor access since a particular region's industry makeup determines how successful that particular region would be at working fully remotely. Regions with a higher concentration of industries such as accommodation and food services, construction, and transportation would experience a larger decrease in labor access, resulting in a more negative economic impact. On the other hand, regions with a larger concentration of industries such as finance, management, and professional services would experience less of a decrease in labor access, resulting in regions with a higher concentration of those industries doing better.

NOTES

1. See https://www.bls.gov/opub/mlr/2021/article/unemployment-rises-in-2020-as -the-country-battles-the-covid-19-pandemic.htm.
2. The extent to which workers share in total economic output.

3. See https://www.brookings.edu/bpea-articles/the-decline-of-the-u-s-labor-share.
4. See https://www.bls.gov/covid19/effects-of-covid-19-pandemic-on-productivity-and-costs-statistics.htm.
5. See https://www.bls.gov/opub/mlr/2020/article/covid-19-shutdowns.htm.
6. See https://www.brookings.edu/research/the-initial-impact-of-covid-19-on-labor-market-outcomes-across-groups-and-the-potential-for-permanent-scarring/.
7. See https://intelligence.weforum.org/monitor/latest-knowledge/eb18fa9099644b5db6b1040f793fa8d0.
8. See https://www.economist.com/graphic-detail/2021/08/20/so-far-ending-pandemic-unemployment-aid-has-not-yielded-extra-jobs.
9. See https://www.washingtonpost.com/business/2021/10/22/states-labor-quitting-turnvoer-jolts/.

REFERENCES

Herring, C. (2009). Does diversity pay? Race, gender, and the business case for diversity. *American Sociological Review* 74(2): 208–24.

Marx, K. ([1867] 2014). *Das Capital*. Createspace Independent Publishers.

McKinsey & Company (2020). The state of AI in 2020. https://www.mckinsey.com/capabilities/quantumblack/our-insights/global-survey-the-state-of-ai-in-2020.

REMI PI+: 8 Major Cities and Rest of US (2021). Version 2.5. Retrieved March 2, 2022.

Slater, S. F., Weigand, R. A., & Zwirlein, T. J. (2008). The business case for commitment to diversity. *Business Horizons* 51(3): 201–9.

9. Neighborhood vulnerability in critical infrastructure and services

Kyle Marks and Joyce Jauer

9.1 INTRODUCTION AND BACKGROUND

The COVID-19 pandemic and the ensuing economic recession are the most recent major shocks to reveal deep inequalities present in cities and towns around the world, including in New York City (NYC). These shocks disproportionately impacted many groups that are historically among the most vulnerable – those who live in crowded housing conditions, those who work in service sector jobs that require face-to-face interactions, and those who rely on public schools not only for education but for childcare needs. The failings of the post-global financial crisis period – including a failure to generate inclusive growth during all but the tail end of the recovery – still live in the memory. In this context, the New York City Economic Development Corporation (EDC) sought to understand vulnerability across the city through a geographic lens. NYC lives in the popular imagination as a city of opportunity, but opportunities are not distributed equally across neighborhoods.

The history of government's impact at the neighborhood level is mixed, with the legacies of redlining, location selection for major highways, and discriminatory lending still visible today. However, governments can also use infrastructure and services to address inequalities and injustices. Equitable provision of public transit, public parks, public libraries, and broadband infrastructure all serves to create cities in which someone's ZIP code does not determine their destiny or their economic outcomes.

The chapter proceeds with a brief introduction to the framework of the Neighborhood Vulnerability research, followed by a literature review, a methodology section, data analysis, and finally, conclusions and recommendations.

9.2 VULNERABILITY IN NYC

EDC views neighborhood-level vulnerability through four main lenses, or "domains." The first of these is Critical Infrastructure and Services (CIS) –

how easy it is for a neighborhood resident to access life's daily needs within a reasonable distance from home. The second of these is Financial and Housing Security – how easy it is for a neighborhood's residents to find good, quality, affordable housing, as well as the ease of building wealth in one's own neighborhood through other means. The third domain is Education and Workforce Development, which reflects not only the educational attainment and workforce prospects of people living in a neighborhood, but also reflects the services and institutions that exist in a neighborhood to help people obtain more education, or to obtain better jobs. Finally, the fourth domain of Job Access and Stability reflects the quantity and quality of jobs that are accessible to a neighborhood's residents within a reasonable commute.

Together these four domains provide a picture of vulnerability in NYC that can be explored in conjunction with other demographic information in one view or dashboard. Each domain is comprised of indicators, most of which can be measured using publicly available data. The 44 core variables are meant to be a litmus test for measuring vulnerability at a neighborhood level and provide a launching point for other research and exploration. These domains are not intended to label or rank neighborhoods but to aid in understanding areas for development.

The focus of this chapter is the CIS domain, which consists of 12 variables (all expressed in percentage terms):

a. Lack of public transit
b. No broadband at home
c. Slow broadband speed
d. Lack of public computer centers
e. Lack of grocery stores
f. Lack of primary care
g. Lack of mental health care
h. Lack of family planning centers
i. Lack of daycare centers
j. Lack of pharmacies
k. Lack of public libraries
l. Lack of public open space access.

9.3   CRITICAL INFRASTRUCTURE AS A KEY COMPONENT OF VULNERABILITY

Lack of or poor access to one or more of these components can present challenges to New York individuals and families, while reliable access can foster prosperity. People need internet access whether at home or at a library to look for and apply for jobs as well as to pursue education. They need grocery stores and pharmacies to maintain health with nutritious food, essential dry goods, and medications. People need access to care whether at local primary care or family planning clinics, and mental and behavioral health have become increasingly important while practicing social distancing. Parents need to have reliable daycare for children and parks to enjoy leisure time. Further, people need to be able to access transit to reach resources outside of their neighborhood.

Literature Review

A survey of the literature on public services supports this perspective and shows how access is important to the health and strength of communities and the people who live in them.

Indicators of critical infrastructure vulnerability

Better broadband availability at the county level is associated with lower employment rates, even after controlling for factors such as race and age (Jayakar and Park, 2013). Within the OECD, countries that began to adopt broadband saw GDP per capita that was 2.7–3.9 percent higher than it had been prior to the adoption of broadband, and "an increase in broadband penetration rate by 10 percentage points raised annual growth in per capita GDP by 0.9–0.15 percentage points" (Czernich, 2011). Higher broadband speeds are also associated with improvements in job growth (Deloitte, 2021). On a household level, a Philadelphia Federal Reserve Bank study found that prime-age workers aged 25–54 with broadband at home participate in the labor force at a much higher rate than prime-age workers without access; the study estimated that 24,000 people in the NYC Metropolitan Statistical Area would enter the labor force if they obtained access to broadband (Sanchez and Scavette, 2021). The need for broadband is no less important for children and young adults in school. Students without home broadband have been found to earn half a letter grade lower than students with access, to have the digital skills of a student four grades below them with access, and to be less likely to plan to attend a college or university (Quello Center Policy Brief, 2020).

For those who lack broadband access at home, public computer centers fulfill a clear need in neighborhoods. According to Lentz et al. (2000), they can help people in applying for jobs, accessing government assistance programs, learning digital skills, filing taxes, or keeping in touch with family over email. A Brooklyn Public Library study on the neighborhood of East New York noted that patrons needed help with printing, sticky keys, creating a resume, uploading/downloading documents; of the patrons observed in the study, 41 percent were seen using one finger to type, 17 percent had trouble operating the mouse, and 9 percent asked for help (Brooklyn Public Library, 2017). In the United

States population aged 16–65, 58 percent lack the skills needed to fulfill more complex tasks in a technology-rich environment (OECD, 2016).

Daycare and childcare

Access to daycare centers is also essential for communities. The U.S. lacks a universal childcare system, and an estimated 93 percent of families with young children in NYC cannot afford center-based care for their infants and toddlers; 80 percent cannot afford less-expensive home-based care (Citizens' Committee for Children of New York, 2020). Daycare and early education are important for both child development and parental labor force participation. An OECD report argues that young children under three, especially those from families living in poverty, can benefit from time away from the home environment because their brain development is more susceptible to family stress and material deprivation.[1] Further, learning and later performance in school are increased by participation in early childcare and education programs. Affordable all-day childcare helps families by enabling more parents to gain employment, bringing in more income and benefits to the household.

According to Modestina et al. (2021), lack of childcare disrupts business operations, affecting companies in addition to families: working parents lost $37 billion in income per year due to inadequate childcare while employers lost $13 billion in productivity per year. The costs were much higher during the PAUSE order:[2] Barron's estimated that closing schools for Covid-19 could cost about $700 billion in lost revenue and productivity, or 3.5 percent of GDP (Beilfuss, 2020).

Transit access

Transportation is another important factor that supports communities and the labor force. The Urban Institute (2020) found that lack of access to public transit disproportionately harms vulnerable populations who depend on it, including seniors, individuals with disabilities, commuters with irregular shifts, Black and low-income workers, women, and young adults – poor access is more harmful to these groups than it would be to a less vulnerable group.

Public transit helps people access services and activities, such as education, employment, shopping, and social eventsas well as alleviates externalities like car congestion and air pollution (Litman, 2014). It is also physically safer for passengers: the American Public Transportation Association (2021) estimated that traveling by public transit is 10 times safer per mile than traveling by automobile.

A policy brief by Health Affairs magazine found that public transit options can improve health and health equity by increasing physical activity, reducing air pollution and traffic accidents, and improving access to employment, medical treatment, nutritious food, essential services, and social linkages

(Heaps et al., 2021). Conversely, transit barriers can lead to missed appointments, delayed treatment, and irregular use of medication, which can cause poor health outcomes (Syed et al., 2013).

Health care and insurance

Access to primary care provides numerous benefits in terms of life expectancy, mortality, and mental health. It can also help to prevent total hospitalizations and emergency admissions equity (World Health Organization, 2018). Primary care has become integral to the overall health system response to the pandemic: both to manage an unexpected surge of demand and to maintain continuity of care for all (OECD, 2021). Further, strong primary health care with multi-disciplinary teams integrated with community health services supports resilience in health systems in the face of future public health emergencies.

Health outcomes are also closely related to insurance coverage. A survey of literature by the U.S. Committee on the Consequences of Uninsurance demonstrates a consistent, positive relationship between health insurance coverage and health-related outcomes including chronic disease management, cancer outcomes, hospital treatment, and mortality. Insurance is associated with greater incidence of preventative care and, consequently, more appropriate use of health care services (Institute of Medicine, 2002). On the other hand, high cost, job loss, and undocumented status can discourage people from seeking medical insurance and care (Tolbert et al., 2020).

Family planning clinics are an important point of access for health care services and have been shown to lead to significant improvements in health and in social and economic well-being. These services help families to anticipate and attain their desired number of children and the spacing and timing of their births, to reduce infant and maternal mortality, to increase maternal health overall, and to improve social and economic conditions of women and their families (Stith et al., 2009; Gipson et al., 2008).

Access to primary care and family planning services reduces the spread of sexually transmitted infections (STI) as well as infertility through the prevention and treatment of STIs. Further, family planning clinics are an important source of non-contraceptive care and offer preventive health services to poor and low-income women such as primary care services, diabetes screening, mental health screening, and referrals for other needed care (Zolna et al., 2016). Studies indicate that these clinics are the entry point or primary source of health care for low-income women (Sonenstein et al., 2004) – one study showed that 61 percent of women visiting family planning clinics (many of whom are low-income) report that the clinic is their usual source for medical care (Frost, 2013). They also have been found to offer more same-day appointments and shorter wait times for an appointment than other primary care clinics (Zolna and Frost, 2016).

The presence of pharmacies in a neighborhood helps to address at least the geographic barrier to accessing prescribed medication. Geographic barriers are associated with lower prescription medicine use overall, and higher out-of-pocket spending (Doloresco et al., 2011). Pharmacies can also be a resource for groceries and dry goods when people do not have good access to a supermarket or between trips; access-burdened households spend more at convenience stores, dollar stores, and pharmacies than those with access (Ver Ploeg et al., 2017).

Social determinants and open space

In addition to health care itself, the social determinants of health are an important component of understanding vulnerability – the wider set of forces shaping the conditions of daily life such as economic policies and systems, political systems and social policies, and social norms are fundamental for reducing longstanding inequities (World Health Organization, 2021). Determinants like socioeconomic status, education, neighborhood and physical environment, employment, and social support networks (Artiga and Hinton, 2018) can be investigated alongside other indicators used by the medical establishment, like disability adjusted life years and incidence of chronic disease, to understand what interventions may make an impact on communities.

Parks and open space produce various economic and non-economic benefits to communities. They can attract visitors who put dollars into local economies; through precipitation capture, they reduce stormwater management costs; and trees can reduce air pollution control costs (The Trust for Public Land, n.d.).

A U.S. Department of the Treasury CDFI Fund report (2011) on the geography of inequitable access to food showed that 60 percent of the NYC population with limited supermarket access lives in a low-income area. NYC's Food Retail Expansion to Support Health (FRESH) program responds to this need by encouraging healthy food retail development in underserved areas throughout the city through tax and zoning code incentives.[3] Certain neighborhoods have greater need depending on the surrounding population and existing retail and can benefit from greater investment in supermarkets and renovation (New York City Economic Development Corporation, 2021). Grocery stores, beyond their potential to create jobs and generate tax revenue, can act "as anchors for further commercial revitalization" within neighborhoods" (Hagan and Rubin, 2013).

It is this sort of targeted research that the dashboard and exploration of vulnerability through the four domains is intended to precipitate, whether related to areas like education, job access and training, housing, or broadband.

9.4 METHODOLOGY AND DATA ANALYSIS

The Neighborhood Vulnerability research project is based on the most recent publicly available data where possible. Data sources vary and come mainly from federal, state, and city agencies: transit access data from the NYC Department of City Planning; broadband and computer center data from the NYC Internet Master Plan; location data for grocery stores, family planning centers, daycare centers, and pharmacies from the New York State Department of Labor;[4] data on Medically Underserved Areas from the U.S. Health Resources and Services Administration; location data for mental healthcare providers from NYC Department of Health and Mental Hygiene; location data for public libraries from the NYC Department of City Planning; and location data for public open spaces from New York State Department of Parks and Recreation.

The function of this domain is to evaluate the relative vulnerability of NYC's neighborhoods in terms of access to various types of critical infrastructure and services. For all variables, except for broadband adoption and broadband speed, access is a spatial metric, determined by the percentage of a neighborhood that lies outside of walkshed of a certain size, typically either ¼ or ½ of a mile from a given point (the location of an establishment).

"Neighborhoods" in the Neighborhood Vulnerability Dashboard are defined as Neighborhood Tabulation Areas (NTAs), a geography created by the NYC Department of City Planning, which are aggregations of census tracts and subsets of the city's 55 Public Use Microdata Areas. There are 188 NTAs in NYC.

To facilitate apples-to-apples comparisons of neighborhood vulnerability across a wide variety of indicators with different scales, units, and distributions, percentiles based on the raw values for each indicator for each neighborhood are calculated. This includes a single percentile value, a composite index, for each of the four domains, based on a weighted average of the percentiles for component indicators within each domain. Weights are based on each indicator's relative power to explain neighborhood vulnerability through the lens of a particular domain. For each indicator, a higher raw value will correspond to a higher percentile, which in turn indicates a higher degree of neighborhood vulnerability. The CIS domain is equal to the sum of the weighted component indicators.

It is important to note that the data analysis in this paper relies heavily on correlation analysis. This analysis is meant to provide inspiration and direction for further research; it is not meant to be used to argue definitively for causation.

Data Analysis

As a reminder, the focus of this chapter is the CIS domain, which consists of 12 variables (expressed in percentages):

a. Lack of public transit
b. No broadband at home
c. Slow broadband speed
d. Lack of public computer centers
e. Lack of grocery stores
f. Lack of primary care
g. Lack of mental health care
h. Lack of family planning centers
i. Lack of daycare centers
j. Lack of pharmacies
k. Lack of public libraries
l. Lack of public open space access.

Again, the calculations are done in such a way that a higher raw value corresponds to higher neighborhood vulnerability. For example, the raw value for Lack of Public Transit reflects the percentage of an NTA's land area that lies outside of a ¼ mile walkshed (Industrial Business Zones are excluded from all spatial calculations).

Of the 12 variables contained within the CIS domain, there is only one for which values (both raw values and percentiles) are positively correlated with the values of all other variables within the domain: Lack of Family Planning Centers. There are only three variables which are negatively correlated with more variables than they are positively correlated with: No Broadband at Home, Slow Broadband Speed, and Lack of Primary Care.

Table 9.1   *Correlation between CIS and other domains*

	Financial and Housing Security	Education and Workforce Development	Job Access and Stability
r value	−0.1	0.256	0.256
r² value	0.01	0.065	0.065

At the domain level, CIS is only weakly correlated with the other domains: a negative relationship with Financial and Housing Security (r^2 of 0.01), and positive relationships with Education and Workforce Development (r^2 of 0.065) and Job Access and Stability (also an r^2 of 0.065) (Table 9.1). One interpretation of this is that CIS captures a type of vulnerability not found in the other domains, which is one of the main justifications for separating vulnerability into four separate domains in the first place.

Density improves likelihood of access to critical infrastructure and services

Most of the indicators in the CIS are spatial metrics, and so it's worth exploring the relationship between access to critical infrastructure and services and neighborhood density. As could be expected, there is a negative correlation between neighborhood population density (people per square mile) and a neighborhood's overall domain value for CIS, with an r^2 value of 0.6216.

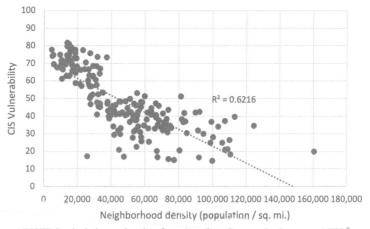

Source: NYCEDC calculations using data from American Community Survey and ESRI ArcGIS.

Figure 9.1   Neighborhood density vs. CIS vulnerability

As can be seen in Figure 9.1, neighborhood density varies much more among neighborhoods with lower vulnerabilities for CIS; neighborhoods with higher levels of vulnerability tend to have relatively low densities. This makes sense: when people are spread out across larger areas, it is less likely that they will live within a certain distance of the infrastructure and services that many people need.

It's also worth looking at the cases in which a neighborhood's density deviates significantly from what would be expected, given the overall relationship between density and access to critical infrastructure and services. The struggles of NYC's housing supply to keep up with housing demand are well-documented,[5, 6] and if the city were to add housing, neighborhoods that represent ideal candidates for increased supply could include those where there is good access to infrastructure and services, but where there is not already high levels of population density. Neighborhoods for which the population density is significantly lower than might be expected given their (low) levels of vulnerability include MN17 (Midtown-Midtown South), MN24 (SoHo-TriBeCa-Civic Center- Little Italy), BK38 (DUMBO-Vinegar Hill-Downtown Brooklyn-Boerum Hill), BK37 (Park Slope-Gowanus), BK25 (Homecrest), and BK09 (Brooklyn Heights-Cobble Hill) (Table 9.2).

Table 9.2   *Largest gaps between CIS vulnerability and expected CIS vulnerability, by NTA*

NTA Code	NTA Name	Density	CIS Vulnerability	Expected* CIS Vulnerability	Difference
MN17	Midtown-Midtown South	25,739	17.3	58.1	−40.8
MN24	SoHo-TriBeCa-Civic Center-Little Italy	47,551	17.0	47.2	−30.1
BK38	DUMBO-Vinegar Hill-Downtown Brooklyn-Boerum Hill	44,682	20.9	48.6	−27.6
BK37	Park Slope-Gowanus	55,051	22.6	43.4	−20.8
BK25	Homecrest	41,835	29.4	50.0	−20.6
BK09	Brooklyn Heights-Cobble Hill	67,514	16.7	37.2	−20.5
BK40	Windsor Terrace	45,330	29.8	48.3	−18.5
MN23	West Village	73,972	15.6	33.9	−18.3
MN40	Upper East Side-Carnegie Hill	77,316	15.1	32.3	−17.2
MN25	Battery Park City-Lower Manhattan	66,974	20.3	37.4	−17.2

Mitigating vulnerability in critical infrastructure with personal vehicles
In neighborhoods with worse access to critical infrastructure and services, there could be certain ways for individuals to mitigate that vulnerability, although these involve costs as well. The most prevalent solution is likely the use, and perhaps ownership, of a personal vehicle. The evidence points to this being the case; whether vehicle availability allows someone to live in a less dense neighborhood, perhaps with lower walkability and access to infrastructure and services, or whether living in that type of neighborhood forces someone to seek access to a personal vehicle.

Figure 9.2 shows a moderate, positive relationship between vulnerability for the CIS domain and the percentage of a neighborhood's population with access to at least one vehicle. It's clear that in neighborhoods with worse access to infrastructure and services, residents are more likely to have access to at least one vehicle; across the city's neighborhoods, the average value for

the percentage of residents with at least one vehicle available is 51.5 percent.
Across the 20 most vulnerable neighborhoods in terms of CIS, that number is
77.6 percent; across the 20 least vulnerable neighborhoods, the corresponding
number is 27.4 percent.

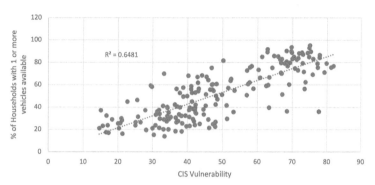

Source: NYCEDC calculations using data from American Community Survey and ESRI
ArcGIS.

Figure 9.2   CIS vulnerability vs. vehicle availability

It is also possible for residents of vulnerable neighborhoods using public
transit to be able to mitigate the cost of low access to other infrastructure and
services. Some neighborhoods have much better transit access than would be
expected, given the typical positive relationship between transit access and
access to other critical infrastructure and services.[7] Neighborhoods that fit
this description include BK93 (Starrett City), BX49 (Pelham Parkway), QN56
(Ozone Park), BX75 (Crotona Park East), and BK23 (West Brighton). It is
possible that in these and other similar neighborhoods, transit access allows
residents to travel outside of a typical walkshed in a manner that is not overly
burdensome or costly.

Internet at home as a means to alleviating multiple vulnerabilities
Some indicators within the CIS domain are most strongly correlated with other
indicators within the same domain. The two indicators within the domain that
relate to broadband, however – percentage with No Broadband at Home, and
percentage with Slow Broadband Speed – are actually more highly correlated
with the overall domain values of the other three domains (the r^2 value of the
association between percentage with No Broadband at Home and overall CIS
is only 0.003, compared to r^2 values of 0.603, 0.211, and 0.472 for associations
with Financial and Housing Security, Education and Workforce Development,
and Job Access and Stability, respectively). Even so, there is no denying that

broadband is an example of critical infrastructure. What this does suggest, is that there could be potential for interventions that improve broadband access to address multiple types of vulnerability. And aside from the potential for any causal relationship, broadband is a fundamental piece of infrastructure, and ideally would not be so strongly correlated with the amount of money in a neighborhood. Figure 9.3 below shows the relationship between the percentage of people in a neighborhood without access to home broadband, and the ratio of the area living wage by household size to the neighborhood's median income for that household size.

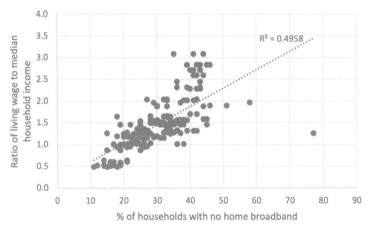

Source: NYCEDC calculations using data from American Community Survey and ESRI ArcGIS.

Figure 9.3   Percentage with no home broadband vs. ratio of living wage to household income

Families need critical infrastructure
Infrastructure can be understood vis-à-vis the built environment, including roads, bridges, and transportation. But those resources can be just as important as others including access to internet, essential services like health care and childcare, and public goods like open space and libraries. Many of these are crucial for families to access nutritious food from convenient grocery stores, to care for and educate children with Pre-K seats and infant daycare centers, and to access medical care whether primary care, family planning, or mental health services.

In this section, the authors explore the relationship among services that support New York families and the potential effects of vulnerabilities as they increase.

Vulnerability in access to daycare aligns with vulnerability in critical infrastructure and services overall with a correlation of 0.5872.[8, 9]

However, there is a far weaker relationship between lack of universal Pre-K and 3-K with CIS vulnerability ($R^2 = 0.0377$). In January 2014, NYC Mayor Bill de Blasio committed to universal Pre-K such that every four-year-old is guaranteed a seat in free, full-day program, tripling enrollment in the subsequent six years (NYC Department of Education, 2021). The city expanded its commitment to include 3-K in 2017, starting in three school districts the next year and six more in the 2019–20 school year. Vulnerability in availability of Pre-K seats will decrease as the 3-K for all program grows, but 58 neighborhoods still have no available seats while 92 percent of NTAs have less than 10 3-K seats per 100 children aged five and under.

Coverage for after-school programs is more disbursed across NYC. Although more established in the city, after-school programs have not been supported by a strong city policy or initiative, unlike Pre-K. Over 900 programs serve K-12 students across the city, but the median percent of an NTA's area within a ¼ mile walkshed from an after-school program center is only 55. Neighborhood accessibility to a center is also positively correlated with the critical infrastructure composite ($R^2 = 0.3826$).

Critical infrastructure and demographics

In addition to the 44 indicators, the Neighborhood Vulnerability Dashboard also contains data for other variables that are not contained within one of the four domains, and for which no value judgments are made (for all other variables in the Dashboard, a higher raw value is assumed to imply a higher level of vulnerability). Within the context of the Dashboard, these variables are referred to as "descriptors"; the descriptors include demographic information, flooding and air pollution risk, and metrics of historical investment. One of the advantages of including these additional variables in the tool is to see how they interact with other indicators, and other domains overall. The data tells us that the strongest negative correlations between the CIS domain and the descriptors are with Air Pollution Exposure, Population Ages 25–39 (%), and Place of Birth: Out of New York State, but in U.S. (%). Put differently, this implies that stronger access to CIS in NYC is associated with higher exposure to air pollution, a higher percentage of people 25–39, and a higher percentage of domestic migrants to NYC (Table 9.3).

This fits with some of the popular narratives of NYC, and of cities in general. Infrastructure and services tend to be more densely packed near the Central Business District, and one tends to expect the center of cities to experience higher levels of pollution. There's also a notion that younger people tend to highly value the conveniences available in denser, walkable neighborhoods with good access to transit and shorter commute times. Domestic migrants

Table 9.3   Correlation between CIS and select Descriptors (r value)

	R value
Air Pollution Exposure (#)	−0.717
Age: 25–39 (%)	−0.678
Place of Birth: Out of NYS, in U.S. (%)	−0.624
Population Count (#)	−0.391
Race: Two or More Races (%)	−0.214

Source: Author calculations; data from NYC Department of City Planning, American Community Survey.

have higher average salaries than NYC residents born in New York State or foreign-born residents, and so can more easily afford to pay for the privilege of having convenient access to services and infrastructure (although better access to infrastructure and services is associated with a higher prevalence of rent burden in a neighborhood). Manhattan, whose neighborhoods tend to be less vulnerable from the perspective of infrastructure and services, can also act as a first port of entry to NYC life: moving from Manhattan to one of the other four boroughs is more common than the reverse journey.

Among individual indicators, those with the strongest correlations with overall CIS itself tend to be those that comprise the domain itself – lack of access to pharmacies, lack of public transit, lack of grocery stores, lack of daycare centers, lack of public computer centers, and so on. Some of the other stronger correlations are with indicators that may be in other domains, but that still capture access or neighborhood density in some way – commute time to Midtown Manhattan, lack of financial services, lack of access to after-school programs, fewer nearby jobs paying $40k or more per year, and average commute time being among these. However, there are other relationships that are perhaps less obvious that are important to examine.

One of these relationships is the relationship between CIS and women's Labor Force Participation (more vulnerability in terms of infrastructure and services is associated with lower women's Labor Force Participation). With an r^2 value of 0.18, and with clear potential for confounding variables and reverse causation, it's impossible to speak strongly about the importance of this relationship without doing further research. Diving deeper into the relationships between women's LFP and other indicators does provide some additional guidance for any subsequent inquiry.

Among indicators within CIS, presence of home broadband, access to daycare centers, access to grocery stores, and faster broadband speeds are a few variables (but far from an exhaustive list) that are associated with higher women's LFP. Again, it bears repeating that it's unclear the extent to which improving broadband access or access to critical services like daycare or grocery would cause improvements in women's LFP, but it is also easy to envision how better broadband access would facilitate applying to jobs or working remotely, and improving access to groceries and daycare could free up a household's time for other pursuits, employment included among those.

It's also worth looking at which indicators might be more important to women's LFP compared to overall LFP, which we can do by looking at the difference between the correlation coefficient (the r value) for an indicator's relationship with women's LFP and the correlation coefficient of that same indicator's relationship with overall LFP. That analysis reveals that indicators with a more positive association with women's LFP compared to overall LFP include (but are not limited to) the following: access to after-school programs, access to daycare programs, access to job training centers, access to grocery stores, and access to public open space. These findings point to interventions that may be useful if there is a desire to increase women's LFP. It may be that, in addition to higher need for a personal vehicle, another cost of high vulnerability with respect to CIS is lower women's labor force participation.

9.5   CONCLUSIONS AND RECOMMENDATIONS

There is a vast array of policies, tools, and interventions available to economic development practitioners at the local level. Vulnerabilities are not distributed evenly across towns and cities, and therefore, any policy, tool, or intervention must consider the importance of place. No two neighborhoods possess either the same historical contexts or the same present-day needs. The goal of EDC's Neighborhood Vulnerability research is to provide a robust first layer of context for those asking the questions of what and where regarding interventions. As a tool and a resource, this is not a silver bullet; it is merely a first stop, and one that will aid in the development of more targeted and incisive research questions.

We have so far examined the specific vulnerabilities associated with a neighborhood's need for CIS. These vulnerabilities are important to consider in isolation, but we have also seen compelling evidence of the interaction between infrastructure and services and other types of neighborhood vulnerability. We have seen how better access can interact with neighborhood density, or with neighborhood wealth. And we engaged with the question of whether improving access to specific infrastructure and services may serve to facilitate increased labor force participation among women and support important services for families.

The significance of critical infrastructure and services plays into the strategy and operations of local government bodies. At NYCEDC, initiatives like the FRESH program, the Harlem River Greenway, and the NYC Ferry are all manifestations of the belief that government tools can be deployed to address neighborhood vulnerability through improvement of infrastructure and services.

These findings do not represent an exhaustive sample of the insights to be gleaned by looking at economic development through the lens of neighborhood vulnerability. This is simply a contribution to a broader conversation, one that we hope will be enriched through the use of vulnerability as a framework.

NOTES

1. See https://www.oecd.org/newsroom/children-paying-a-high-price-for-inequality.htm.
2. March 22, 2020 to May 28, 2020.
3. See https://edc.nyc/program/food-retail-expansion-support-health-fresh.
4. Some location data requires special permissions and training using Quarterly Census of Employment and Wages data.
5. See https://www1.nyc.gov/assets/planning/download/pdf/planning-level/housing-economy/nyc-geography-jobs2-1019.pdf.
6. See https://greaterdc.urban.org/sites/default/files/publication/83656/2000907-strategies-for-increasing-housing-supply-in-high-cost-cities-dc-case-study_2.pdf.
7. Defined by a weighted average of the 11 non-transit indicators within the Critical Infrastructure and Services domain.
8. Critical Infrastructure Vulnerability less Lack of Daycare compared to Lack of Daycare.
9. The composite indicator, Critical Infrastructure and Services domain, is recalculated for comparison with a component indicator to exclude the component indicator (domain – weighted indicator vs. indicator).

REFERENCES

American Public Transportation Association (2021). Public Transportation Facts. https://www.apta.com/news-publications/public-transportation-facts/.

Artiga, S. and Elizabeth Hinton (2018). Beyond Health Care: The Role of Social Determinants in Promoting Health and Health Equity. *Kaiser Family Foundation.* https://www.kff.org/racial-equity-and-health-policy/issue-brief/beyond-health-care-the-role-of-social-determinants-in-promoting-health-and-health-equity/.

Beilfuss, L. (2020). Keeping Schools Closed Could Cost the US Economy at least $700 Billion. *Barron's.* https://www.barrons.com/articles/the-next-big-test-for-the-economy-getting-america-back-to-school-51598044647.

Blumenthal, P., John R. McGinty, and Rolf Pendall (2016). Strategies for Increasing Housing Supply in High-Cost Cities. *Urban Institute.* https://greaterdc.urban.org/sites/default/files/publication/83656/2000907-strategies-for-increasing-housing-supply-in-high-cost-cities-dc-case-study_2.pdf.

Brooklyn Public Library (2017). East New York's Digital Access Needs: Findings from the Community Need Assessment for the BklynConnect Pilot Project. https://www.bklynlibrary.org/sites/default/files/documents/general/EastNY_DigitalAccessNeeds_web.pdf.

Citizens' Committee for Children of New York (2020). Community-Level Data Show How Deeply Unaffordable Child Care Is For NYC Families With Young Children. https://cccnewyork.org/press-and-media/community-level-data-show-how-deeply -unaffordable-child-care-is-for-nyc-families-with-young-children/.

Czernich, N., et al. (2011). Broadband Infrastructure and Economic Growth. *The Economic Journal*, 121(552), 505–32. www.jstor.org/stable/41236989.

Deloitte (2021). Broadband for All: Charting a Path to Economic Growth. https:// www2.deloitte.com/content/dam/Deloitte/us/Documents/process-and-operations/us -broadband-for-all-economic-growth.pdf.

Doloresco, F., et al. (2011). Projecting Future Drug Expenditures: 2011. *American Journal of Health-System Pharmacy*, 68(10). https://pubmed.ncbi.nlm.nih.gov/ 21546644/.

Food Retail Expansion to Support Health (FRESH) (n.d.). *NYCEDC.* https://edc.nyc/ program/food-retail expansion-support-health-fresh.

Frost, J.J. (2013). U.S. Women's Use of Sexual and Reproductive Health Services: Trends, Sources of Care and Factors Associated with Use, 1995–2010. *Guttmacher Institute.* https://www.guttmacher.org/report/us-womens-use-sexual-and-reproductive -health-services-trends-sources-care-and-factors.

Gipson, J.D., Michael A. Koenig, and Michelle J Hindin (2008). The Effects of Unintended Pregnancy on Infant, Child, and Parental Health: A Review of the Literature. *Studies in Family Planning*, 39(1), 18–38. https://pubmed.ncbi.nlm.nih .gov/18540521/.

Hagan, E., and Rubin, V. (2013). Economic and Community Development Outcomes of Healthy Food Retail. *Policy Link.*

Heaps, W., Erin Abramsohn, and Elizabeth Skillen (2021). Public Transportation in the US: A Driver of Health and Equity. *Health Affairs.* https://www.healthaffairs.org/ do/10.1377/hpb20210630.810356/full/.

Institute of Medicine (US) Committee on the Consequences of Uninsurance (2002). Effects of Health Insurance on Health. *National Academies Press (US).* https://www .ncbi.nlm.nih.gov/books/NBK220636/.

Jayakar, K. and Eun-A Park. (2013). Broadband Availability and Employment: An Analysis of County-Level Data from the National Broadband Map. *Journal of Information Policy*, 3, 181–200. www.jstor.org/stable/10.5325/jinfopoli.3.2013 .0181.

Lentz, B., et al. (2000). Structuring Access: The Role of Public Access Centers in the 'Digital Divide'. *Moody College of Communication at the University of Texas at Austin.* https://moody.utexas.edu/sites/default/files/structuring_access_2000.pdf.

Modestina, A.S., et al. (2021). Childcare is a Business Issue. *Harvard Business Review.* https://hbr.org/2021/04/childcare-is-a-business-issue.

NYC Department of Education (2021). Pre-K for All. http://teachnyc.net/pathways-to -teaching/early-childhood-education/all-about.

OECD (2016). Policy Brief on the Future of Work: Skills for a Digital World. https:// www.oecd.org/employment/emp/Skills-for-a-Digital-World.pdf.

OECD (2019). Children Paying a High Price for Inequality. https://www.oecd.org/ newsroom/children-paying-a-high-price-for-inequality.htm.

OECD (2021). Strengthening the frontline: How Primary Health Care Helps Health Systems Adapt during the COVID 19 Pandemic. https://www.oecd.org/coronavirus/ policy-responses/strengthening-the-frontline-how-primary-health-care-helps-health -systems-adapt-during-the-covid-19-pandemic-9a5ae6da/.

Quello Center Policy Brief 01-20 (2020). Broadband and Student Performance Gaps. *Michigan State University.* https://quello.msu.edu/wp-content/uploads/2020/03/ Quello-Center-Policy-Brief-01-20.pdf.

Sanchez, A. and Adam Scavette (2021). Broadband Subscription, Computer Access, and Labor Market Attachment across U.S. Metros. *Federal Reserve Bank of Philadelphia.* https://www.philadelphiafed.org/-/media/frbp/assets/community-development/reports/ broadband-subscription-computer-access-and-labor-market-attachment-across-us -metros.pdf.

Sonenstein, F.L., Shilpa Punja, and Cynthia Scarcella (2004). Future Directions for Family Planning Research: A Framework for Title X Family Planning Service Delivery Improvement Research. *Urban Institute.* http://webarchive.urban.org/ UploadedPDF/311062_family_planning.pdf.

Stith, B.A. and Clayton E. Wright (Eds.) (2009). *A Review of the HHS Family Planning Program: Mission, Management, and Measurement of Results. Institute of Medicine (US) Committee on a Comprehensive Review of the HHS Office of Family Planning Title X Program.* National Academies Press (US). https://www.ncbi.nlm.nih.gov/ books/NBK215219/.

Syed, S.T., Ben S. Gerber, and Lisa K. Sharp (2013). Traveling Towards Disease: Transportation Barriers to Health Care Access. *J. Community Health*, 38(5), 976–93. https://www.ncbi.nlm.nih.gov/pmc/articles/PMC4265215/.

The Geography of Jobs (2019). *NYC Department of City Planning.* https://www1 .nyc.gov/assets/planning/download/pdf/planning-level/housing-economy/nyc -geography-jobs2-1019.pdf.

The Trust for Public Land (n.d.). Economic & Health Benefits. https://www.tpl.org/ economic-health-benefits.

Todd, L. (2014). Transportation and the Quality of Life. *Encyclopedia of Quality of Life and Well-Being Research.* https://doi.org/10.1007/978-94-007-0753-5_3053.

Tolbert, J., Kendal Orgera, and Anthony Damico (2020). Key Facts about the Uninsured Population. *Kaiser Family Foundation.* https://www.kff.org/uninsured/ issue-brief/key-facts-about-the-uninsured-population/.

Urban Institute (2020). The Unequal Commute: Examining Inequities in Four Metro Areas' Transportation Systems, 6 October. https://www.urban.org/features/unequal -commute.

U.S. Department of the Treasury CDFI Fund (2011). The Geography of Inequitable Access to Healthy & Affordable Food in the United States. https://www.reinvestment .com/wp-content/uploads/2015/12/Searching_For_Markets-Report_2011.pdf.

Ver Ploeg, M., Elizabeth Larimore, and Parke Wilde (2017). The Influence of Foodstore Access on Grocery Shopping and Food Spending. *US Department of Agriculture.* https://www.ers.usda.gov/webdocs/publications/85442/eib180_summary.pdf?v=0.

World Health Organization (2018). Building the Economic Case for Primary Health Care: A Scoping Review. https://www.who.int/docs/default-source/primary-health -care-conference/phc---economic-case.pdf?sfvrsn=8d0105b8_2.

World Health Organization (2021). Social Determinants of Health. https://www.who .int/health-topics/social-determinants-of-health#tab=tab_1.

Zolna, M.R. and Jennifer J Frost (2016). Publicly Funded Family Planning Clinics in 2015: Patterns and Trends in Service Delivery Practices and Protocols. *Guttmacher Institute.* https://www.guttmacher.org/report/publicly-funded-family-planning-clinic -survey-2015.

10. Clusters and regional transformation: establishing actionable forward agendas

Ifor Ffowcs-Williams

10.1   BACKGROUND

Building regional economies demands a focused approach, especially after external shocks such as COVID-19. In any region, sectors and their businesses are not equal in terms of transformational potential. A starting point is within the traded side of a region's economy ... the businesses that are already bringing wealth by servicing more distant customers.

There will be patterns within the traded segment. These patterns may originate from a raw material, a cultural tradition, a skill, a chance event or demanding customers. Similar businesses often emerge in response to a distinct regional need. With time, the specialisations and competitiveness to service more distant customers may develop. It is these specialisations, with their clusters of businesses, that differentiate regions.

In many regions, around a third of jobs are in the traded segment. This is where there is more innovation, higher productivity, more start-ups. A resilient ecosystem successfully grounds the scale-up businesses, a key to generating within the region well-paying jobs.

Retaining high growth businesses within the region is supported by relevant broad, horizontal capabilities, such as in IT or freight logistics. These capabilities can underpin several vertical specialisations, several clusters. Taken together, these capabilities form a resilient regional innovation system when they draw on diversity in skills and backgrounds and tight teamwork.

While clusters are a natural occurrence, their development does not need to be left to chance. Many countries now have two to three decades of practical cluster engagement. The author's hands-on cluster development experience extends to six continents and over 50 countries. These combined experiences are drawn on in structuring this chapter.

Firstly, the logic for cluster development is introduced as a framework for regional transformation. Then three overarching design principles are presented for public agencies that are introducing a cluster development intervention. An approach to selecting the clusters that merit public support is advanced. Then, cluster development organisations are introduced, with their triple helix governance and broad forward agendas. Finally, the umbrella structure that supports several clustering initiatives is addressed.

10.2 CLUSTERS AS ENABLERS AND PLATFORMS

Within a month of COVID-19 reaching Barcelona, Catalonia's clusters were in transition. The Fashion Cluster was coordinating the manufacture of medical gowns and masks. In the Lighting Cluster, firms were collaborating to manufacture respirators. The Kid's Cluster was active in improving families' experiences at home. The Edutech Cluster's immediate response was to provide an online education framework for school kids. Two of Catalonia's clusters, Railgroup and Foodservice, partnered to design COVID-free spaces for public transport and restaurants.

The Catalan clusters were also within a month sharing their experiences. Online seminars on telework were underway between the clusters, along with pooling experiences on the rapidly evolving business environment. These exchanges were taking place amongst senior players within the key drivers of Catalan's economy. In total, 30 clusters are under development in Catalonia, contributing 30 per cent of the region's GDP.

The rapid responses to COVID-19 that were achieved in Catalonia were also visible elsewhere. Germany's Biosaxony Cluster (TCI Network, 2020) established a network of 3D printing service firms to supply clinics and other healthcare providers with missing materials. France's technical textiles cluster, in Lyon, within a month was producing protective masks. Ecuador's financial services cluster was quick off the mark in enabling the adoption of digital payment solutions by over 1,000 small Quito retailers. In Medellin, Colombia, the fashion cluster supported casual wear manufacturers in rapidly converting to specialised sanitary garments. Some of these companies are now marketing anti-viral casual wear.

Cluster Excellence Denmark, the organisation facilitating knowledge sharing among Denmark's clusters, has highlighted that clustering initiatives around the world are well equipped to support transformation: 'Before the COVID-19 crisis, clusters had a key role in helping to transform the companies to circular economy, digitalization, industry 4.0 etc.' (Cluster Excellence Denmark, 2020).

Tested by the sudden arrival of COVID-19, clusters and clustering initiatives have been well placed to respond to external shocks, to support transformation. The clustering initiatives in Catalonia, Denmark, and elsewhere are also bringing together groups of business and support organisations to respond to other disruptions, climate change, digitalisation, the green economy, emerging technologies, and to support more equitable growth.

There are solid foundations for the economic development focus seen across Europe. Multiple strands of evidence demonstrate that strong regional economies are centred on clusters. Alfred Marshall (1890) observed that regional concentrations in specific industries created advantages. Jane Jacobs' (1984) insight in *Cities and the Wealth of Nations* emphasizes the micro rather than the macro, with cities, not nations, as the key economic unit. The dynamics of Silicon Valley have been contrasted with the (then) dysfunctional Boston region in AnnaLee Saxenian's (1994) *Regional Advantage.*

Michael Porter provided clarity in *The Competitive Advantage of Nations* (1998) that frontier firms are not randomly scattered within a nation but are geographically clustered. Cooke and Morgan, in *The Associational Economy* (2000), conclude that innovation support should primarily be directed at and through the regional state level. Giacomo Becattini (2002) drew on his extensive research into Italy's industrial districts to emphasise social proximity as a precursor to economic growth.

Edward Glaeser's *The Triumph of the City* (2011) underlined the exceptionally tight geography of innovation. Charles Landry in *Cities of Ambition* (2015) stressed the need to identify and then orchestrate around a city's unique resources. OECD in a Regional Development paper (2021) demonstrated that cities with autonomy and low horizontal fragmentation are particularly productive .

The accumulated evidence is clear, even 'weightless' activities as for example in Hollywood, Bollywood, and Wellington's Wellywood are grounded within strong, regional clusters. Spillovers and the diffusion of tacit information have a tight geography.

Each of the clusters that have been mentioned is centred on a natural occurrence. No public agency has 'created' any of them. Within Europe, 3,000 clusters have been identified. As the European Commission highlights, these clusters matter.[1] They account for one in four jobs, particularly the better paying jobs. International evidence is clear from both advanced and developing economies: 'regions that were home to dynamic clusters, and the companies that were rooted in such clusters, did better' (Ketels, 2016). Clusters are an essential block in building a modern economy.

Europe has accumulated extensive experience in regional development with a cluster focus. These platforms, with strong support from the European Commission, have become a focal point in developing collective responses to change.

Compared with European Union countries, cluster engagement in the US has been limited, under-resourced and has underdelivered. 'Cluster initiatives in the U.S. regions have, for the most part, failed to live up to their expected potential' (Brookings Institution, 2021). In part, responding with scale to COVID-19, the US is developing fresh approaches to regional development with $3 billion being made available through the Build Back Better Act to support regional economic clusters (Center for American Progress, 2021).

Similarly, the United Kingdom has been a laggard in substantially engaging around clusters as a focus for regional development and building more inclusive and resilient economies. In the UK, a lead private sector group, the Confederation of British Industry (2021), has presented the case for cluster development as a central strategy to 'level up the regions' and is establishing a new 'Centre for Thriving Regions'.

10.3   CLUSTER DEVELOPMENT IN PRACTICE

Since the early 2000s, cluster development has become, in many countries, a mainstream approach for stimulating economic growth. This approach can enable remote, disadvantages regions and their small and medium-sized enterprises (SMEs) to garner the competitiveness and critical mass to service distant customers. The examples in Table 10.1 show the wide range of activities underway around the world. These initiatives provide a coordination and mobilising mechanism and, through addressing ecosystem imperfections, are lifting productivity and upgrading the competitiveness of the cluster's businesses.

Table 10.1   Examples, cluster development initiatives

Australia	Brisbane: Mining services, Robotics; Perth: Subsea, Hydrogen Technology
Austria	Lower Austria: E-Mobility, Food, Green Building, Mechatronics; Upper Austria: Cleantech, Medical Technology, Furniture & Timber
Belgium	Flanders: Agrofood, Blue Cluster, Energy, Logistics & Transport, Materials, Sustainable Chemistry; Wallonia: Biotech; Limburg: Bike Valley
Canada	Nova Scotia: Oceans; Quebec: Aerospace, AI, Aluminum, Digital Arts, Fashion; Saskatchewan: Protein; Vancouver: Digital Tech, Cleantech
Colombia	Bogota: Cosmetics, Dairy, Gastronomy, Jewelry, Leather, Music; Medellin: Medical tourism, Sustainable Energy, Textiles, Tourism
Denmark	Copenhagen: Fintec, Maritime & Logistics, Medicon Valley; Odense: Robotics, Welfare Tech; Herning: Lifestyle & Design; Struer: Sound cluster
France	Paris: Digital, Finance Innovation, Medicine, Road Safety, Mobility; Lyon: Aerospace, Digital, Healthcare, Lighting, Mobility, Technical Textiles

Germany	Hamburg: Aviation, Creative, Healthcare, Life Sciences, Media/IT; Berlin: Optics/Photonics, Healthcare, Logistics, ICT/Media/Creative
Iceland	Reykjavik: Oceans, Renewable Energy, Tourism
Netherlands	Eindhoven: Augmented Reality, Design, Photonics, Sports Tech, IT; Wageningen: Food Valley; Horn: Seed Valley
New Zealand	Christchurch: Agribusiness, Health; Queenstown: Tourism Tech
Norway	Bergen: Ocean Technology; Hordaland: Seafood Innovation; Møre: Blue Maritime; Oslo: Cancer Cluster; Trondheim: Ocean Autonomy Cluster
Pakistan	Lahore: Leather footwear, Textiles; Sialkot: Surgical instruments
South Africa	Cape Town: Fine Food, Furniture, IT, Textiles, Oil & Gas, Renewables; Durban: Automotive, Chemicals, Green, Maritime
Spain	Basque Country: Aerospace, Agrofood, Bioscience, ICT, Railway, Steel; Catalonia: Beauty, Foodservice, Gourmet Foods, Kid's, Packaging, Sports
Sweden	Gävleborg: GIS; Hudiksvall: Fiber Optics; Mälardalen: Robotics; Örnsköldsvik: Biorefinery; Uppsala: Life Sciences; Värmland: Paper

While some of these clustering initiatives may appear similar, a closer examination often reveals differentiation through specialisation. As the specialisation of a cluster develops, opportunities for extending the served geographic market arise.

10.4   SELECTING CLUSTERS FOR PUBLIC SUPPORT

The first design principle relates to how clusters are selected for public support. Two common approaches are top-down analysis to identify the most promising growth sectors, and bottom-up open competitions. Top-down analysis is principally suited for cities and regions with a tight geography. For more extensive regions, public competitions have become a preferred approach, often at the national level, including Australia, Canada, France, Germany, Norway, and Sweden. A selection-by-competition approach is also suitable for large conurbations, such as New York, Sao Paulo, Sydney, or Tokyo.

Cluster development is at times introduced by a public agency as another economic development project, in parallel to generic, across-sector initiatives such as workforce training, investment and talent attraction, export development, innovation hubs, and 'smart cities'. Alternatively, cluster development is introduced as a centre-stage approach. Then, cluster development provides a high-level integration framework across a spectrum of business support activities. Successful cluster development initiatives address the coordination failures that reach across public agencies, academia, and business.

Hosting a competition upgrades the economic development agenda from supporting a few cluster projects to more fundamentally placing emphasis on transforming behaviour patterns through collaboration. Importantly, this bottom-up approach ensures that the cluster is a willing occupant in the driver's seat from the start. Alternatively, a (top-down) sponsoring organisation determines which clusters are to be supported and at times imposes its support onto an unreceptive agglomeration. Political leaders may dream about creating the next Silicon Valley, yet another me-too cluster. Business leaders understand the region's current strengths.

Hosting cluster competitions lets the market determine the cluster's shape in terms of a functional region and a specialisation. International experience is that the proposals of many competition winners are frequently much broader than conventional 'sector' development approaches. Many of the initiatives that fail to win support through the competition gather sufficient momentum to garner alternative support, albeit at a lower level.

Cluster competitions are usually introduced with extensive promotion to position the relevance of cluster development around a region's specialisations. Wide-ranging presentations and discussions are held with business organisations, community leaders, and universities.

When cluster development is being introduced, business attention needs to be captured. Norway and Sweden offered their priority clusters five to ten years of public co-funding to galvanise attention. Canada captured the attention of business, academic and civic leaders to cluster development by offering $950 million in co-funding over five years. This funding was shared amongst just five competition winners.

10.5 COMMENCING A CLUSTER DEVELOPMENT INITIATIVE

A common practice in financing clustering initiatives is co-funding of three, five, and even ten years. Public agencies frequently take the lead in initiating the intervention, usually contributing at least half of the funds at the start up. For many European clusters, annual co-funding from public agencies is around $250,000–$1.5 million per cluster. The public funding to individual clusters should not be equal. Norway offers three levels of support with differing time commitments and holds an annual competition to select further clusters for support. The balance of funding may come from other agencies and the private sector, with some in-kind contributions. Securing funding from a mix of sources, locked in for a minimum of three years, is a major strength that provides the platform for resilient interventions.

Cluster Development Organisations

In Europe, well over 1,000 clustering initiatives are underway. The cornerstone of each intervention is a cluster development organisation that is introduced as a meso structure, a not-for-profit intermediary between individual firms and public agencies. Such meso organisations provide the necessary neutral home for coordination and mobilisation amongst the wide range of cluster stakeholders. Cluster development organisations are change agencies and strongly benefit when they are not directly attached to any one stakeholder, such as a large business, a public agency, a university or an industry association.

The main application of funding is to underpin the cluster organization, staffed by a small team and headed by a cluster manager. This person is primarily a catalyst and a connector. As will be described, the activities and roles of this small team of change agents can be extensive.

From Agency Clutter to Alignment

An array of business support organisations has important roles in the development of any cluster, but often there is support agency clutter that includes piecemeal, uncoordinated, and at times, random government support. In developing countries, donor support, while welcomed, can add to this clutter. Key support organisations include the relevant national and state/provincial agencies. National agencies may have responsibilities that include trade and investment policy and setting standards.

State/provincial/municipal responsibilities can cover workforce training, investment attraction, export support, access to research universities, labour regulations, start-ups and SME development, industry estates, technology centres and common user facilities. These are the aspects that are often critical in upgrading competitiveness. However, the engagement of these agencies is frequently with individual firms, rather than clusters and ecosystems.

Support organisations also include academic institutions (from high schools and vocational training through to universities and public R&D) and from the private sector, industry associations, and chambers of commerce.

The Inter-American Development Bank (2016), drawing on its cluster development experience in Argentina, Brazil, Colombia, and other countries, identifies that aligning this array of support organisations around a cluster's forward agenda is one of the most complex activities that the cluster manager undertakes. A response is the formation of an informal 'Cluster Ignition Team' that brings together the relevant support organisations for a cluster. Frequently, this group of people, engaging with similar businesses, will not have met.

From Agglomeration Clumps to Business Co-opetition

Effective cluster development initiatives also address the isolation of firms that are often found within regional agglomerations. Moving from clumps of firms working individually and in competition, to a 'co-opetition'culture, with businesses naturally competing and simultaneously collaborating, requires careful facilitation by the cluster development team.

Business collaboration is typically in non-strategic areas and can be cluster-wide (e.g. technical training, establishing the cluster's international profile) or amongst small groups of businesses joining forces, for example, to purchase raw materials, tender jointly, or establish an export consortium. While firms may well know of each other, substantive engagement can often be assisted by a neutral broker, such as a cluster manager. Trust builds as businesses engage.

Initial Cluster Diagnosis

A short and sharp review, identifying the cluster's growth impediments and opportunities, is often led by the cluster manager, rather than a consultant or a specialist analyst. This allows the cluster manager to establish a facilitative, honest broker role from the start of the intervention. There are two agendas in play in undertaking this review. Firstly, an overt agenda, understanding the opportunities and challenges facing the cluster's core and support businesses. The review also needs to identify the key support organisations and the individuals within them, that either are, or could, offer support to the businesses. Through this review, the cluster manager is directly understanding of the cluster's development issues.

Secondly, a covert agenda, establishing a personal, open relationship between the cluster manager and the cluster stakeholders, particularly the business CEOs. The cluster manager should use this initial review to start identifying the cluster's hot spots, the segments where the cluster's businesses are particularly successful and competitive. The businesses within the cluster will not be equal in terms of growth aspirations and the competencies to grow. Possibly 10-20 per cent of the cluster's firms can be considered the lead businesses. It is these businesses, particularly within the cluster's hot spots, that the cluster development team needs to focus on. Meeting with the lead businesses individually provides the cluster manager with a first assessment of the potential leaders for the initiative, those that could subsequently be invited to participate on project teams and possibly on the cluster's leadership team.

The necessary insights and information are gathered through a semi-structured, face-to-face discussion with the CEO. Mail questionnaires do not provide the quality of insights that are required and fail to give the opportunity of establishing personal connections.

To address the covert agenda, an extensive range of interviews are often required. To start identifying the cluster's lead businesses, members of the Cluster Ignition Team should be invited to indicate, from their perspective, which businesses merit interviewing. The open-ended discussion topics for this interview will vary from cluster to cluster. Aspects can include:

- How do you differentiate from your competitors?
- Does your firm have specialist suppliers?
- What is one thing that you can't do by yourself?
- What is holding you back from doubling sales?
- How can a world-class reputation for the XYZ cluster be established?
- Who are the business leaders that you particularly respect?

This is not an extensive academic exercise covering all elements. It provides the base for a common understanding of the cluster's development obstacles and opportunities. The findings from the review should be presented at a cluster-wide workshop and early low-hanging-fruit projects discussed. The process is geared towards action.

Many politicians and public agencies are keen to see lengthy diagnostic reports. As cluster outsiders, they require an understanding of the cluster's current situation. In contrast, the cluster's insiders, especially the businesses, are seeking action on the forward agendas and the early delivery of benefits. Effective cluster development needs to satisfy both needs.

Broad Forward Agendas

The rapid response to the review is the development of a broad portfolio of needs-driven projects and services. For any cluster, there is no one silver bullet; a range of issues will need to be addressed in upgrading competitiveness. This necessitates coordinated support from the many support organisations who ideally are already engaged through the Cluster Ignition Team. Early delivery on low-hanging-fruit projects helps build the momentum for more substantive projects later.

Collaborative projects are a clustering initiative's engine room and are designed around the needs of groups of firms. As such, they are bottom-up activities, not top-down, determined by a remote agency. The cluster review will have identified issues, many of which will be specific to that cluster. The response to these issues is a portfolio of action projects. Some of these projects will have urgency, as short-term quick fixes. Many projects will be open to all, such as workshops to introduce e-commerce or energy efficiency audits, a training programme, or a briefing on an export market.

Some projects will be private and amongst smaller groups of firms, such as sharing an export manager, joint purchasing, co-investing in a new facility, collaborating on freight logistics, and so on. Several projects are likely to be long-term, perhaps a collaborative R&D project in exploring new materials or developing a strategy for a priority export market. At times, projects will be competing, exploring alternatives, learning by doing, with tight feedback loops. A strong clustering initiative has tensions.

While resilient clusters focus on endogenous growth, many take a very targeted approach to investment attraction, centred on filling gaps in the cluster's ecosystem. Moving from 'What can we offer?' to 'What do we need?' demands a deep understanding of the cluster.

Opportunities for diversification often emerge at the cluster's periphery, with resilient diversification drawing on deep specialisations. A collaborative project could be exploring new market applications for the cluster's competencies. Finally, projects that address wicked problems could benefit from mission-type collaboration with partners from beyond the immediate cluster.

Within each of these dimensions to cluster projects, businesses are choosing to hunt as a pack to achieve outcomes that are beyond their reach in isolation. The cluster management team is active in identifying and kick-starting these projects, but ideally is not the project manager for every activity. While forward agendas are specific to each cluster, frequent aspects include those listed in Table 10.2.

Table 10.2   Examples, cluster development forward agendas

Building the cluster community	Facilitating silo removal amongst businesses and support organisations; assisting firms navigate through support agency clutter; developing informal & formal business links, building a co-opetition/co-specialisation culture, enabling businesses to learn from each other, circulation of tacit information, spillovers, diffusion of ideas & practices; collaborative responses to COVID-19, digital transformation, the circular economy; engaging with community newcomers.
Skills development	Needs-driven technical & management training; needs-driven tertiary course development; graduate projects with the cluster's businesses; school partnerships; training the disadvantaged.
Technology	Needs-driven, collaborative, R&D; R&D centres; university links; technology mapping, foresight.
Start-ups & scale-ups	Business mentoring; specialised incubators; seed funding & venture capital; local supply chain development; grounding the scale-ups.
Internationalisation	Establishing international connections and cluster-to-cluster links; cluster branding; export development; knowledge links with related international institutions; international talent and student attraction within the cluster's domain.
Investment, two-way	Finely targeted investment attraction, addressing ecosystem gaps. Importing exporters. Outward investment, especially to related clusters.

Connecting to related clusters	Supporting business-to-business (B2B) links, especially for SMEs. Within the region, building the region's innovation system. Within the country, establishing bottom-up national agendas & mission orientated approaches to grand challenges. With related clusters globally, two-way investment & knowledge links.
Physical infrastructure	Cluster specific incubators, precincts, technology parks, centres of excellence, one-stop-service-centre, common user facilities.
Finance	Facilitating equity and debt funding, venture capital, angels, seed funding.
Cost reduction	Joint purchasing of raw materials, packaging, transport services …

Many projects are organised around the cluster's lead businesses; the identified businesses that have the potential to make a substantive difference. However, participation should be open to others.

Projects have differing demands on the cluster organisation. Most projects will just require the time of the cluster manager, such as facilitating the development of an export consortium. Drawing on knowledge of individual businesses, potential common issues and collaborative agendas are identified, and then, the cluster manager uses his/her neutral corner to bring together possible participants for a roundtable discussion.

More substantive projects will need external resources for delivery, such as from an export development agency, a training institute, or a public R&D centre. The cluster manager needs to have strong personal connections with such partners, facilitated through the Cluster Ignition Team. Project implementation is facilitated by co-designing such projects with the delivery organisation.

Successful cluster organisations have funding at hand to facilitate quick engagement on small-scale projects, such as:

- Hosting regular events, providing opportunities for the cluster's stakeholders to meet, a key component in building the trust, the social capital, and the cluster's community. While a guest speaker may be the drawcard for an event, the prime objective is providing occasions for the cluster's stakeholders to mix and mingle.
- Developing the cluster's website.
- Supporting an exploratory export trade mission, an inward buyer's mission.
- Designing a training course; bringing in technical or market specialists.
- Preparing a feasibility study for a common user facility, a hub, or a specialised business incubator.

A cornerstone project for many clusters is establishing a one-stop service hub or common facility centre. Cluster service hubs provide a key 'Institution for Collaboration' for many clusters. They are usually introduced once cluster development is well underway; they are not a low-hanging-fruit project.

Successful hubs can provide the all-important physical visibility to the cluster's stakeholders, demonstrating to politicians and international customers the cluster's significance. Hubs provide a neutral meeting place for the cluster's stakeholders, for training events, for trade shows, for customer interaction, including international buyers. The range of services offered expands as needs are clarified. When a hub is in place, it is often the base from which a hands-on cluster organisation operates.

There is emphasis in many countries on building a cluster's specialised physical infrastructure, such as cluster-specific incubators, precincts, and science parks. This is a relatively quick-fix aspect of cluster development. More relevant (more complicated and longer term) for many clusters is establishing the specialised knowledge infrastructure, with coordination from high schools to vocational training graduates, PhDs, and public R&D. However, even more critical and complex is building the social infrastructure, the personal relationships amongst the cluster's stakeholders. This is where a cluster development team really comes into play.

10.6 GOVERNANCE AND PERFORMANCE MEASURES

The governance of successful clustering initiatives is firmly business-led. Business CEOs are the majority on the cluster's board and take the chair. A point of difference to an industry association is that governance also includes senior participation from the other triple helix actors – relevant public agencies and academia. For some clusters, governance is extended to quadruple helix, including society at large and customers. Even as the main funder, most public agencies accept that they do not have the entrepreneurial zest, flexibility, risk appetite, or speed to directly manage a clustering intervention. Independence fosters sustainable initiatives.

A range of backgrounds and gender diversity are strengths. Strong debates are expected as board members integrate different insights and knowledge. The confidence of politicians and public agencies needs to be earned so that these boards are turned to for advice, rather than individuals, and possibly favoured, business leaders. By having a triple or quadruple helix governance arrangement, credibility is gained far more quickly as stakeholders see that issues are being addressed from all sides.

The cluster board has the autonomy to rank priorities and needs to be equipped with the resources to engage. Public agencies and funders do not determine the cluster's forward priorities but should partner in establishing that agenda. The focus is on action through collaborative engagement, rather than making recommendations for others to deliberate on. As such, the board is a decision-making organisation, not an advisory one. The culture of a clustering initiative is strategic doing. It is not paralysis by analysis.

While metrics need to be in place to establish the success of a clustering initiative, it is hard to establish direct attribution from public investment in achieving outcomes. For example, it is unrealistic to claim the number of jobs or start-ups that have been created are the direct result of the public investment or the clustering intervention.

That said, hard numbers should be gathered at the start of a cluster development intervention. The metrics should be relevant to the cluster and demonstrate change over time, such as the number of employees and professionally trained staff, the number of firms, total sales volume, percentage of international sales, and so on. This hard data is usually gathered through cluster surveys, rather than the (over analysis) analysis of (broad) public statistics. Published statistics are gathered by sector and political region. Clusters are broader than sectors and have functional regions that are unlikely to align with regional boundaries.

Most of the cluster's projects should have metrics attached that facilitate evaluation, such as to train employees in a new process, to assist companies in developing a first export market, and to support companies in establishing their social media interfaces.

In reviewing the progress of a clustering intervention, evidence is needed that demonstrates behaviour changes. Success for the cluster organisation will, in a large part, be that it has created the environment that surfaces this evidence. Drawing on international experiences, a range of success indicators follow (Table 10.3). None should be considered in isolation.

Table 10.3   Cluster development success elements

Cluster governance	A triple helix, business-led, governance entity in place, integrating different perspectives, setting the forward agendas. Not an 'Old Boy's Club'. Drawing on the wisdom of the crowd. The cluster organisation is self-determining and then engaging. And resourced to do so.
Cluster management team	Energetic relationship builders. Addressing coordination failures. Identifying opportunities for B2B collaboration. Attracting quality investments, private and public. Earning the respect of key cluster stakeholders and the wider community; accepted as an insider, a strategic guide, a critical friend.
Project portfolio	Broad forward agendas with a wide portfolio of projects underway. Some projects cluster-wide, others more focused. Rapid engagement on small-scale projects, accepting failures. Projects are more than what an industry association could deliver.

Silo removal amongst businesses	Trust amongst businesses has increased. Rivalry centred on differentiation. Culture of co-opetition & co-specialisation. Active business participation in collaborative projects.
Silo removal amongst support organisations	Support organisation clutter has been removed, alignment around business needs, bringing their resources to support cluster projects. High schools, vocational training institutions and universities closely responding to cluster needs, with specific facilities & programmes.
Cluster profile	Enhanced through frequent & extensive communications, social media. Strong awareness within the home region & well beyond. Reaching out internationally, e.g. online presence in relevant languages, inward & outward missions, establishing export beachheads.
Co-funding & co-resourcing	Businesses contributing to the costs of the cluster organisation through an annual fee, and to relevant projects. Businesses participating because the initiative adds value, is making a difference to their bottom lines. Co-resourcing by public agencies, academic institutions.

With support from the European Commission, an international cluster benchmarking facility has been established in Berlin. The base for this benchmarking comes from over 1,000 clustering initiatives from 45 countries. The European Secretariat for Cluster Analysis (ESCA) awards Bronze, Silver or Gold quality labels.[2] Achieving a Gold Label has become an international mark of distinction for a cluster. This benchmarking uses 31 criteria, with a three-point scale: excellent performance level, potential for improvements, or minimal criteria not reached. The criteria used reinforce the elements that contribute to a strong, internationally competitive cluster and include:

- Cluster organisation's age & legal form
- Cluster's degree of specialisation within its technology area
- Influence of business, academia & public agencies on the cluster's agenda
- Documentation of the cluster's strategy
- Media visibility
- Cluster organisation's web presence
- Entrepreneurship development
- Collaborative technology development
- Integration into regional & national innovation systems
- Cooperation with clusters in other countries
- Cluster organisation's financial sustainability
- Number of cluster participants per employee of the cluster organisation
- Maturity of the cluster management
- Activities and services of the cluster management
- Cluster participants' satisfaction surveys.

Cluster Support Structures

The final design principle addresses the umbrella structure that selects and supports the clustering initiatives. These structures, with a small and senior team, are at times housed within a specific public agency, such as with responsibility for Science & Technology, Innovation, or Export Development. A consequence of such delivery structures is that the host agency can have an undue influence over the forward agendas of the clustering initiatives. Some countries have developed partnership structures for cluster development, bringing together relevant agencies, with delivery being the responsibility of one agency.

Effective support structures offer more than just funding to the selected clusters. An important aspect is to influence the multiplicity of support organisations, providing them with up to date information on business transformation needs and garnering their resources. A further role is to establish the preferred legal framework for cluster organisations as not-for-profit meso institutions. An ongoing activity of these support structures is the training of cluster managers and (importantly) training cluster board members.

Clusters provide building blocks to wider engagement. No cluster is an island. Coordination is needed across clusters where there are common, bottom-up agendas supporting the development of the region's innovation system. Regional clusters provide bottom-up input into national agendas. Many initiatives are linking with related clusters around the world, to accelerate their SMEs into international markets, to support two-way investments, and to draw on international knowledge that is absorbable by the cluster's businesses.

Finally, this umbrella facility has the responsibility to review the clustering initiatives, and to establish the measurement and evaluation approaches. Should difficulties arise with a clustering initiative, the umbrella support structure may need to step in.

Red Lights on Cluster Development

At times, political support is centred on wanna-be clusters, often in the fashionable information, communication, and technology (ICT), eco, creative, and nano areas. Occasionly, a cluster is narrowly limited to a political region, or to SMEs, or an ethnic group. Some 'clustering initiatives' are little more than dressed-up real estate development; or the prime funder predetermines the cluster's forward agenda and expects visible evidence of transformation within months. Much to the frustration of participating businesses, funders have been known to view cluster analysis and report writing as the end deliverable.

At times, the appointed cluster manager is better suited to back-room analysis than front-room relationship building. Governance of a fast-moving clustering initiative can be severely hampered by a dominance of public agency and industry association officials.

10.7 CONCLUSION

Cluster development interventions have been introduced in many countries as a low-cost, high-impact route to building regional economies, centred on regional strengths. These initiatives, when placed centre stage and adequately resourced, have successfully pivoted groups of businesses and their regions in adjusting to dislocations, including the arrival of COVID-19. Resilient initiatives evolve and adapt, offering fresh opportunities for newcomers. Cluster development provides a community-wide platform, enabling stakeholders to collaborate in designing their future.

With an emphasis on endogenous growth, equitable cluster development enhances the ecosystem potential through the inclusion of minorities, collaborative learning, reducing gender barriers and facilitating start-ups that challenge the existing elite.

NOTES

1. See https://ec.europa.eu/growth/industry/policy/cluster_en.
2. See https://www.cluster-analysis.org/.

REFERENCES

Becattini, Giacomo (2002). *From Marshall's to the Italian "Industrial Districts": A Brief Critical Reconstruction, in Complexity and Industrial Clusters*. Springer.
Brookings Institution (2021, September). A new federal giant should make regional leaders rethink their industry clusters. https://www.brookings.edu/blog/the-avenue/2021/09/01/a-new-federal-grant-should-make-regional-leaders-rethink-their-industry-clusters/.
Centre for American Progress (2021, November 23). https://americanprogress.org/article/build-back-rural-new-investments-in-rural-capacity-people-and-innovation/.
Cluster Excellence Denmark (2020, April). Rethinking Innovation, Danish Clusters' Response to the Covid-19 Crisis. https://clustercollaboration.eu/sites/default/files/news_attachment/rethinking_innovation_-_danish_clusters_response_to_the_covid-19_crisis.pdf.
Cooke, Philip and Morgan, Kevin (2000). *The Associational Economy*. Oxford University Press.
Glaeser, Edward (2011). *Triumph of the City*. Penguin.
Inter-American Development Bank (2016). The Impact Evaluation of Cluster Development Programs: Methods and Practices, ed. Alessandro Maffioli, Carlo

Pietrobelli, and Rodolfo Stucchi. https://publications.iadb.org/en/impact-evaluation -cluster-development-programs-methods-and-practices.

Jacobs, Jane (1984). *Cities and the Wealth of Nations*. Pelican.

Ketels, C. (2016). Foreword, *Cluster Development Handbook*. https://www.clusternavigators .com/product/cluster-development-handbook.

Landry, Charles (2015). *Cities of Ambition*. Comedia.

Make the UK a World leader in Cluster Development (2021, November 22). Confederation of British Industry. https://www.cbi.org.uk/our-campaigns/make-the -uk-a-world-leader-in-cluster-development/.

Marshall, Alfred (1890). *The Principles of Economics*. Macmillan.

OECD (2021). A comprehensive approach to understanding urban productivity effects of local governments. Regional Development Papers #11.

Porter, Michael E. (1998). *The Competitive Advantage of Nations*. Free Press.

Saxenian, AnnaLee (1994). *Regional Advantage: Culture and Competition in Silicon Valley and Route 128*. Harvard University Press.

TCI Network (2020, June). Recovery Playbook, Helping Today. Preparing for Tomorrow – A Guide for Economic Development Organisations and Cluster Organisations. https://tci-network.org/events/tci-recovery-playbook/.

11. The global visitor economy and resilience challenge: Mallorca's destination resurgence in perspective

Fergus T. Maclaren and Bartomeu Deya Canals

11.1 INTRODUCTION

In 2019, there were 1.5 billion international tourist arrivals, representing the 10th consecutive year of sustained growth (United Nations World Tourism Organization [UNWTO], 2020a). Travel and tourism was the third largest export sector of the global economy, and for some countries, it represented over 20 per cent of their GDP. While sustaining the livelihoods dependent on the sector throughout the pandemic has been deemed a priority, rebuilding visitor economies is also an opportunity for transformation. This includes leveraging tourism's impact on destinations visited and building more resilient communities and businesses through innovation, digitalization, sustainability, and partnerships (United Nations Development Programme [UNDP], 2020).

Prior to the advent of COVID-19, high-profile destinations were more concerned about overtourism and the impacts on destinations and quality of life. Aspects affecting communities living within and on the periphery of these tourism venues included:

- Operational challenges: Limited organizational capacity and financial resources; dealing with irregular and not always accountable levels of governance.
- Site sustainability: Visitor attraction and management; participation of underrepresented groups; and maintenance of traditional cultural use and activities.
- Community resilience: Dealing with pressures to leave traditional neighbourhoods, occupations, and residential areas; tourism sector's ability to respond to and withstand unforeseen circumstances like global pandemics, financial crises, natural disasters, and regional conflicts.

The COVID-19 crisis has fully exposed the fragility of the global visitor economy, and the dependence countries have placed on deriving benefits from tourism industry investments. Local communities that depend on the continuous flow of monies to sustain well-being, infrastructure, and services are now bereft.

This chapter examines the phenomenon of sustainable tourism, its emergence and application over the past 30 years; and how the global tourism sector has been severely debilitated by COVID-19 and is now focused on a tandem recovery approach of sustainability and resilience. The case study of Mallorca is representative of a high-profile, mass tourism destination whose image and attractiveness were suffering under the weight of overtourism; whose tourism reliant economy has been battered by changing COVID-19 regulations and circumstances; and is now continuing on its path to a more sustainable and resilient visitor economy, that is balancing out its risk exposure to tourism and branching out into other sectors such as agriculture, traditional crafts, and longer term experiences.

By taking this approach, the intent is to demonstrate how sustainable tourism can be applied, the challenges that the explosive growth in the sector has created, and how a more sustainable and resilient model can emerge out of the global COVID-19 calamity.

The chapter is framed to address how destinations are dealing with sustainability and resiliency challenges, and a case study on Mallorca. In the next section, we examine the visitor economy and the shift towards sustainability, followed by the advent of COVID-19 and the challenge of establishing destination resilience. A case study on Mallorca's reorientation as a sustainable and resilient tourism destination is discussed, before we end with concluding thoughts.

11.2   THE VISITOR ECONOMY AND THE SHIFT TOWARDS SUSTAINABILITY

Tourism's Growth and Impacts Since 1950

Tourism is one of those unique sectors where there is the potential to create economic value for resources whose conservation would otherwise be seen as having no financial value; such resources include wildlife, natural and protected areas, and tangible (built) and intangible (traditions and customs) cultural heritage. Tourism can also provide an economically, socially, and environmentally sound growth alternative for countries that does not involve resource extraction, nor 'smokestack' industries, and the accompanying infrastructure and services to support them. Government and industry investment in the sector, combined with the lower cost of access due to factors such as package holidays, low-cost air carriers, and relaxing of visa restrictions have subsequently witnessed the rise of global tourism arrivals by 5,600 per cent since 1950.

With those positive attributes in mind, there are a number of challenges facing what has become known as the 'visitor economy' and the ability to manage it in a sustainable and resilient manner. The World Travel and Tourism Council (WTTC) defines the visitor economy as any direct, indirect, and induced economic activity resulting from visitors' interactions with their destination (WTTC, 2020). This activity includes direct consumption of goods and services paid by people who visit a destination, activity generated indirectly from supply chains and services to the industry, construction, and so on, and additional induced activity from what people who work, directly or indirectly, serving visitors spend in the local economy. This takes into account broader economic activity than has been historically defined as tourism and events, encompassing the direct and indirect economic contributions from visitors travelling outside of their usual domicile for holiday, leisure and events and festivals, business, conventions and exhibitions, education, to visit friends and relatives and for employment (Balding et al., 2012).

In the post-2008 economic recession era, the visitor economy for many of the more popular destinations in Europe, North America, and Asia were characterized by mass tourism and ever-increasing growth in visitor numbers. This was driven, among other factors, by an increase in inexpensive package holidays, discount air carriers, and a digital ecosystem that provided ready access to competitive pricing relevant to airfares, accommodation, and rental cars.

The response from local communities to tourism growth
There have been a number of ways that destinations have tried to respond, either through bylaws, regulations and/or restrictions on tourism numbers and behaviours. One approach that integrates input from different sectors of the visitor economy and communities is the Tourism Social Entrepreneur (TSE) Framework. This is defined as: 'a process that uses tourism to create innovative solutions to immediate social, environmental and economic problems in destinations by mobilizing the ideas, capacities, resources and social agreements, from within or outside the destination, required for its sustainable social transformation' (Sheldon, Pollock, & Daniele, 2017).

Tourism social entrepreneurs are thus deemed as the change agents in a destination's social entrepreneurship system; the people who bring their vision, characteristics, and ideas to solve the social problem and bring about the transformation of the tourist destination. Tourism social enterprises are organizations created by the entrepreneurs as private, semi-private organizations or foundations dedicated to solving the social problems in the destination.

Tourism relies on various enterprises (i.e. the visitor economy) to mobilize the industry (Solvoll, Alsos, & Bulanova, 2015); that provides tourism businesses with a significant role in delivering desired community development outcomes. There are five types of TSE categories based on service offerings, namely: 'intermediaries, accommodation providers, destination – [and] community-based tourism operators and tourism institutions' (Sigala, 2016).

Linking TSE with sustainability, de Lange and Dodds (2017) assert that the adoption of social entrepreneurship in tourism:

- stimulates the sustainability of the industry, because social entrepreneurship offers tourists alternative yet sustainable tourism products and services;
- places pressures on existing traditional tourism enterprises to follow responsible tourism practices;
- serves as a foundation for other entrepreneurial activities for local development;
- enables the instigation of policies and regulations that can induce positive environmental and social outcomes; and
- promotes the development of local economies and draws global interest.

For their sustainability visions to be realized, tourism social entrepreneurs need to undertake the challenging tasks to engage, influence and forge meaningful relationships with local community and institutions and other organizations and civic society organizations. The premise and structure for these interactions are rooted in an international scale that has been in development since 1992, with the formulation and application of the concept of sustainable tourism, as outlined in the following section.

Integrating equity, resilience, and sustainability in the visitor economy: conceptual perspectives

The concept of sustainable tourism is rooted in the United Nations Conference on Environment and Development (UNCED), also known as the Earth Summit, which was convened in Rio de Janeiro, Brazil in 1992. Its subsequent Agenda 21 that emanated from the event was a programme of action agreed upon by 182 governments, to chart a sustainable future for the planet. The UNWTO defines sustainable tourism as: 'Tourism that takes full account of its current and future economic, social and environmental impacts, addressing the needs of visitors, the industry, the environment and host communities.'

Sustainable tourism, in turn, should:

- Make optimal use of environmental resources that constitute a key element in tourism development, maintaining essential ecological processes, and helping to conserve natural heritage and biodiversity.

- Respect the socio-cultural authenticity of host communities, conserve their built and living cultural heritage and traditional values, and contribute to inter-cultural understanding and tolerance.
- Ensure viable, long-term economic operations, providing socio-economic benefits to all stakeholders that are fairly distributed, including stable employment and income-earning opportunities and social services to host communities, and contributing to poverty alleviation (UNWTO, 2020b).

While there has been a 30-year basis for sustainable tourism to develop, and be applied, there are still difficulties when it comes to quantifying sustainability in the sector. First of all, there is a question as to which 'pillars' are an appropriate basis and measure. The World Commission on Environment and Development's Brundtland Report's original definition of sustainable development was: 'development that meets the needs of the present without compromising the ability of future generations to meet their own needs' (World Commission on Environment and Development, 1987). The original intention was to have three pillars from which to evaluate the degree of sustainability occurring in an individual sector: economic growth, social inclusion, and environmental balance.

The Brundtland Report, however, also acknowledged that: 'We have the power to reconcile human affairs with natural laws and to thrive in the process … In these our cultural and spiritual heritages can reinforce our economic interests and survival imperatives' (World Commission on Environment and Development, 1987). The advent of UNESCO's Universal Declaration on Cultural Diversity (2001), UNESCO's Convention on the Diversity of Cultural Expressions (2005), and Agenda 21 for Culture (2004) posited that the lack of consideration of the cultural dimension of development hinders the possibility of achieving sustainable development, peace, and well-being. Hence, there has been an ongoing effort to include culture as the fourth pillar of sustainable development (UCLG, 2010).

The Rio+20 outcome document 'The Future We Want' includes sustainable tourism as contributing to green growth. The four-pillar approach for tourism sustainability is necessary, however, as it captures those elements to enhance (economic growth, social inclusion), to reduce the negative impacts (environmental balance), and the key attributes of tangible and intangible heritage at destinations (culture).

The United Nations has intended to address different sustainability facets in the tourism sector with the International Year of Ecotourism in 2002, and the development of the Sustainable Tourism Programme in 2008 by the UNESCO World Heritage Centre. There was also the adoption and use of the 2030 United Nations Sustainable Development Goals (SDGs) in 2015 to encourage more sustainable forms of tourism. Specifically, there are four SDG targets out of the 165 total that correlate to tourism and cultural heritage. These targets include:

- 8.9 – By 2030 devise and implement policies to promote sustainable tourism which creates jobs, promotes local culture and products.
- 12b – Develop and implement tools to monitor sustainable development impacts for sustainable tourism which creates jobs, promotes local culture and products.
- 14.7 – By 2030 increase the economic benefits to Small Island Development States (SIDS) and Least Developed Countries (LDCs) from the sustainable use of marine resources, including through sustainable management of fisheries, aquaculture and tourism.
- 11.4 – Strengthen efforts to protect and safeguard the world's cultural and natural heritage.

The first two of these SDG targets (8.9 and 12b) are focused on supporting sustainable livelihoods and unique intangible cultural heritage; the third (14.7) is concerned with the conservation and sustainable use of marine resources; and the fourth target (11.4) supports the preservation of cultural resources, of which tourism may contribute sustaining revenues and employment. The sustainability dissonance between these targets is that where the development and expansion of a visitor economy (i.e. any direct, indirect, and induced economic activity resulting from visitors' interactions with their destination) (WTTC, 2020) has provided the revenue necessary to preserve monuments, historic sites, and intangible cultural heritage, the increasing volumes of tourists can also result in significant damage and demands on these same resources (McClimon, 2019).

In 2017, with the sponsorship of the UNWTO, there was a more specific, targeted approach to tourism and sustainability, driven by these SDG targets, incorporating and aligning the elements of the four sustainability pillars: cultural, economic, environmental, and social. The 2017 International Year of Sustainable Tourism for Development (IYSTD)[1] promoted tourism's role in the following five key areas:

- Inclusive and sustainable economic growth
- Social inclusiveness, employment, and poverty reduction
- Resource efficiency, environmental protection, and climate change
- Cultural values, diversity, and heritage
- Mutual understanding, peace, and security.

In the pursuit of sustainability, all five of the IYSTD themes have resonated as touchstones, as tourism authorities endeavour to rebuild, renew, and rejuvenate their visitor economies after the debilitating impacts of COVID-19.

11.3   COVID-19 AND DESTINATION RESILIENCE

The Pre-COVID Visitor Economy

The global tourism industry was already facing a number of challenges prior to COVID, particularly overtourism, which entered the destination management lexicon in 2018 when it was coined by the digital travel publication, Skift as follows:

> A new construct to look at potential hazards to popular destinations worldwide, as the dynamic forces that power tourism often inflict unavoidable negative consequences if not managed well. In some countries, this can lead to a decline in tourism as a sustainable framework is never put into place for coping with the economic, environmental, and sociocultural effects of tourism. The impact on local residents cannot be understated either. (Skift, 2018)

Overtourism subsequently generated a number of impacts including:

- Overcrowding and creating a negative destination image, particularly at high profile World Heritage sites such as Amsterdam, Venice, and Dubrovnik in Europe.
- A disproportionate impact on marginalized groups in host communities on vulnerable populations (e.g. the poor, youth, older people, and women), where costs of goods, services, and housing become unaffordable or reduced due to constantly increasing prices and rents and diminishing availability due to conversion to short-term rental platforms like Airbnb.
- Demands on sites affected their physical and environmental integrity, to the point that some destinations had to be closed indeterminately, such as Ko Phi Leh island in Thailand (film location for the *The Beach* produced in 2000) and Boracay in the Philippines.
- Inconsiderate tourist behaviour affected visitor experience and site conservation efforts, causing some destinations like Italian cities Venice and Florence to initiate 'Enjoy and Respect' social media campaigns, while the 'Palau Pledge' was introduced to encourage visitors to act in an ecologically and culturally responsible way on the South Pacific island.
- Governments were developing ways to instil improved visitor access controls and management, including timed and controlled entries to famed international destinations like Peru's Machu Picchu; Croatia's Dubrovnik will only accept two cruise ships a day, with a maximum of 5,000 passengers allowed.
- Economic leakage was becoming a significant problem for destinations that were experiencing what was becoming known as low- or zero-dollar tourism, where visitors on tour packages travel to specific destinations with

accommodations and amenities owned by foreign entities, and apart from employee salaries, a large proportion of the revenues returns to the visitors' countries of origin. This model has been similarly used in the global cruise industry, where points of entry and shore tours are controlled and segregated from local operators by cruise companies.

Despite these ongoing issues, tourism can function well at destinations when there is a mostly consistent flow of visitors whose interests, needs, and expectations can be met by local operators and associated services. Due to the global spread of COVID, and the subsequent external and internal travel restrictions across several countries, there is a loss of confidence and ability to travel that are within and outside of a destination's control. Travel advisories, inconsistent and uneven visitor flows, control of movement outside national borders, and the sudden, extreme loss of revenue have hobbled tourism dependent economies, particularly in emerging destinations, where financial support for the sector can be minimal, and there may be little opportunity to generate revenue elsewhere at the destination.

The WTTC has estimated that the sector's contribution to global GDP fell from nearly US$9.2 trillion in 2019, to just US$4.7 trillion in 2020, with 62 million travel and tourism jobs lost. Global sector capital investment dropped by almost one third (29.7 per cent) resulting in a decline of US$986 billion in 2019, to US$693 billion in 2020 (WTTC, 2021). This economic collapse in global tourism from COVID has resulted in several concerns pertaining to sustainability on the considerable investments that have been made in the planning, development, integration, and infrastructure in visitor economies. These include:

- Economic risk of tourism never returning to the same levels of growth and consistent revenue generation to sustain local tax bases, employment, and industry.
- Social risk of loss of key employment sector and ability to support other sectors such as health and education.
- Environmental risk of loss of biodiversity and potential inability to provide sufficient protective measures and anti-poaching controls.
- Cultural risk of diminished revenues to preserve and maintain sites and the associated communities, landscapes, and traditions that support them.

There are also the critical, longer-term risks that are already emanating from climate change. Higher temperatures are driving extraordinary environmental changes that can affect tourism to destinations: the melting of polar ice sheets and glaciers; thawing of Arctic tundra; increases in extreme weather events, including more severe storms, floods, and droughts; accelerating sea-level rise and coastal erosion; desertification; more and larger wildfires; and changes in species distribution and ecosystems. As far back as 2005, a survey by the UNESCO World Heritage Centre found that for 72 per cent of World Heritage properties for which responses were received from States Parties, climate change was already acknowledged as a threat to natural and cultural heritage (UNESCO, 2007). Hence, destination and visitor economy resilience need to be considered for the immediate and longer-term to address these risks.

The Building Back Better Strategy

One approach for destinations is the building back better (BBB) strategy aimed at reducing the risk to people and communities in the wake of future disasters and shocks. The BBB approach integrates disaster risk reduction measures into the restoration of physical infrastructure, social systems and shelter, and the revitalization of livelihoods, economies, and the environment (UNDRR, 2017). Given existing pre-COVID issues in the global tourism sector, there has been an intention to build in sustainability and resilience into the tourism sector to deal with future concerns related to pandemics, natural disasters, and conflicts, as well as climate change. There is also a need to take risk-based measures that can both anticipate potential challenges and develop a response protocol to do so as rapidly and effectively as possible (Croce, 2018).

The UNWTO has articulated an initiative to guide countries as they recover and rebuild from the devastating impacts of COVID is the sustainable tourism strategy that was launched in June 2021: *One Planet Vision for the Responsible Recovery of the Tourism Sector*. The strategy is structured around six lines of action to guide responsible tourism recovery for people, planet, and prosperity:

- Public health: Integrate epidemiological indicators (i.e. evidence-based monitoring mechanisms) in tourism, connect hygiene (i.e. social distancing and safety protocols) with sustainability, and restore trust through communication (i.e. transparent and proactive communication on health and safety measures).
- Social inclusion: Channel targeted support towards vulnerable groups (i.e. targeted support for a more inclusive recovery), channel long-term support to small- and medium-sized enterprises (i.e. support businesses to diversify their customer base and revenue streams), and repurpose tourism as a supporter for the community (i.e. create stronger local value chains to bring social and economic benefits to local communities).
- Biodiversity conservation: Capture the value of conservation through tourism (i.e. support monitoring mechanisms that would capture conservation's contribution and the value of ecosystem services), support conservation efforts through tourism (i.e. recognize tourism's role to sustain conservation and fight illegal wildlife trade), and invest in nature-based

solutions for sustainable tourism (i.e. support natural resources approaches to conserve water, coral reefs, wetlands, mangroves, coastlines, and foster disaster resilience).

• Climate action: Monitor and report CO2 emissions from tourism operations (i.e. develop monitoring mechanisms for destinations to understand emissions across the value chain), accelerate the decarbonization of tourism operations (i.e. enhance mitigation efforts in the tourism sector investments to develop low carbon transportation options and greener infrastructure and amenities), and engage the tourism sector in carbon removal (i.e. cut emissions to achieve industry carbon neutrality by 2050).

• Circular economy: Invest in transforming tourism value chains (i.e. support integration to promote innovation and the creation of new sustainable business models), prioritize sustainable food approaches for circularity (i.e. mainstream food loss and waste reduction) and shift towards a circularity of plastics in tourism.

• Governance and finance: Measure beyond economic impacts (i.e. align with goals on resource efficiency, climate change and biodiversity, and ensure that the needs of host communities are well integrated in destination management), steer recovery funds towards better tourism (i.e. balance the urgent support from COVID losses needed for business survival, job retention and the restart of tourism operations with longer-term goals such as the protection of ecosystems and climate change), and consolidate partnerships for implementation (i.e. enhance collaboration between key stakeholders along the destination's tourism value chain) (UNWTO, 2021a).

A relevant example of transition from a traditional pre-COVID mass tourism model is the high-profile Spanish island of Mallorca. Through careful planning and integrated initiatives, it has successfully undertaken a strategy to transform to a more sustainable and resilient destination, that would be a useful model for other destinations to consider emulating as they recover and 'build back better'.

11.4   CASE STUDY: MALLORCA AS A SUSTAINABLE AND RESILIENT TOURISM DESTINATION

Mallorca is the largest of Spain's Balearic Islands, located in the western Mediterranean Sea. The island has a land mass of 3,640 square kilometres. It has become one of the main tourism destinations in Europe, combining the conservation of the natural and historic heritage with the necessary modernity that its inhabitants and visitors need. Mallorca has always been a leading destination and example of mass tourism, eventually becoming viewed as a somewhat spoiled, overtouristed and even obsolete in comparison to other destinations in the Mediterranean basin over the past decade (Global Sustainable Tourism Council [GSTC], 2020). This was realized, however, to be a negative disinformation campaign promoted by competitor destinations that were undertaking the same level of tourism development in the region.

The Island, however, has a magical attraction for the most diverse tourism segments and accommodates all levels of people. From the beginning of the twentieth century, Mallorca has been a pioneer in tourism, thanks in part to its combined idyllic mountain and seaside landscapes, and the hospitality and adaptability of native Mallorquins, contributing to its success as a destination.

The beginning of tourism in Mallorca was basically for adventurers and artists seeking inspiration. The person who 'put the island in the map' was British poet and author Robert Graves who came first in 1929 and remained on the island until his death in 1985. For native Mallorquins, the testimony that his son William often quotes has a deep meaning:[2]

> When in 1929 Robert Graves left England after a "complicated domestic crisis" with his then companion the American poet Laura Riding, he had nowhere in mind to settle. He had just written *Goodbye to All That*. In France they called in their friend the poet Gertrude Stein who told them "Majorca is a Paradise if you can stand it". It required self-discipline not to sit in a café and admire the island. (p. 10)

In Mallorca, there was almost no industry, and original tourism development efforts meant a transfer of workers from the countryside. To augment these numbers, it was necessary to intake many workers from other regions of Spain as the local labour market was insufficient. In spite of the somewhat hard conditions of work, for many, working in tourism was an improvement compared with the past jobs and for women even an opportunity to get more independence and decent or real jobs.

This situation has been regulated in the past decades with very strict labour agreements between companies and unions to safeguard working conditions. Seasonality has even been regulated so that many workers receive public compensation in the months that businesses (hotels, restaurants, etc.) are closed. A present example of the authorities and social agents' commitment to equality and decent work conditions for women is the new Tourism Law that is due for approval this year (2022) (Box 11.1). It is commonly accepted that the chambermaids (mainly women in Mallorca) are a collective with hard physical working conditions especially after years of doing that activity. The new law will require that the 4- and 5-star hotels adapt beds with elevators to make their work less hard.

BOX 11.1 BALEARIC ISLANDS SUSTAINABLE TOURISM LAW

The Law, adopted in January 2022 focuses both on the improvement employee working conditions as well as the following sustainability initiatives:

- Replace fuel oil boilers for natural gas or electric models, to enhance property energy efficiency, while reducing annual emissions by 57,600 kilograms of CO_2 per hotel.
- Remodel the hotel classification and the stars system, which define the quality standard of each hotel, to account for and highlight circularity measures, the use of renewable energies and the optimization of energy consumption.
- Install water saving equipment (especially in the clients' bathrooms).
- Promote the use of QR codes in order to limit the use of paper.
- Remove the use of individual (one use) amenities in the rooms (toiletries) provided by accommodations to reduce waste.
- Encourage and favour the implementation of circular economy measures to foster the use of local products and the reuse of waste.

Source: https://thepointsguy.com/news/new-balearic-islands-sustainability-tourism-laws/.

Mallorca has one of the world's oldest tourist boards that was established in 1905. Mallorquins learnt a long time ago the meaning of 'hospitality business', which has helped to both lead and advance many shifts in destination planning, management, and promotion worldwide with many entrepreneurs, particularly in the hotel and accommodation domain, which has expanded its global footprint across all five continents.

Miquel Vicens, former president of the Mallorca Tourism Board, wrote in the foreword of the book edited to celebrate the centenary (*Historia del Fomento del Turismo de Mallorca 1905–2005*):

> Tourism is an instrument of peace and understanding. I am convinced that the wars that Europe suffered in the last century today would not be possible for the mere fact that entire generations of tourists have visited and met their neighbouring hosts or tourists who were previously enemies. ... Tourism is the second largest economic activity in the world and one of the strongest because it satisfies two innate aspirations of humanity: the thirst of knowledge and the pursuit of happiness. (p. 8)

In the interwar years, Mallorca was viewed as a paradise, yet still a humble island with an agriculture-based economy, impacted by depopulation with many persons forced to emigrate to Europe or South America due to the spread and impacts of the Spanish Civil War. Tourism began its expansion after

World War II in the 1950s, due primarily to the creation of package holidays and charter flights with European countries, primarily the United Kingdom. Within a few decades, resorts expanded in the island and Mallorca's visitor economy and GDP grew steadily.

The idyllic 'corners' of the island discovered by the first visitors were somewhat saved but other coastal areas grew excessively. With 40 per cent of its land protected, with many unspoiled landscapes, Mallorca's 550 kilometres of coastline is the most protected of the European Mediterranean countries. As well, UNESCO declared the Serra de Tramuntana's cultural landscape, which accounts for 22 per cent of the island's surface, as a World Heritage site in 2011.

Cultural tourism was an important segment before the world heritage nomination, but after that, the island entered a new dimension, first to withdraw or defeat critics that used Mallorca and created the concept of 'Balearization' as an example of inappropriate tourism development, which later reinforced the point that natural and cultural heritage protection on the island had always been a serious issue in the wake of tourism development.

Some 11.8 million visitors flooded Mallorca in 2019, dwarfing the local population of under a million. The cost of living has skyrocketed, and the affordable housing supply limited, a trend aggravated by the conversion of family homes into vacation rentals. Environmental impacts have been grave. Tourism pushed water usage to the brink. An average of 1,094 flights landed on the island each day between May and October, and, some days also brought as many as 17,000 cruise ship passengers.

Mallorca is better prepared than most destinations to face the post-pandemic era, in part due its investment in time, effort, and resources in researching, innovating, and rethinking tourism. Some of the broad measures that had been taken to combat visitor saturation since 2015 include application of a Sustainable Tourism Tax (dedicated since 2016 to environmental issues and tourism projects), greater control of licences for vacation rentals such as by Airbnb, limitations on the use of alcohol in party areas, and stricter sanctions for those who do not comply (Box 11.2).

The Balearic government's Sustainable Tourism Tax was the first of its kind for a destination in Europe. Its aim is to make the tourists active stakeholders of the necessary investments to compensate the impact that tourism has on the land and local environments. The revenues generated from this tax are destined for environmental projects that meet current sustainable tourism preferences and to improve or adapt infrastructure to reduce environmental impacts. To guarantee transparency and participatory management, the Balearic authorities established the Commission for the Promotion of Sustainable Tourism, with representatives from different tourism and social sectors to assess and select the investment projects that the Sustainable Tourism Tax finances (Balearics Government, 2018).

BOX 11.2 MALLORCA'S TOURISM STRATEGIC PLAN 2022–23

In 2019, the Mallorcan Tourism Authorities presented the 'Mallorca Tourism Strategic Plan 2020–23', with clearly defined actions and objectives that were updated once the pandemic affected the plan's directives. Within the framework of the document, the main products and destination values to sustainably promote are: Culture and Heritage, Sport and Active Tourism, Premium, and MICE. The accompanying main visitor segments are: Families, Couples, University Students (millennials), Senior Tourists, and Corporate entities. The target markets are in four groups: Germany, UK, Spain, and the rest of the world.

Source: Tourism Department, Consell de Mallorca (2020).

The plan was ably complemented and supported by the work of the University of the Balearic Islands School of Tourism and Hotel Management and private research institutions such as the IMPULSA Foundation. The innovative and deep tourism 'know how' was demonstrated with the first project worldwide to integrate circular economy in the hotel business undertaken by this Foundation.

Through the formulation and research of the circular economy in the hotel business, with UNWTO support, IMPULSA Foundation presented a project with high-profile international hotelier GRUPO IBEROSTAR to implement a strategic framework to guide the hotel management circularity. The strategy is based upon three pillars:

- The management of available resources in terms of investment, innovation, and governance.
- The modernization of internal processes in the consumption of materials and resources.
- The implication of the main stakeholders as the employees, suppliers, and clients

Source: Fundacion Impulsa (2020).

A connected example of the sustainability commitment of the Island's tourism sector is the 'Guide of Good Practices in Corporative Social Responsibility' distributed to the hotels by the Mallorca Hotel Federation. With the motto '*know, act, transform*', the guide was created with the purpose of helping hotel companies in their journey towards their transformation to sustainability (Mallorca Hotel Federation, 2020). A clear example of the real application of these recommendations is by the family-owned accommodations company, Garden Hotels. They support the local community by:

- Prioritizing purchases from local suppliers, reaching 80 per cent of the total being bought.
- Promoting local and seasonal produce for consumption at the hotel.
- Promoting organic produce in Mallorca by buying these products and with the creation of organic gardens at their hotels.
- Promoting local traditions and culture amongst their clientele to both appreciate and participate.
- Organizing beach clean-up days to increase awareness of the importance of respecting the local environment (Garden Hotels, 2021).

Other factors that have focused on sustainability as part of the Mallorca's tourism offer include:

- The most advanced waste management law in Spain, whose intention is to ban or significantly reduce the use of plastics and promote waste selection to facilitate the best use and recycling.
- Innovative laws applicable across the Balearic Islands related to the reduction of climate change impacts by the investment and installment of more sustainable forms of energy (e.g. solar, wind, and geothermal).
- The concerns related to undesirable tourism behaviour in some areas of the island have been tackled by regulating business licences for night activities, alcohol consumption, and noise allowance in public areas, as well as accommodation or rentals.
- Airbnb and other rental operators are now required to have a licence with certain quality requirements and also to pay the Sustainable Tourism Tax.

One of the key international approaches to support these measures was Mallorca's successful designation as Sustainable Tourism Observatory designation (Box 11.3).

BOX 11.3 MALLORCA'S TOURISM OBSERVATORY

A more formalized approach has been undertaken with the creation and validation of the Mallorca's application to become a member of the International Network of Sustainable Tourism Observatories (INSTO) by the UNWTO in June 2021. Mallorcan tourism authorities, along with most of the stakeholders in the visitor economy, are aware that this Observatory will reinforce the island's commitment to sustainability as is reflected on the candidature folder:

- Tourism is Mallorca's principal economic engine.
- Natural resources are not infinite.
- Need to preserve and restore the island's cultural and natural heritage.
- Adapting to change is a must and innovative tourism systems need to be designed.
- Lessening the negative impacts of tourism across Mallorca is imperative.

The Observatory will systematically apply information management, evaluation, and surveillance techniques to assessing tourism sustainability on the island. By belonging to this network, Mallorca will be able to provide key resources for tourism managers and planners, as well as all stakeholders, to strengthen institutional capacity, policymaking, and strategy development. The Observatory will also play a fundamental role in monitoring and dealing with issues like job creation and sustainable production and consumption, public health and safety and security, human rights, quality education, and inequalities.

Source: UNWTO (2021b).

In 2019, three of Europe's top-five tourist destinations were Spanish (based on nights spent at tourist accommodations), and the country's tourism sector was worth $200 billion, or 14.3 per cent of the national GDP. McKinsey forecasts that domestic tourism in Spain might not return to pre-pandemic levels until 2024, and inbound international tourism by 2025, if recovery is muted by recurrent bouts of the virus. Subsequently, by the time the sector recovers, Spain may have amassed cumulative GDP losses of $300 billion, and up to 4.4 million jobs might be eliminated (Binggeli et al., 2021).

As of January 2022, the Balearic Islands were identified as Spain's fourth least affected autonomous region in terms of COVID-19 contamination, after the Canary Islands, Madrid and Andalucia, according to figures from the Ministry of Health (Ministerio de Sanidad, 2021).

COVID-19, nevertheless, has had a significant impact on the island's economy. This is due in large part to major visitor origin countries travel restrictions such as the United Kingdom's 'Traffic Light' system – a green, amber, and red list of countries all summer, with each colour meaning different rules around testing and quarantining (Malbon & James, 2021).

Almost 2.5 million passengers travelled through Mallorca's airport in July 2021, almost 50 per cent less than in July 2019. The hotel association estimates the average occupancy rate on the island in summer 2021 at 65 per cent, whereas in normal years, everything is booked out in August, with just two-thirds of the approximately 700 hotels open.

McKinsey underlines five factors that will determine how fast Spain's tourism sector could recover from the pandemic: attractiveness of domestic destinations, availability of air transport, health and hygiene (i.e. need to upgrade health standards and number of hospital beds per capita), importance of business travel, and sustainability. To the last point, it is noted that 'Travelers are increasingly conscious about the size of their carbon footprint when they travel and may base their travel decisions on environmental issues … According to the Yale Center for Environmental Law & Policy, Spain's environmental performance index ranks 14th internationally (Binggeli et al., 2021).

What COVID has accelerated is the application of sustainability and safety measures that have been on tourism authorities' agenda for long and now are a reality. To increase social distancing and visitor loads, Mallorcan authorities have exercised traffic limitations in some areas like the Formentor peninsula. Now, private vehicles cannot enter the area and bus shuttles drive the visitors around, reducing air and noise pollution, while easing traffic flows (Balearics Government, 2019). That being said, domestic tourism demand on the island has seen COVID limitations increase the carrying capacity controls of the island's most visited areas. This includes the mobile app 'Safe Beaches', an innovative tool developed to provide real time information on crowd levels at beaches, and the accompanying current safety measures and protocols (Majorca Daily Bulletin, 2020).

Nevertheless, the experience and know-how of Mallorcan enterprises and society give the island a certain advantage to adapt and better position for the new challenges to its tourism-dependent economy. Most of the measures adopted or projected were indeed researched or planned before COVID and now that should be a competitive advantage. Now, despite the presence of COVID, the island has begun to respond, at least partially, to revising some 60 years of mass tourism practice. The post-COVID adaptation is based on four pillars: Infrastructure or Operative Capacity, Companies, Professionals, and Residents/Tourists. The Mallorcan government has adapted the Finhava platform to enable the integration of these different facets to reduce the environmental impacts of the island's visitor economy (Box 11.4).

BOX 11.4 FINHAVA DIGITAL CIRCULAR ECONOMY PLATFORM

Finhava enables traceability of the entire food cycle. Hotels produce organic matter derived from consumption, which is transported to the Tirme facilities – Tirme is the company responsible for waste recycling in Mallorca. It is transformed into an ecological compound and farmers make use of the compound for fertilizing crops. Farmers' products are then reintroduced into the process and the circular economy cycle is closed.

The Council of Mallorca is using the Finhava platform in promoting the circular economy, local agriculture, and sustainable tourism. The Council stated that this platform traces the routes of food consumed in hotels participating in the project, calculates the carbon footprint, measures the energy produced, evaluates the volume of food waste, and transforms this into an ecological compound for cultivation purposes. In addition, it facilitates interaction between all those along the consumption chain and guarantees the origin of raw material throughout the process, thereby promoting 'sustainable, local and ecological agriculture and measuring its economic and environmental effects'.

At the presentation in Sa Pobla, the Council's president, Senora Catalina Cladera, said that the platform closes the circle of sustainability between producers in the primary sector and large consumers, such as the hotel sector. She also referred to the Council's commitment to making Mallorca 'a benchmark for the circular economy, as reflected in the "Mallorca Circular" plan'.

This includes 24 projects backed by 800 million euros from the European Union's Next Generation Fund. These are to develop a new model of circular production and consumption, which minimizes waste and has the tourism sector as a driving force.

Cladera added that 'ecological transition is especially urgent in vulnerable areas, such as the islands', which need to have energy autonomy. Sustainability is not only a political and business commitment; it is also an attraction for travellers. Knowledge and innovation capacity can turn sustainable tourism into 'the economic lever for change towards a greener, fairer and more resilient Mallorca, and with a tourism that cares for the environment, promotes Mallorcan product, creates quality employment and distributes wealth equitably'.

Source: https://www.majorcadailybulletin.com/news/local/2022/01/19/96035/balearic-government-sets-out-tourism-model-the-future.html.

The full range of initiatives being undertaken are furthering the sustainability path that Mallorca has been pursuing to change its direction from the over-tourism impacts of almost 60 years of mass tourism growth and development, towards becoming a sector that is both more resilient and puts local communities first. In general, domestic opposition to tourism is limited because most of the island's GDP and visitor economy is related directly or indirectly to tourism. The COVID crisis, however, has aroused sentiments in Mallorcan government and society that nothing can be taken for granted and that recovery and rejuvenation measures using BBB should be geared towards new approaches to foster resilience in the sector.

11.5   CONCLUDING THOUGHTS

In the post-COVID era, if the global tourism sector is to establish itself as such a key driver of change, it could also become a role model for a new approach to economic development that puts the valorization of intangibles, such as the conservation, preservation, and protection of cultures or the environment, at the heart of economic development. Natural and cultural resources are the lifeblood of tourism, and while tourism contributes on one side to protect the natural and cultural heritage of a destination, not last securing its value, visibility, and profitability, it can also become the main cause of its own disruption. Sustainability, especially its social and environmental pillars, is probably the most manifest paradox of this global sector.

Some high-profile destinations and their residents, such as Mallorca, were becoming weary of the continuous growth cycle that was straining infrastructure, natural and cultural heritage resources, and quality of life. By embarking on sustainability measures across its visitor economy, tourism authorities on the island were generating more revenue from the Sustainable Tourism Tax to pay for environmental remediation projects; the Guide of Good Practices in Corporative Social Responsibility was providing a more sustainable operational framework for the sector; and the implementation of the Mallorca Sustainable Tourism Observatory is geared towards improving tourism data and management, to improve the broad brush of sustainability initiatives across the Island. These initiatives will be reinforced with the implementation of the new Balaeric Islands Sustainable Tourism Law.

COVID has accelerated and underscored the importance of transforming tourism at a major destination. These same approaches can be applied elsewhere and at emerging destinations, whose visitor economies have been severely impacted by the global pandemic and are looking for successful examples where sustainability and resilience measures can work in a scalable manner.

NOTES

1.   See https://www.unwto.org/tourism4development2017.

2.   A. Nicholas (2019). 'Majorca is a Paradise if you can stand it'. https://www
      .thelocal.es/20191129/opinion-why-mallorca-is-a-paradise-for-writers-if-you
      -can-stand-it/.

REFERENCES

Balding, R., Baird, B., King, J. & Chipchase, S. (2012). *Final Report of the Visitor
    Economy Taskforce: A Plan to Double Overnight Visitor Expenditure to NSW
    by 2020*. https://www.business.nsw.gov.au/__data/assets/pdf_file/0003/24375/VET
    _finalreport_20120810.pdf.
Balearics Government (2019). *Ley de Cambio Climatico y Transición Energetica. Ley
    De Residuos*. http://www.caib.es/pidip2front/jsp/es/ficha-convocatoria/strongspan
    -stylecolornavyconsell-de-govern-spanstrongla-primera-ley-de-residuos-de-las-illes
    -balears-pretende-poner-freno-al-uso-indiscriminado-de-plaacutesticosnbspnbsp#.
Balearics Government (2018). *Sustainable Tourism Tax*. http://www.illessostenibles
    .travel/en/sustainable-tourism-tax/what-is-its.
Binggeli, U., Caballero, J., Constantin, M. & Köpke, S. (2021, 23 April). Spain's travel
    sector can't afford to wait to recover. What can stakeholders do? *McKinsey*. https://
    www.mckinsey.com/industries/travel-logistics-and-infrastructure/our-insights/
    spains-travel-sector-cant-afford-to-wait-to-recover-what-can-stakeholders-do.
Croce, V. (2018). With growth comes accountability: could a leisure activity turn into
    a driver for sustainable growth? *Journal of Tourism Futures*, 4(3), 218–32. https://
    doi.org/10.1108/JTF-04-2018-0020.
de Lange, D. & Dodds, R. (2017). Increasing sustainable tourism through social
    entrepreneurship. *International Journal of Contemporary Hospitality Management*,
    29(7), 1977–2002. https://doi.org/10.1108/IJCHM-02-2016-0096.
Garden Hotels (2021). *Corporate Social Responsibility*. https://www.gardenhotels
    .com/en/corporative-responsibility/.
Fundacion Impulsa (2020). *La economía circular abre una ventana de oportunidad
    para la reformulación del turismo en Baleares*. https://www.impulsabalears.org/
    index.php/estructura/91-noticias/1178-la-econom%C3%ADa-circular-abre-una
    -ventana-de-oportunidad-para-reformulaci%C3%B3n-del-turismo-en-balears.
GSTC [Global Sustainable Tourism Council] (2020). Mallorca tries to tame tourism.
    Destination Stewardship Report, 1(2). https://www.gstcouncil.org/mallorca-tries-to
    -tame-tourism/.
Majorca Daily Bulletin (2020). *App Safe Beaches*. https://www.majorcadailybulletin
    .com/news/local/2020/10/31/74179/safe-beaches-app-rolled-out-across-mallorca
    .html.
Malbon, A. & James, S. (2021, 17 September). Does the traffic light system for travel
    still exist? *Conde Nast Traveller*. https://www.cntraveller.com/article/traffic-light
    -system-travel-green-countries.
Mallorca Hotel Federation (2020). *Guia de BuenasPracticasenResponsabilidad
    Social Corporativa*. http://www.fehm.info/storage/app/media/Boletin%2028%20de
    %20mayo/guia-de-buenas-practicas-en-rsc-del-sector-hotelero-de-mallorca-formato
    -digital.pdf.
McClimon, T.J. (2019). The future of preservation is sustainable tourism. Forbes. https://
    www.forbes.com/sites/timothyjmcclimon/2019/12/09/the-future-of-preservation-is
    -sustainable-tourism/?sh=7296401b6ea5.

Ministerio de Sanidad (2021). *El coronavirus en España: mapas y últimos datos de los casos y su evolución.* https://www.eldiario.es/sociedad/mapa-datos-coronavirus -espana-comunidades-autonomas-septiembre-20_1_1039633.html.

Sheldon, P., Pollock A. & Daniele, R. (2017). Social entrepreneurship and tourism: setting the stage, in P. Sheldon and R. Daniele (Eds), *Social Entrepreneurship and Tourism Philosophy and Practice* (p. 4). Springer. http://internal.khntusg .com.ua/fulltext/Springer/1%D0%91%D0%9C/2017_Book_SocialEntrepreneursh ipAndTouri.pdf.

Sigala, M. (2016). Learning with the market: a market approach and framework for developing social entrepreneurship in tourism and hospitality. *International Journal of Contemporary Hospitality Management*, 28(6), 1245–86. https://doi.org/10.1108/ IJCHM-06-2014-0285.

Skift (2018). *The Genesis of Overtourism: Why We Came Up With the Term and What's Happened Since.* https://skift.com/2018/08/14/the-genesis-of-overtourism-why-we -came-up-with-the-term-and-whats-happened-since/.

Solvoll, S., Alsos, G. A. &Bulanova, O. (2015). Tourism entrepreneurship – review and future directions. *Scandinavian Journal of Hospitality and Tourism*, 15(sup1), 120–37. https://doi.org/10.1080/15022250.2015.1065592.

Tourism Department, Consell de Mallorca (2020). *Tourism Strategical Plan 2020–2023.* https://en.nexmallorca.com/.

UCLG [United Cities and Local Governments] (2010). *Culture: Fourth Pillar of Sustainable Development.* https://www.agenda21culture.net/sites/default/files/files/ documents/en/zz_culture4pillarsd_eng.pdf.

UNDP [United Nations Development Programme] (2020, August). *Policy Brief: COVID-19 and Transforming Tou*rism. https://unsdg.un.org/resources/policy-brief -covid-19-and-transforming-tourism

UNDRR [United Nations Office for Disaster Risk Reduction] (2017). *Report of the Open-Ended Intergovernmental Expert Working Group on Indicators and Terminology Relating to Disaster Risk Reduction.* https://www.preventionweb.net/ publication/report-open-ended-intergovernmental-expert-working-group-indicators -and-terminology.

UNESCO [United Nations Education, Science and Cultural Organization] (2007). Climate change and world heritage: report on predicting and managing the impacts of climate change on world heritage and strategy to assist states parties to implement appropriate management response. *World Heritage Report 22.* https://whc.unesco .org/document/8977.

UNWTO [United Nations World Tourism Organization] (2019). *Balearic Islands Poised to Become First Tourism Destination Developed under 2030 Agenda.* https:// www.unwto.org/global/press-release/2019-04-11/balearic-islands-poised-become -first-tourism-destination-developed-under-20.

UNWTO [United Nations World Tourism Organization] (2020a). *COVID-19 and Tourism: Tourism in Pre-Pandemic Times.* https://www.unwto.org/covid-19-and -tourism-2020.

UNWTO [United Nations World Tourism Organization] (2020b). *Sustainable Development.* https://www.unwto.org/sustainable-development.

UNWTO [United Nations World Tourism Organization] (2021a). *One Planet Vision For A Responsible Recovery of the Tourism Sector.* https://webunwto.s3.eu-west -1.amazonaws.com/s3fs-public/2020-06/one-planet-vision-responsible-recovery-of -the-tourism-sector.pdf.

UNWTO [United Nations World Tourism Organization] (2021b). *Mallorca Joins UNWTO's Network of Sustainable Tourism Observatories.* https://www.unwto.org/news/mallorca-joins-unwto-s-network-of-sustainable-tourism-observatories.

World Commission on Environment and Development (1987). *Our Common Future.* https://sustainabledevelopment.un.org/content/documents/5987our-common-future.pdf.

WTTC [World Travel and Tourism Council] (2021). *Investing in Travel & Tourism.* https://wttc.org/News-Article/New-WTTC-report-provides-vital-investment-recommendations-for-the-Travel-Tourism-sector-post-pandemic.

WTTC [World Travel and Tourism Council] (2020). *Economic Impact Reports.* https://wttc.org/Research/Economic-Impact.

12. Innovation and value creation in Canada's ocean sector: a blue economy imperative

Fred Olayele

12.1 INTRODUCTION

At 243,042 km, Canada has the longest total coastline in the world. With abundant ocean resources and deep capabilities, the country is a global leader in coastal and marine sciences, technology, and innovation. Its coastline stretches along the Pacific Ocean in the west, the Atlantic Ocean in the east, and the Arctic Ocean in the north. The Canadian ocean economy is worth $31.7 billion, with about 300,000 jobs in fisheries and aquaculture, energy, shipping, tourism, and recreation (Fisheries and Oceans Canada, 2021). This provides a unique opportunity for startups and small and medium-sized enterprises (SMEs) to scale up and break into global and regional value chains.

One in five Canadians live in coastal communities; the potential of the ocean economy is enormous. With an ocean economy worth only one percent of national output, this presents a huge opportunity for Canada – both commercially and in terms of its ability to influence the emerging, new global political economy. However, sustainable value creation in the sector requires a blue economy paradigm that recognizes the opportunities and challenges associated with simultaneously achieving environmentally responsible, commercially profitable, and socially acceptable outcomes. This makes the argument for a policy and business modernization architecture that prioritizes diversification and value addition in the ocean sector compelling, particularly through inclusive economic development programming anchored on sustainable marine-based technologies.

Whether in the context of deploying cutting-edge technologies in aquaculture production or fostering climate change mitigation and adaptation through ocean-based climate solutions such as marine protected areas, Canada recognizes the key role of the natural environment in building a sustainable blue economy. Healthy oceans and coastal ecosystems in the context of a sustainable and resilient blue economy are important for food production, climate resilience, and the socioeconomic well-being of coastal communities. From exploitation and conservation to protection and allied issues, the ocean has become a key focus in the discourse on the transition to net-zero emissions.

The 2020 Speech from the Throne (Government of Canada, 2020) corroborates the country's policy position on the blue economy, "...the Government will look at continuing to grow Canada's ocean economy to create opportunities for fishers and coastal communities, while advancing reconciliation and conservation objectives. Investing in the Blue Economy will help Canada prosper." The World Bank (2017) defines the blue economy as the "sustainable use of ocean resources for economic growth, improved livelihoods, and jobs while preserving the health of ocean ecosystem."

In addition to emerging industries and activities driven by cutting-edge developments in science and technology – such as offshore energy and marine biotechnology – Canada's blue economy consists of traditional ocean-based sectors such as commercial fishing, aquaculture, seafood processing, marine shipping, port activities, shipbuilding, and coastal tourism.

In terms of blue economy best practices, structural factors and political economy nuances in Europe make comparisons with Canada in certain segments somewhat difficult. Nonetheless, it is not lost on us that countries such as Norway and Iceland are exemplars in the global ocean innovation economy. This makes the case for policy diffusion quite compelling.

In light of the ongoing rapid pace of digitalization, maximizing Canada's share of the global ocean innovation economy requires a critical assessment of the current business environment, along with solutions that can address market access and competitiveness challenges. For context, in recent years, Canada has prioritized investments in innovations capable of fostering productivity and sustainability in the exploitation of ocean resources, but more work remains to be done.[1]

Among others, positioning the blue economy for sustainable growth and prosperity in Canada will require:

- Increasing private sector and innovative financing
- Attracting top talent and addressing labour shortages
- Prioritizing skills development and intellectual capital
- Helping ocean technology startups and SMEs scale up and internationalize
- Increasing participation by Indigenous communities and underrepresented groups
- Recognizing shifting patterns in global trade and geopolitics and their implications for diversification and global market access
- Aligning Canada's trade and development priorities with the ongoing structural shifts in global value chains

• Improving the business environment through incremental innovations in the business and policy modernization architecture

The knowledge economy, through cutting-edge research and technological innovations, continues to drive economic competitiveness and social progress. Increasingly, clusters are becoming an important vehicle in the development of the entrepreneurial ecosystem, by driving innovation at scale. Considering the growing need to deepen Canada's innovation economy as a strategy to complement efforts targeted at diversifying its trade towards emerging and non-traditional high-growth markets, the role of innovation ecosystems in unlocking value in the marine sector cannot be overemphasized. This is the focus of this chapter.

The remainder of the chapter is organized as follows. Section 12.2 discusses Canada's diversification imperative in the context of lagging productivity. The third section examines the role of agglomeration economies, through the innovation cluster framework, in the development of the Canadian ocean innovation ecosystem. Section 12.4 highlights important considerations in the internationalization-innovation nexus, while the last section concludes.

12.2   VALUE CREATION AND THE PRODUCTIVITY IMPERATIVE

To diversify successfully, Canadian startups and SMEs in the ocean sector require a nuanced understanding of where the opportunities lie, and how to successfully break into global and regional value chains. This is important for maximizing the benefits and opportunities that flow from trade – particularly for underrepresented groups such as women, low-income earners, young entrepreneurs, and Indigenous peoples in coastal communities. Programmatic interventions must prioritize these demographics, while supporting the entrepreneurs among them to develop the capacity to scale up their enterprises and access global markets.

Lagging Productivity

Productivity growth lies at the heart of economic prosperity; it remains a key source of growth and competitiveness. Unfortunately, productivity growth in Canada in the last two decades has remained sluggish (Gu, 2018). Compared to the U.S., Canada witnessed lackluster performance on labour productivity growth over this period, with much of the lagging performance due to sub-par innovation outcomes, mainly due to multifactor productivity gap (Lee and Tang, 2000; Baldwin et al. 2008).

Greenspon et al. (2021) question why Canada, a more open economy, has a smaller measured linkage between productivity and wages, compared to the U.S. The authors attribute this, in part, to Canada's dependence on natural resources vis-à-vis the impact of commodity price supercycles on terms of trade, exchange rate, inflation, wages, and employment. Riddell et al. (2016), in a strand of literature that questions the potency of raising labour supply to drive economic growth, caution that while this strategy has its merits, raising immigration and population – and ultimately the labour supply – may not materially translate to a higher standard of living.

Robson and Mahboubi (2018) echo the above sentiment and argue that while immigration can ease, but not materially alter the age structure of the population over time, other policies that complement immigration are necessary to ensure Canada's competitiveness. This has implications for the productivity growth debate. In the same vein, this narrative continues to generate concerns for policymakers, who understand that raising productivity growth will lead to higher wages and decent standards of living for Canadian workers – particularly those at the lower end of the income distribution. To move the needle, a nuanced perspective on inclusive economic development in the context of the blue economy, beckons.

Value Creation in the Ocean Sector

Canada's ocean economy was heralded by the earliest European fishing expeditions and settlement based largely on fisheries and naval installations in the 17th century. Over time, commercial fishing, aquaculture, fish processing, shipbuilding, and marine transportation have all become the economic engine for coastal communities in the country.

As well, as digital technologies continue to drive economic change in the global digital economy, ocean technology-driven and emerging sectors like tourism, biotechnologies, specialized manufacturing, and offshore oil and gas exploration and development provide sustainable value creation opportunities. This offers a long-term value-creation paradigm, based on a robust blue economy approach that resolves the inherent tensions in balancing economic, social, and environmental priorities.

The Canadian ocean economy generates over $30 billion a year, with significant innovation and job creation in key sectors and across the provinces and territories. In exploring the economic impact and inter-industry comparability of the marine sectors across Canada, a nuanced view of three key segments is key: a) sectors directly involved (e.g., commercial fishing, manufacturing, construction, and tourism); b) ocean-based private sector activities (including extractive and non-extractive uses); and c) activities of government and non-government organizations (NGOs) covering safety, research, and allied responsibilities.

At \$34 billion in 2020[2], the private sector contributed 78 percent of total marine sector output at \$26.8 billion, with fishing and seafood, transportation, and oil and gas contributing the largest shares. National defence and fisheries and ocean-related activities in the public sector, universities, and environmental NGOs accounted for the other 22 percent (Table 12.1).

Table 12.1   Canada's ocean GDP by sector, 2020 ($millions)

Marine Sector	2019	2020
Private sector	**31,227**	**26,797**
Seafood	**7,652**	**6,505**
Commercial fishing	3,687	2,839
Aquaculture	1,241	1,160
Fish processing	2,724	2,506
Offshore oil & gas	**8,177**	**5,903**
Transportation	**7,210**	**7,222**
Marine Transportation	3,024	2,963
Support activities for marine transportation	4,186	4,259
Tourism & recreation	**4,860**	**3,728**
Manufacturing & construction	**3,328**	**3,438**
Ship and boat building	2,308	2,151
Ports and harbours construction	1,020	1,287
Public sector	**6,798**	**7,417**
National Defence	3,282	3,811
Fisheries & Oceans	2,120	2,092
Other federal departments	597	638
Provincial/Territorial departments	299	312
Universities and ENGOs	500	564
Total marine economy	**38,025**	**34,214**
Total economy	**2,313,563**	**2,209,681**

Source: Statistics Canada and Fisheries and Oceans Canada

In terms of the number of jobs created in the marine economy, the 2020 results are similar to the GDP figures with 74 percent and 26 percent contributions by the private and public sectors, respectively. Transportation, fishing and seafood, and tourism and recreation emerged as the top three sectors in the private sector, while national defence and fisheries and oceans were ahead in the public sector (Table 12.2).

Table 12.2   Canada's ocean employment by sector, 2020 (number of jobs)

Marine Sector	2019	2020
Private sector	**243,752**	**216,818**
Seafood	**64,926**	**55,639**
Commercial fishing	25,769	19,642
Aquaculture	9,568	8,810
Fish processing	29,589	27,187
Offshore oil & gas	**15,134**	**10,925**
Transportation	**65,922**	**66,108**
Marine Transportation	27,044	26,534
Support activities for marine transportation	38,878	39,573
Tourism & recreation	**64,147**	**49,239**
Manufacturing & construction	**33,623**	**34,907**
Ship and boat building	22,146	20,660
Ports and harbours construction	11,477	14,247
Public sector	**70,345**	**76,694**
National Defence	35,044	40,633
Fisheries & Oceans	22,528	22,200
Other federal departments	5,171	5,531
Provincial/Territorial departments	2,705	2,819
Universities and ENGOs	4,897	5,511
Total marine economy	**314,097**	**293,513**
Total economy	**19,121,200**	**18,043,800**

Source: Statistics Canada and Fisheries and Oceans Canada

With oceans spanning its west, north, and east coasts, Canadians are influenced in many ways by the Pacific, Arctic, and Atlantic Oceans. Not only do Canada's three oceans host a wide variety of habitats that support vast marine ecosystems, but growth and prosperity in many neighbourhoods depend largely on ocean industries, with one in five Canadians living in coastal communities. The direct, indirect, and induced impacts of the ocean economy are presented in Tables 12.3 and 12.4.

Table 12.3   Canada's ocean economic impact, 2020 (GDP by sector, $millions)

Marine Sector	Direct	Indirect	Induced	Total
Private sector	**15,190**	**6,574**	**5,033**	**26,797**
Seafood	**3,746**	**1,621**	**1,138**	**6,505**
Commercial fishing	1,887	568	385	2,839
Aquaculture	530	441	188	1,160
Fish processing	1,329	612	565	2,506
Offshore oil & gas	**4,752**	**807**	**343**	**5,903**
Transportation	**3,356**	**2,036**	**1,831**	**7,222**
Marine Transportation	1,444	717	802	2,963
Support activities for marine transportation	1,912	1,318	1,029	4,259
Tourism & recreation	**1,755**	**1,105**	**869**	**3,728**
Manufacturing & construction	**1,581**	**1,005**	**852**	**3,438**
Ship and boat building	916	682	552	2,151
Ports and harbours construction	665	322	300	1,287
Public sector	**3,886**	**1,332**	**2,199**	**7,417**
National Defence	2,188	415	1,208	3,811
Fisheries & Oceans	861	603	627	2,092
Other federal departments	335	134	169	638
Provincial/Territorial departments	127	116	69	312
Universities and ENGOs	374	64	126	564
Total marine economy	**19,076**	**7,906**	**7,233**	**34,214**

Source: Statistics Canada and Fisheries and Oceans Canada

While direct impact occurs in the ocean sector itself, indirect and induced impacts are due to activities in other industries but are attributable to the direct impact. Of the $26.8 billion total output generated in the private sector in 2020, direct, indirect, and induced impacts accounted for 56.7 percent, 24.5 percent, and 18.8 percent respectively. In the public sector, the corresponding shares were direct (52 percent), indirect (18 percent), and induced (30 percent), respectively.

Table 12.4   Canada's ocean economic impact, 2020 (employment by sector, number of jobs)

Marine Sector	Direct	Indirect	Induced	Total
Private sector	**108,815**	**62,654**	**45,349**	**216,818**
Seafood	**28,939**	**16,072**	**10,629**	**55,639**

Marine Sector	Direct	Indirect	Induced	Total
Commercial fishing	10,191	5,811	3,639	19,642
Aquaculture	2,744	4,403	1,664	8,810
Fish processing	16,004	5,858	5,325	27,187
Offshore oil & gas	**1,248**	**6,592**	**3,085**	**10,925**
Transportation	**30,359**	**19,491**	**16,258**	**66,108**
Marine Transportation	13,558	5,837	7,139	26,534
Support activities for marine transportation	16,801	13,653	9,119	39,573
Tourism & recreation	**30,660**	**10,958**	**7,620**	**49,239**
Manufacturing & construction	**17,609**	**9,541**	**7,757**	**34,907**
Ship and boat building	8,905	6,745	5,010	20,660
Ports and harbours construction	8,704	2,796	2,748	14,247
Public sector	**42,068**	**14,721**	**19,906**	**76,694**
National Defence	25,237	4,344	11,052	40,633
Fisheries & Oceans	9,661	6,950	5,589	22,200
Other federal departments	2,473	1,559	1,500	5,531
Provincial/Territorial departments	1,078	1,107	634	2,819
Universities and ENGOs	3,618	762	1,131	5,511
Total marine economy	**150,883**	**77,374**	**65,255**	**293,513**

Source: Statistics Canada and Fisheries and Oceans Canada

On the job creation front, the relevant shares were direct (50 percent), indirect (29 percent), and induced (21 percent) in the private sector, and direct (55 percent), indirect (19 percent), and induced (26 percent) in the public sector, respectively.

Maritime Trade and Diversification

A quintessential small open economy, Canada relies significantly on international trade to drive economic growth and foster social inclusion. Trade accounts for 66 percent of Canada's annual output, particularly in large export-oriented primary goods sectors. While top exports are in energy products, motor vehicles and parts, and consumer goods, ocean-related economic activity generates significant direct and indirect impacts across industries, with benefits in every province and territory.

Canada's ocean sectors are concentrated in Atlantic Canada, Quebec, British Columbia, and the Arctic region. In addition to a burgeoning ocean technology sector, which continues to power innovation with its industrial, technical, and scientific diversity, traditional and primary ocean economic activities include marine shipping, offshore oil and gas, fish and seafood processing, commercial fishing, Indigenous fisheries and traditional livelihoods, shipbuilding, aquaculture, and recreation and tourism. While the Pacific Ocean is critical to trade with the Asia Pacific region, Canada's Arctic region presents a huge opportunity for making advances in the blue economy in the context of land-based natural resource exploration, Indigenous fisheries and traditional livelihoods, increased access for shipping vessels, and unique tourism experiences (Fisheries and Oceans Canada, 2021).

With several ocean tech companies and some of the world's best ocean research and innovation taking place in Canada, the case for maximizing Canada's share of a rapidly growing and dynamic ocean export market is compelling. As part of its trade diversification agenda, the Canadian government's inclusive approach to trade is committed to supporting all segments of society in taking advantage of the economic opportunities flowing from trade and investment.

Table 12.5   *Top destinations for Canada's fish and seafood exports, 2021[3]*

Destination	Exports ($ billion)	Share of exports (%)
U.S.	6.18	70.3
China	1.12	12.7
EU (ex UK)	0.45	5.2
Others	1.04	11.8
Total	**8.79**	**100**

Source: Statistics Canada and Fisheries and Oceans Canada

Table 12.5 provides a snapshot of Canada's exports in the seafood sector in 2021, with the U.S. (70.3 percent), China (12.7 percent), and the EU excluding the UK (5.2 percent) accounting for 88 percent of Canada's total $8.79 billion fish and seafood exports.

For context, the Canada-United States-Mexico Agreement (CUSMA) replaced the North American Free Trade Agreement (NAFTA) and entered into force on July 1, 2020. After NAFTA entered into force in 1994, Canada increasingly became more dependent on trade with the U.S., with 75 percent of its exports going to its southern neighbour (Council on Foreign Relations, 2020).

The risks associated with such over-reliance on bilateral trade with the U.S., at the expense of multilateral trade with other regions of the world, became evident during the renegotiations that culminated in CUSMA. While CUSMA preserves key parts of the original NAFTA provisions, the revised trilateral trade pact includes a slew of new rules aimed at integrating recent developments in technology and trade practices.

The U.S. remains Canada's major source of inward foreign direct investment (FDI) stock, with Canada's southern neighbour holding over 80 percent of its inward FDI stock until 1970. However, this share has gradually fallen over the years, from two thirds in the late 1980s, to less than one half in 2012, with further declines afterwards (44 percent in 2020). In the same vein, compared to decades ago, Canadian inward FDI is now more geographically diverse, with 40 percent from Europe and 10 percent from Asia and Oceania (Government of Canada, 2021).

The literature on the beneficial impacts of innovation and FDI on the Canadian economy is extensive. Among other benefits, compared to domestic investment, FDI accounts for higher productivity spillovers (Tang and Wang, 2020), higher wages (Breau and Brown, 2011), and industry-agnostic upskilling (Souare and Zhou, 2014). Rao and Zhing (2018) corroborate this: for every 10 percent increase in inward FDI stock in Canada, construction investment rises by 3.1 percent, machinery and equipment investment by 1.3 percent, R&D expenditure by 1.7 percent, and the share of the university-educated workforce by 0.4 percent.

One key lesson for Canada from the renegotiated pact is the need for trade and investment diversification. The disruptive trade policies in the Trump era constituted, in many ways, a clarion call for Canada to consider other emerging markets and diversify its trade beyond the U.S. (Helliwell, 2002). While trade diversification helps in minimizing asymmetric shocks with varying degrees of severity for the Canadian economy, investment diversification deepens innovation and commercial linkages and helps integrate Canadian firms into global value chains to take advantage of opportunities in fast growing markets.

12.3 INNOVATION CLUSTERS AND THE OCEAN ECONOMY

The ocean innovation economy cuts across many sectors and derives its primary value from digital technologies, the availability of top talent, startup and growth capital, intellectual capital, creativity, the presence of large firms, and a robust ecosystem capable of connecting startups to programs and funds for expansion. As established in the preceding sections, with abundant ocean resources and deep capabilities, Canada is a global leader in coastal and marine sciences, technology, and innovation.

Given contemporary challenges in addressing Canada's productivity gap, the need for deepening its innovation economy by bringing together industry, research, investors, government, and Indigenous stakeholders cannot be overemphasized. This model is already operationalized through the Canadian innovation superclusters, anchored on robust private–public partnerships.[4] This is discussed further below.

Theoretical Underpinning

Clusters are essentially anchored on robust private–public partnerships, with transaction costs at the core of the institutional design. Williamson (1981) argues that five key factors explain the optimum structure needed to achieve economic efficiency by minimizing the costs of exchange: frequency, asset specificity, uncertainty, bounded rationality, and opportunistic behavior.

Before it became a popular framework for understanding innovation policies, Etzkowitz (1993) and Etzkowitz and Leydesdorff (1995) refined earlier concepts and developed the triple helix model of university-industry-government interactions. This has become popular as a strategy to foster synergistic outcomes that drive innovation based on lower transaction costs. At its core, the triple helix model is essentially about taking advantage of the triadic relationship in the university-industry-government nexus and the knowledge-based modern economy to create value and advance innovation economies.

Over time, the practical relevance of the triple helix concept in explaining regional innovation has been challenged. In the context of the gradual shift of the analytical framework of superclusters from the triple helix, the poor performance of the latter in explaining emerging entrepreneurial patterns is one key observation. Among others, Lindberg et al. (2014) argue in favor of the quadruple helix model that incorporates civil society as the fourth helix. This is based on the notion that civil society actors can navigate the complexities associated with the commercial-political-scientific community by leveraging their non-profit status to advance initiatives that would traditionally face hurdles in becoming operational.

Canada's Ocean Supercluster

With transaction costs at the core, Canada's five innovation clusters leverage digital technologies for value creation across regional innovation ecosystems. In many ways, the Canadian supercluster system explains the innovation imperative in the context of the productivity challenge discussed above. Canada understood that it was lagging in terms of productivity and that it needed to catch up. It then made a deliberate choice to recalibrate and build its innovation economy from the ground up. In some sense, this is a policy design aimed at incentivizing SMEs and large companies to collaborate and boost high-growth sectors in the innovation economy.

In 2018, the Canadian superclusters were launched as a 10-year innovation system comprised of five superclusters spread across five regions of the country based on existing regional innovation ecosystems. The Ocean Supercluster[5] is one of these (see Box 12.1).

BOX 12.1   CANADA'S REGIONAL CLUSTERS

Digital Technology Supercluster

* Core elements: Using virtual, mixed, and augmented reality, data, and quantum computing to solve productivity, health, and sustainability challenges.
* Economic impacts: $5 billion in GDP and 13,500 jobs over 10 years.
* Partners: Boeing, Deloitte, D-Wave Systems, Microsoft, and Telus Communications.

Protein Industries Supercluster

* Core elements: Evolving agricultural production with plant genomics and novel processing.
* Economic impacts: $50 billion in GDP and 50,000 jobs over 10 years.
* Partners: AGT Food and Ingredients, Maple Leaf.
* DowDuPont, Dot Technology, and Roquette.

Next Generation Manufacturing Supercluster

* Core elements: Designing next-generation manufacturing companies by adopting advanced processes and developing and deploying new technologies like robotics and 3D printing.
* Economic impacts: $13.5 billion in GDP and 13,500 jobs over 10 years.
* Partners: AutoDesk, Clearpath, Linamar, Myant, University of Waterloo.

AI-Powered Supply Chains Supercluster

* Core elements: Building the supply chains of the future using artificial intelligence and robotic technologies.
* Economic impacts: $16.5 billion in GDP and 16,000 jobs over 10 years.
* Partners: Aldo, BCG, CGI, Cisco, Intel, PwC, Shopify.

Ocean Supercluster

* Core elements: Solving global challenges like how to meet energy demands through marine renewable energy, fisheries, aquaculture, oil and gas, defence, shipbuilding, and transportation.
* Economic impacts: $14 billion in GDP and 3,000 jobs over 10 years.
* Partners: Cuna del Mar, Emera, Palaerospace, Smartice, Dalhousie University.

Canada's Ocean Supercluster accounts for a significant proportion of the Canadian activity in the sector. A pan-Canadian, industry-led supercluster with close to 500 member organizations from coast-to-coast-to-coast, it has become a catalyst for growth and opportunity in the Canadian ocean sector, working with its members across different ocean sectors and regions to accelerate the development and commercialization of made in Canada innovation targeted at solving some of the world's biggest ocean challenges.[6]

Based in Atlantic Canada, the Ocean Supercluster is tapping the combined strengths of the industries operating in Canada's oceans, including marine renewable energy, fisheries, aquaculture, oil and gas, defence, shipbuilding, transportation, and ocean technology. By harnessing emerging technologies, this Supercluster is digitizing and optimizing marine operations, maximizing sustainable approaches to resources, and increasing safety for those operating in marine environments.

In addition to driving wealth generation, environmental sustainability, and the protection of Indigenous and non-Indigenous cultures and ways of life, Canada's coastlines on the Atlantic, Pacific, and Arctic Oceans play a significant role in fostering economic diversification and inclusive growth by driving international trade, contributing to food security, and helping coastal and Indigenous communities remain resilient and vibrant.

The Canadian government overarching objective is anchored on the expectation that following recent funding, the clusters:

> will continue to grow their innovation ecosystems, promote investment in innovation and commercialization, expand their national and global presence, collaborate to deepen their impact, act as a catalyst for skills and talent development, and continue to support the growth and scale-up of Canadian small and medium-sized enterprises.[7]

12.4 KEY TAKEAWAYS AND LESSONS FOR POLICY MODERNIZATION

The interdependence of climate, ocean and marine ecosystems, biodiversity, and people is key to mapping the key elements of ocean-centric knowledge mobilization and innovation activities. Not only is this important for leveraging blue economy best practices to achieve environmentally responsible, commercially profitable, and socially acceptable outcomes in the ocean economy, but it could also support policymakers and other stakeholders in the Canadian innovation ecosystem to understand key interlinkages, foster comprehensive and coordinated synergies in the blue economy, and accelerate the policy innovation process.

The capacity to innovate remains key for economic stability and resilience, particularly after a major disruption. Such innovation and transformation capacity explains how, in the aftermath of the 2008 financial crisis, policymakers in many jurisdictions across the world recognized the need to diversify their economies away from dominant sectors to enable them to become more resistant and resilient to future exogenous shocks.

In a regional context, the economic structures of the Atlantic, Pacific, and Arctic regions in Canada can help catalyze reinvention to achieve more resilient and diversified economic outcomes vis-à-vis technology-led innovation and early-stage entrepreneurship. Strategic investments in pathways for increased access to established and high-growth, emerging overseas markets that are better positioned to thrive in the "new normal" cannot be overemphasized.

The future of the ocean innovation economy depends largely on private sector financing insofar as the business model is anchored on technology-driven outcomes with high-growth potential. While government grants, subsidies, early-stage funding, turbocharging, and the use of industrial policy funding to steer ocean-based businesses are in order, they are not a substitute for sustainable commercial finance and private sector investments.

The ability to attract top talent and retain skilled workers is central to regional economic success and building the foundations for a well-functioning innovation ecosystem. Accelerated investment in digital infrastructure, resilience, and public–private partnerships to help lower transaction costs for startups and SMEs operating with thin margins will also go a long way in fostering sustainable value creation.

Given the rapidly evolving global political economy and Canada's high degree of economic openness, with the right support and appropriate incentive framework, startups and SMEs operating in the ocean sector can increase their global trade and investment shares, thereby scaling up, diversifying, retaining, and building market access in a sustainable manner.

Equity is not just a social justice issue; it is, in fact, an economic and business imperative. Fostering an equitable regime that addresses barriers limiting meaningful participation by Indigenous peoples, women, and other historically underrepresented populations can go a long way in maximizing workforce participation and solving, in a sustainable manner, perennial labour shortages and supply constraints.

With increased interdependencies between trade and FDI – because of the complex dynamics of global value chains – federal, provincial, and municipal stakeholders in the Canadian ocean innovation ecosystem need a more coherent multistakeholder blue economy knowledge mobilization, dissemination, and implementation framework. It is important to map the complex processes around the supply of inputs, access to knowledge and new markets, and service offerings to consumers.

In addition to the commercial ramifications, programmatic interventions in the ocean sector should be aligned with Canada's international development efforts, in the context of fighting climate change through nature-based solutions, supporting food and nutritional security, advancing gender equality, and building resilience.

In many ways, the analysis above underscores a value creation approach that situates Canada in the context of the ongoing shifts in global trade patterns and geopolitics, as well as what these mean for diversification and global market access for startups and SMEs with limited ability to compete on the world stage. On the foreign policy front, this also implies that Canada must assess and recalibrate its trade and development priorities with the ongoing structural shifts in global value chains.

12.5 CONCLUDING REMARKS

The discussion above offers a compelling argument for supporting policy-makers and other stakeholders by mapping core linkages and innovation opportunities in the Canadian ocean sector under a blue economy paradigm. The timing for mobilizing knowledge around Canada's innovation capabilities on the global stage has never been more important.

Policy and business modernization efforts targeted at blue economy commercialization opportunities will go a long way in helping Canadian firms to create value in a sustainable way and develop the competitive edge required to maximize existing opportunities across and within sectors. This is particularly important for the adoption of blue economy paradigms to achieve sustainability in the use of marine resources, in addition to the social, institutional, political economy, and equity dimensions of the ocean economy.

NOTES

1. See https://www.dfo-mpo.gc.ca/about-notre-sujet/blue-economy-economie-bleue/ engagement-paper-document-mobilisation/heard-entendu-eng.html.
2. The 2019 figures are included in Tables 12.1 and 12.2 for context in light of the impact of COVID-19 on total output in 2020.
3. Seafood is the most popular food commodity traded in the world.
4. See https://ised-isde.canada.ca/site/global-innovation-clusters/en.
5. See https://oceansupercluster.ca/.
6. Ibid.
7. See https://ised-isde.canada.ca/site/global-innovation-clusters/en.

REFERENCES

Baldwin, J.R., A. Fisher, W. Gu, F.C. Lee, and B. Robidoux (2008). Capital Intensity in Canada and the United States, 1987 to 2003. Statistics Canada Catalogue No. 15-206-X. Ottawa, Ontario. *The Canadian Productivity Review*. No. 18.

Breau, S. and W.M. Brown (2011). Global Links: Exporting, Foreign Direct Investment, and Wages: Evidence from the Canadian Manufacturing Sector. *Statistics Canada*.

Council on Foreign Relations (2020). NAFTA and the USMCA: Weighing the Impact of North American Trade. Available at https://www.cfr.org/backgrounder/naftas-economic-impact.

Etzkowitz, H. (1993). Technology Transfer: The Second Academic Revolution. *Technology Access Report*, 6: 7–9.

Etzkowitz, H. and L. Leydesdorff (1995). The Triple Helix—University-Industry-Government Relations: A Laboratory for Knowledge-Based Economic Development. *EASST Review*, 14: 14–19.

Fisheries and Oceans Canada (2021). Blue Economy Strategy Engagement Paper, *Government of Canada*. Available at https://www.dfo-mpo.gc.ca/about-notre-sujet/blue-economy-economie-bleue/engagement-paper-document-mobilisation/part1-eng.html.

Government of Canada (2020). Speech from the Throne. Available at https://www.canada.ca/content/dam/pco-bcp/documents/pm/SFT_2020_EN_WEB.pdf.

Government of Canada (2021). State of Trade 2021: A Closer Look at Foreign Direct Investment (FDI). Available at https://www.international.gc.ca/transparency-transparence/state-trade-commerce-international/2021.aspx?lang=eng.

Green, D., C. Riddell, and F. St.-Hillaire (eds) (2016). *Income Inequality: The Canadian Story*. Montreal: IRPP.

Greenspon, J., A. Stansbury, and L.H. Summers (2021). Productivity and Pay in the United States and Canada. International Productivity Monitor 41.

Gu, W. (2018). Accounting for Slower Productivity Growth in the Canadian Business Sector after 2000: Do Measurement Issues Matter? *Statistics Canada*. Available at https://publications.gc.ca/site/eng/9.860576/publication.html.

Helliwell, J. (2002). *Globalisation and Well-Being*. UBC Press, Vancouver, British Columbia.

IPCC [Intergovernmental Panel on Climate Change] (2022). Climate Change 2022: Impacts, Adaptation and Vulnerability. Available at https://www.ipcc.ch/report/ar6/wg3/.

Lee, F.C. and J. Tang (2000). Productivity Levels and International Competitiveness between Canada and the United States. *American Economic Review* (papers and proceedings), 90(2): 168–71.

Lindberg, M., M. Lindgren, and J. Packendorff (2014). Quadruple Helix as a way to Bridge the Gender Gap in Entrepreneurship? A Case Study of an Innovation System Project in the Baltic Sea Region. *Journal of the Knowledge Economy*, 5(1): 94–113.

Rao, S. and Q. Zhing (2018). Macroeconomic Impacts of Inward and Outward FDI in Canada. *Transnational Corporations Review*, 11(1): 80–96.

Robson, W.B.P. and P. Mahboubi (2018). Inflated Expectations: More Immigrants Can't Solve Canada's Aging Problem on Their Own. *C.D. Howe Institute*, e-Brief: Demographics and Immigration.

Souare, M. and B. Zhou (2016). Foreign-Affiliate Presence and Skilled Labour Demand. *International Economics and Economics Policy*, 13: 233–254.

Tang, J. and W. Wang (2020). Why Are Multinationals More Productive than Non-multinationals? Evidence from Canada. *Statistics Canada*.

Williamson, O. (1981). The Economics of Organization: The Transaction Cost Approach. *American Journal of Sociology*, 87(3): 548–77. Available at http://www.jstor.org/stable/2778934.

World Bank (2017). What is the Blue Economy? Available at https://www.worldbank.org/en/news/infographic/2017/06/06/blue-economy.

Index